designing
culture

designing
culture

The Technological
Imagination at Work

anne **balsamo**

Duke University Press
Durham & London 2011

© 2011 Duke University Press
All rights reserved

Printed in the United States of America
on acid-free paper ∞

Typeset in Arno Pro and Helvetica Neue
by Keystone Typesetting, Inc.

Library of Congress
Cataloging-in-Publication Data
appear on the last printed page
of this book.

contents

*Women of the World Talk Back:
An Interactive Multimedia Documentary* (enclosed DVD)

contents of **designingculture.net**

EXHIBIT: XFR: Experiments in the Future of Reading
- ○ Twelve videos of speculative reading devices
- ○ *What Would McLuhan Say?*

WALLS: Interactive Wall Books
- ○ *Episodes in the History of Reading*
- ○ *Deslizate en el Tiempo: Episodios en la Historia de la Comunicatión*
- ○ *Science for All Ages: Magnificent Developments in the History of Science and Technology*

MAPS: Mapping the Technological Imagination
- ○ *Learning to Love the Questions*
- ○ *Teaching Original Synners*
- ○ *The Distributed Museum: The Cultural Work of Museums in a Digital Age*

VIDEOS: Primers on TechnoCulture
- ○ *Tools for the Asking*
- ○ *How a Robot Got its Groove: Gendering the Technological Imagination*
- ○ *DIY Culture: Making Community, Making the Future at Makers' Faire*

BLOG: designing :: technolculture
- ○ Observations about design, culture, and technology
- ○ Digital portfolio of Anne Balsamo

illustrations

Figures

Tables

acknowledgments

 Throughout my teaching career, I have often been hijacked by questions posed by students. During the 1990s, I taught in the masters' program for Information Design and Technology (IDT) at Georgia Institute of Technology. One day during a class discussion, a student asked, "Why do we have to read cultural theory if we want to become webmasters?" (This was the heady days of the early web, a time when webmasters were paid six-digit salaries and academic institutions scrambled to design new programs to prepare and credential students to shape the emerging industry.) I don't remember which of the IDT students asked the question (although Katie Albers and John Canning are likely suspects), but it inspired me to take on a broad project of new research and personal retooling, which has now lasted more than 15 years.

The time that passed between that initial question and the publication of this book took the form of a journey, one marked by a series of intellectual and creative adventures. Mary Hocks has been an intellectual traveling companion since the beginning. What started as a shared interest in exploring the possibilities of using digital media for feminist activism, evolved into a set of shared understandings about technology, culture, and more importantly, friendships. She remains my dearest confidant who continues to inspire me with her own intellectual adventures.

When the adventures span such a long time, there are many debts of gratitude. My beloved editor and friend, Ken Wissoker, is one of those people who not only provided early encouragement about the scope of the book, but also patiently guided me in actually getting it done. And when I write "patiently," I mean it. I felt Ken's interest in the project even when I wasn't writing; he kept gentle pressure on me to persevere, and to work my way through what this book was to become via the process of writing it. It's difficult to describe how important it was to me to know that, even though he strongly wanted me to complete this thing, he was respectful and understanding of the arduous process I (apparently) had to go through to do so.

And then there are the two collaborators who have taught me how to think more complexly about technology and culture. My collaborative relationship with Scott Minneman—first a colleague at Xerox PARC, then one of the cofounders of Onomy Labs—has been transformative. Among the many things he taught me was the importance of remaining calm in the face of technological troubles. Along with Dale MacDonald, another PARC colleague and Onomy co-founder, they have homesteaded my brain. I am smarter when I think with them and through them. There is nothing I enjoy more than our collaborations, in whatever form they take: building a company; sussing out clients; stressing over finances; handholding during personal crises; or designing new stuff. Dale has been the programming wizard for the *Designing Culture* website; he not only understood the transmedia nature of this book project, but also invented ways to make it manifest on the web.

I have been privileged to have support for my ideas, my professional activities, and my intellectual passions from several people who served as mentors and idea cheerleaders, and when necessary, as tender critics. As one of the co-founders of a new field of digital humanities, Cathy Davidson has been a steadfast guide, sounding board, and supporter, who serves as a model of how to live the life of the mind while engaged in what needs doing in the world. She has never failed to be there when I have asked for honest professional advice or an encouraging word. Our mutual friend, David Goldberg, is a dream collaborator: conspiring with him on HASTAC, SECT, or any of his own brilliant efforts to transform the humanities in a digital age has always been easy and effortless; he is simply a joy to work with. Both Cathy and David are creative community builders, impressive and inspiring to watch in action. Closer to home at USC, I enjoy the camaraderie of Tara McPherson, who has to be one of the most intellectually generous colleagues a woman could ever want. As the editor of *Vectors*, she has thoughtfully guided my thinking on the design of new scholarly genres. As a friend, she keeps my spirits nourished. Through my collaborations with these three scholars, I learned to think in more nuanced ways about the connection between my narrow set of interests and the abiding questions of the humanities. They are creative co-conspirators who take deep joy in pushing boundaries: of what scholarship looks like in a digital age; of what it means to be an engaged intellectual; and of the work of the academy in a 2.0 world.

Two people in particular provided guidance in the most gentle of ways, by just talking to me about what needs doing in the world. My conversations with them ranged widely and wildly, and unfolded over many years. They have been the teachers of my adult mind, who guided my education *after* the Ph.D. was done. I still miss Rich Gold, my manager at Xerox PARC, who died in 2003. Rich was the one who first suggested I think about leaving the academy, because he didn't believe that "it was the place where I was going to learn what I needed to, to really make a difference in the world." He recognized my passion for a set of questions, and challenged me to follow the questions and not a career path. So I did; I will never regret it, even if the road has been a bit bumpy. If there was ever someone who modeled passion in the pursuit of the big questions of "what needs doing in the world," it is John Seely Brown. At first I knew him as my boss at PARC, then he became a friend, but he has always been a mentor who listens keenly and deeply, not only on the individual level, but the global as well. He watches the world to see what needs doing. In conversation, he has an uncanny ability to guide you to making the connections between parochial interests and the things that really matter, and every time, he made me feel like it was my insight all along.

I could write pages expressing my gratitude for the many acts of encouragement, guidance, and friendship that contributed to this book effort, but I fear that this will delay the production even longer. So here I mention just those who made a difference along the way: Lucy Suchman, Paula Treichler, Larry Grossberg, Cary Nelson, Mark Meadows, Roddey Reid,

Lisa Bloom, Meaghan Morris, Bob Markley, Curtis White, Gail Hawisher, Karen Barad, Willard Uncapher, Andreas Larsson, Tobias Larsson, Ellen Wartella, Stuart Moulthrop, Nancy Kaplan, Alan Liu, Timothy Roscoe, Beau Takahara, Holly Kruse, Jennifer Curran, Marina LaPalma, Anne Wysocki, Guillermo Gomez-Pena, Carolena Ponce deLeon, Niklas Damiras, Sha Xin Wei, Helga Wild, Brian Janusiak, Eric Siegel, Patrick Swennson, John Palfrey, Carl Mitcham, and Carl and Lynn Jensen. Thanks especially to Julie Klein who read the entire manuscript and provided supportive feedback.

I have to call out special thanks to my colleagues at University of Southern California. I am fortunate to have so many who are actively and creatively engaged with digital culture. Their work inspires and challenges me to think differently. At the Institute for Multimedia Literacy, I thank Holly Willis, Virginia Kuhn, David Lopez, and Lisa Tripp. At the Interactive Media Division: Steve Anderson, Mark Bolas, Scott Fisher, Marientina Gotsis, Perry Hoberman, Michael Naimark, and Peggy Weil. Other USC colleagues have been generous with their encouragement for this project: Mimi Ito, Bruce Zuckerman, Doug Thomas, Nancy Lutkehaus, Milind Tambe, and especially, the late Anne Friedberg.

My colleagues at Xerox PARC were thoughtful company during the creation of the XFR museum exhibit: Maribeth Back; Banny Banerjee; Mark Bernstein; Mark Chow; Matt Gorbet; Steve Harrison; Polly Zelleweger; and Anita Borg and Mark Weiser (both for too short a time).

There is a special group of colleagues who belong to Erstic (that dream of a name), who offered timely feedback on the organizing theoretical framework of the book: Charles Acland; Marty Allor; Ron Greene; Gil Rodman; Kim Sawchuk; Greg Siegworth; Jennifer Slack; Jonathan Stern; Will Straw; Ted Striphas; and Greg Wise.

In a similar way, colleagues at Stanford University helped clarify my thinking about issues relating to the role of design in and across the disciplines: Penny Eckert; Pam Davis; Tim Lenoir; Haun Saussy; Jeffrey Schnapp; Fred Turner; and Patience Young.

Several students helped with the research, digital media production, and manuscript editing. At USC, these were Lisa Walsh, Jean Beaty, Susan Jack, Pragya Tomar, Maura Klosterman, Susana Bautista, and John Brennan; at Stanford, Lilly Irani, and Karis Eklund. As a graduate research assistant, Veronica Paredes took on the task of revising and updating the

Women of the World Talk Back interactive application. She was single-handedly responsible for bringing it up to date as a cross-platform DVD. Her work was not simply technologically skillful; she engaged the material with intelligence and a designer's eye. Cara Wallis read the entire manuscript to provide critical feedback at the most timely stage: when I simply couldn't write one more word. In the gentlest manner, and with a new set of questions, she encouraged me to go through it one more time.

Some of the research reported in this book was supported by a generous grant from the John D. and Catherine T. MacArthur Foundation as part of the Digital Media and Learning initiative. I thank Connie Yowell, Director of Education in the Foundation's Program on Human and Community Development, for her support of this work.

The Designing Culture website was created by Scott Mahoy and Dale McDonald, and Eric Kabisch worked on one of the applications for an earlier version. Scott Mahoy created the beautiful graphic and flash designs for the site, while Dale MacDonald turned interactivity designs into web experiences. I also thank Craig Dietrich, my co-author/designer on the "Learning to Love the Questions" application, and Ray Vichot, who edited the video materials.

Last, but not least, I must express my gratitude to my family and friends who offered steadfast support during the adventure and, when the going got tough, rallied around me to keep my spirits nourished: to Donna Hunt-Dussé for providing a space for creative art-making that kept me grounded during the Bay Area days and for being a friend through thick and thin; and to Alison Clark for texting me when I stayed quiet for too long. I'm especially thankful to Ana Reyes, Deirdre West, Robert Ruilly, Andy Jimenez, Sean Daly, Mark Bolas, and Perry Hoberman, for being there during the most difficult year, which helped make it the most wonderful year for friendship and community; to my beloved sister Rose Balsamo, for always being my family; and to my niece Amanda Balsamo, for her amazon spirit and creative 2.0 intelligence. She reminds me that there are new questions waiting in the wings. Thanks, finally, to Rich Gossweiler for showing up at exactly the right time.

designing
culture

Taking Culture Seriously in The Age of Innovation

 We are in the midst of a frenzy of innovation. Technological innovation has been called the single most significant driver for the development of national competitiveness for countries across the globe.[1] While the position of the United States has fallen in the global rankings that measure investment in innovation (from first in 2005, to seventh in 2007), countries such as Denmark, Sweden, and Singapore are leading the way in cultivating complex socio-technical and political systems that foster innovation based on the development and deployment of new technologies.[2] But technological innovation is not simply the concern of national governments, it is also the preoccupation of increasing numbers of individuals who display their inventiveness as *YouTube* videos, *FaceBook* games, and pithy blog entries. Terms such as DIY, *the Maker's Movement*, and *prosumer markets* identify cultural zones where personally motivated individuals fabricate innovative applications that contribute to the plentitude of digital cultures. In between government-initiated national projects and new popular social movements lies the middle zone of the creative industries, an emergent cultural formation in-

An Index of Culture and Technology (07.07.07)

o Amount per capita in U.S. dollars Singapore is poised to invest in incentives to develop the nation as a global hub for innovations in Interactive Digital Media: **74.**[3]

o Amount per capita allocated in the FY2007 U.S. budget for the "American Competitiveness Initiative" intended to boost U.S. innovation through R&D, education, and entrepreneurship: **19.**[4]

o The number of pixels color-coded as Kashmir territory by Microsoft designers as part of a map of India included in a Windows 95 plug-in: **8.**[5]

o Estimated loss of revenue for Microsoft when the Indian government banned the product for designating the disputed territory as belonging to the Kashmiri people: **$3,000,000.**[6]

o Number of YouTube videos uploaded on a daily basis: **65,000.**[7]

o Number of on-line scholarly journals that accept submissions that include embedded video materials: **5.**[8]

o Number of academic programs (worldwide) in culture and technology: **7.**[9]

o Number of graduate schools (worldwide) of culture and technology: **1.**[10]

o Number of Google hits for the phrase "technological innovation and economic growth": **14,500.**

o Number of Google hits for the phrase "technological innovation and cultural enhancement": **0.**

volving the capitalist transformation of art practice into creative labor for the purpose of fostering innovation—especially in the area of new media— as a consumer commodity. The emergence of the creative industries has garnered significant attention from cultural critics, whose evaluations of the political implications of this new formation, which gives rise to new class identities (the no-collar worker), new work practices (e-lancing), and new organizational forms (Jelly work events), are all over the map.[11] I call attention to these examples as evidence for my claim that whether it manifests through the launch of new national initiatives, as popular cultural movements, or new work practices, innovation has become the dominant zeitgeist of the early twenty-first century.

In this project I discuss the practices of a professional group of technological makers (of which I've been a member) who were—at least for part of the story—employed in the business of technological innovation. Given the index items mentioned above, there are several frames of analysis I could employ in this effort, but do not. For instance, I am not going to situate the work I describe in this book as part of a U.S. national project on innovation; I am not going to offer explicit comments about the ideological implications of the creative industries; and I am not going to spend much time teasing-out the distinctions between professional versus amateur innovation. The historically literate understand that the distinction between "professional" and "amateur"—especially as agents of technological innovation—has always been about struggles for privileged legitimacy. The official histories of science and technology are full of accounts of significant contributions by so-called *amateur* scientists and technologists, as well as the accounts of how the demarcation between *professional* and *amateur* has been institutionalized, politicized, and deployed in the service of the consolidation of power. The distinction is one of the enabling conditions that literally wrote women out of the official histories of technology (Stanley, 1995). In point of fact, the membrane that separates professional from amateur science has always been leaky. While it would be fascinating to explore the shifts that have generated the rise of the "prosumer" as an ultramodern cultural agent, this is not my focus here. What I am going to do is describe and analyze a series of efforts and projects that were explicitly designed to produce cultural innovations using, what were at the time, cutting-edge technologies. My aim is to argue for the importance of taking culture seriously in the process of technological innovation and to illustrate through references to specific projects how this may be done. I hope to demonstrate how innovation could be even more innovative in its scope of vision for the future if it were to take culture as a precondition and horizon of creative effort.

In the popular business press, the common understanding of innovation focuses almost exclusively on its technological dimension: and relatedly, the *value* of innovation rests solely on the basis of economic payoff (or costs). Where the term "invention" refers to a novel idea or thing, innovation implies the creation of unique arrangements that provides the basis for a reorganization of the way things *will be* in the future: in this sense, all innovations rearrange culture. But, as was true for the misinformed Microsoft products referred to in the above index, the recognition of this fact often does not happen until well after the innovation has propagated throughout various quarters.[12] How is it that discussions about technological innovation in the twenty-first century continue to bracket conversations about culture?

While the unintended consequences of new technologies are difficult to predict before they unfold, many people still seem to be surprised by the fact that technological innovations have cultural consequences. This persistent blind spot is symptomatic of an impoverished understanding of the relationship between technology and culture. As cultural theorists, Jennifer Slack and Greg Wise (2005: 6) explain, the dominant perception—what they refer to as the "received view of the relationship between culture and technology"—is that culture and technology are separate domains of human life. This received view is well represented in common understandings about technology that, for example, see it as the main "engine of progress," and that propagate beliefs in technological determinism, along with the myth that people have little or no control over technology writ large. Holding tight to the received view significantly impacts the imagined process of technological innovation. Like blinders on racehorses, it literally limits the vision of the track ahead. As a consequence, the range of possibilities for a technology-under-development is narrowed. This narrowed perspective sets up the conditions whereby technological failures are attributed (in a most unsatisfactory manner) to both unintended consequences and unforeseen circumstances. Continuing to bifurcate the technological from the cultural not only makes probable consequences unthinkable, but also severely limits the imaginative space of innovation in the first place.

It is not currently common to pursue technological innovation for the purposes of cultural enhancement, as the search results I reported in the above index reveal; yet, even the most cursory review of the major innovations to emerge over the past two decades provides ample evidence that the significance of impact isn't tied simply to technological dimensions or economic payoff, but to the breadth of an innovation's social and cultural repercussions. The invention of novel devices, applications, and tools necessarily involve the manifestation of an array of human practices: new languages; new body-based habits; new modes of interactivity; new forms of sociality; new forms of agency; new ways of knowing; new ways of living and dying. Recent advancements in computing, media forms, networked communication systems, material sciences, and biotechnology, have not simply rearranged the technological infrastructure of human life, they have reconfigured what it means to be human by reconfiguring the spaces of possibility for the formation of social relationships, as well as for the production of human life. As I stated earlier, the overarching argument of this book asserts that culture needs to be taken seriously in the practice of technological innovation. Moreover, I argue that those who engage in technological innovation are not simply involved in the creation of unique consumer goods, digital applications, gadgets, and gizmos, but also in the process of designing the technocultures of the future. This leads me to assert that the *real* business of technological innovation is the reproduction of technocultures over time.

I use the word "culture" throughout this project to indicate a socially shared symbolic system of signs and meanings. This project is deeply informed by a rich tradition of cultural studies that is strongly interdisciplinary in its approach to "culture as a whole way of life" (Williams, 1981). In its early formation, cultural studies bridged the analytical divide between sociology (as the study of practices) and literary theory (as the study of expressive forms). As it developed into a robust scholarly field, cultural studies encompassed insights, key concepts, and methods from anthropology, art history, media studies, and political economy.[13] It is by now, 2009, a mature tradition in the humanities. This book seeks to extend the questions, methods, and analytics of cultural studies to those disciplines and domains of human practice that are centrally engaged in technological innovation. I consider this a meeting that is long overdue. Following the lead of Slack and Wise (2002; 2005), I try to avoid setting the terms "technology" and "culture" in opposition in favor of developing a concept that formulates technology and culture as a specific unity; the term for this unity is "technoculture." In this project I address one aspect of the dynamic formation of contemporary technoculture that involves specific groups of people who engage in particular practices for the purposes of creating technological innovation. These groups of people include the many collaborators I have worked with on the design of innovative digital experiences, as well as those designers and technologists who created the inspiration and prior art for these innovations. My point is to illuminate the details of situations when matters of culture were overtly discussed in the negotiations among design participants, and resulted in the manifestation of something called an "innovation."

Bruce Sterling, the author and public intellectual who, in his book *Shaping Things* (2005), turns his well-honed imagination for science fiction to the project of unpacking the contours of contemporary technoculture, provides another vector of inspiration for this project when he speculates about the changing relationship between people and objects.[14] In his case, the privileged object of theoretical fascination is the "gizmo," an explicitly designed object-form that manifests the fecundity of digital information. Living in a gizmo technoculture requires significant investments of time and attention. "What impact," he asks, "does this have on us?" He describes the cognitive conundrum of living in a gizmo epoch: "It may dawn on you that you are surrounded by a manufactured environment. You may further come to understand that you are not living in a centrally planned society, where class distinctions and rationing declare who has access to the hardware. Instead, you are living in a gaudy, market-driven society whose material culture is highly unstable and radically contingent. You're surrounded by gadgets. Who can tell you how to think about gadgets, what to say about them—what they mean, how that feels?" (29). From Sterling's vantage point, the opportunity costs of attending to the information-fecundity of gizmos are too great, and more importantly, not sustainable over time. In an effort to elaborate what is needed to harness these excesses, Sterling fixes his vision on one of the key elements of technoculture: the role of design and designers in creating the infrastructure of sustainability. To elaborate how technoculture is reproduced in the development of technological innovation, I (like Sterling) focus my attention on designers and designing practices. Designers work the scene of technological emergence: they hack the present to create the conditions of the future.[15] Throughout this book, I discuss various design projects for which the designers explicitly considered issues of culture throughout their designing processes.

The process of technocultural innovation is the stage for the performance of two critical practices: 1) the exercise of the *technological imagination*; and 2) the work of *cultural reproduction*. In order to elaborate these practices, let me begin with an assertion: the wellspring of technological innovation is the exercise of the technological imagination.[16] This is a mindset that enables people to think with technology, to transform what is known into what is possible. This imagination is performative: it improvises within constraints to create something new. It is through the exercise of their technological imaginations that people engage the materiality of the world, creating the conditions for future world-making. In the active engagement between human beings and technological elements, culture too is reworked through the development of new narratives, new myths, new rituals, new modes of expression, and new knowledges that make the innovations meaningful. When people participate in the activities of producing "innovation," their technological imaginations are engaged in a complex process of meaning-making whereby both technology and culture are created anew. What gets reproduced is a particular (and historically specific) form of technoculture.

I examine how the exercise of the technological imagination reproduces cultural understandings at every turn. For this reason, I assert that cultivating and shaping the technological imagination is a cultural imperative of the highest order; yet, as the opening index statements attest, there are few places in the world where one can learn how to engage in practices of technological development that consider the cultural aspects of an intended innovation *from the onset*. Based on an analysis of how imagination unfolds throughout the designing process, I speculate about what is required to educate and inspire imaginations that are as ingenious in creating new democratic cultural possibilities as they are in creating new kinds of technologies and digital media. I seek nothing less than the transformation of current educational programs and the development of new learning strategies adequate to the task of inspiring culturally attuned technological imaginations.

The education of the technological imagination is not just the business of engineers and computer scientists; on the contrary, it is the responsibility of educators across the curriculum. In making this argument, I address the interests of distinct groups of readers: I hope to inspire my colleagues in the humanities to engage with digital technologies, both for the purpose of developing new insights about contemporary technoculture, and for the purpose of imagining new possibilities for collaborative multidisciplinary projects of technocultural innovation. For my colleagues who identify themselves as technologists—computer scientists, engineers, interactive media researchers, digital artists—I hope to illuminate how the theoretical frameworks and analytical methods of the humanities can serve as resources for the creation of socially effective and engaging technocultural projects. For all my readers, I seek to clarify a set of understandings about the nature of technology, the practices of technology design, and the logics of technoculture more broadly. One objective for this project is to encourage the creation of productive collaborations among humanists, artists, and technologists, through which each can appreciate the particular contribution of the others in the efforts of designing culture. To do so requires the creation of a set of shared understandings about the nature of technology, the logics of technological innovation, the dynamics of cultural reproduction, and the notion of technoculture itself.

Ten Lessons about Technoculture Innovation

These lessons summarize key insights that emerged during the process of collaboratively designing new technologies—the efforts that I discuss in each chapter of this book. Comprising key concepts and assertions, these lessons are intended to serve as the foundation for a culturally attuned technological imagination.

Lesson #1: Innovations Are Historically Constituted

What counts as an innovation is historically relative because they are constituted within particular technocultural formations. These formations emerge at certain historical moments in response to a wide range of influences—economic, political, and institutional—through interactions among people, and between people and the matter of the world. Cultural formations are dynamic phenomena; they are neither preordained nor randomly assembled. They are structured in a particular way, with an internal organization that is, in turn, integrated into a broader social order. This broader social order is always historically constituted; therefore technoculture must be understood as a historically specific formation: it is contingent on particular historical actions and forces, but not necessarily determined by them.[17] Innovations coalesce through specific practices of cultural reproduction—the processes whereby culture is renewed, reenacted, and regenerated.[18]

Lesson #2: Innovations Are Not Objects

Innovations are not really things, but are better understood as assemblages of practices, materialities, and affordances. The assemblage is made up of diverse elements each of which contributes something to the overall meaning of the innovation. Some of the elements that contribute are recognizable as material objects, such as physical artifacts, tools, and hardware devices—things common-sensically referred to as "technologies." Other elements include infrastructures, which may be material, such as highways and power lines, or intangible and immaterial, such as codes or technical standards.[19] Equally significant are the social elements that contribute to the overall meaning of an innovation, including the social practices through which technologies take shape, the rituals and habits engendered by innovative devices, and the social structures that congeal through the use of machines, the consumption of products, the imposition of laws, and the enactment of policies.[20] This leads scholars in the social studies of science and technology to assert that every technology is, at its most fundamental, a socio-technical construction.[21] Humanists extend this analysis by noting that every technology also involves the expression of cultural understandings in the form of narratives, myths, values, and truth claims. Instead of seeing innovations as bounded objects, this lesson argues that they are better understood as hybrid socio-technical-cultural assemblages.[22]

Lesson #3: Innovation Is an Articulatory and Performative Process

The creation of new technologies requires the involvement of many people who contribute distinct forms of labor: intellectual; artistic; managerial; representational; communicative; physical; emotional; and funereal (the disposal or dismantling of the technology at its end-of-life). Their efforts and labor must be integrated: tasks require coordination; communication must be facilitated; resources must be acquired, maintained, allocated, and dispersed; end users must be identified, recruited, and trained. All these functions—coordination, facilitation, acquisition, maintenance, allocation, recruitment, and dispersion—are articulatory practices: they are the processes whereby the activities of individuals are organized as part of a collective effort identified as "innovation."[23]

At a fundamental level, the process of innovation involves a wide range of expressive practices whereby meanings are created for the technology-under-development.[24] It's not just the case that technological innovation involves the creation of new meanings, but that an innovation inevitably replicates previous meanings at the same time that it makes possible the expression of new meanings. Communication scholar Klaus Krippendorf (1995: 156) describes the fundamental paradox of the designing process as an oscillation between "the aim of making something new and different from what was there before, and the desire to have it make sense, to be recognizable and understandable."[25] As he rightly points out, innovation cannot be so novel that it makes no sense at all. To be comprehended, an innovation must draw on understandings that are already in circulation within the particular technocultures of users, consumers, and participants; at the same time it must perform novelty through the creation of new possibilities, expressed in the language, desires, dreams, and phantasms of needs. The term "articulation" is useful here in part because of its double meaning: articulation is both a process (of meaning-making) and a production. As a process of meaning construction, articulation describes the practice of forging associations among signifying elements.[26] The meaning of an element is established in part through its semiotic relationship to other elements of an ensemble. The articulations among elements produce a formation. The formation, in this case, is an innovation. In this sense, innovation is performed through acts of articulation.

Lesson #4: Innovation Manifests the Dual Logic
of Technological Reproduction

There is a doubled logic at the heart of all technological innovation: technologies not only replicate previous elements—for example, codes, standards, forms of knowledge, and conventions—they also bring new elements into existence through the development of new materials, the creation of new functionalities, or the novel combination of prior components. In this sense, the process of technological innovation is reproductive: every technology replicates previous possibilities and makes new ones manifest. Reproduction, as anthropologist Marilyn Strathern (1992) reminds us, involves two processes: 1) of *replication*, when original (parental) material is duplicated; and 2) of *expression*, when the combination of original material takes a shape within a new context.[27] This "turn to reproduction" reminds us that formations do not get set in place once, and only once, but that the articulations among elements must be reproduced over time and over place.[28] This is how technologies can logically manifest multiple and contradictory effects. To embrace this understanding is to forgo the metaphysical debates that posit technology as either fully autonomous and completely determining in its effects, or a mere tool in the hands of a human operator. Once the binary either-or proposition is established as the frame for discussion, all further attempts at complex thinking about the nature of technology bog down in an effort to establish a singular essence of technology.[29] A culturally attuned technological imagination not only grasps the doubled-nature of technology—as determining and determined, as both autonomous of, and subservient to, human goals— but also holds this contradiction throughout the process of technology development.

Lesson #5: Designing Is an Important Process of Cultural Reproduction

Although there are many people who contribute to the production of an innovation, there are particular participants who are designated as creative agents, namely designers and engineers. Designing involves a full range of expressive practices: story telling, sketching, sculpting, image making, storyboarding, semantic mapping, composing, ventriloquizing, and word-smithing (among others).[30] In engaging in these practices, designers manifest creativity. Creativity is a cultural construct: what counts as creativity or novelty varies from culture to culture, and in this sense, culture is the generative mainspring of creativity.[31] Designers serve as cultural mediators by translating among languages, materials, and people, to produce— among other things—taste, meaning, desire, and coherence (Bourdieu, 1984). Through the practices of designing, cultural beliefs are materially reproduced, identities are established, and social relations are codified.[32] Culture is both a resource for, and an outcome of, the designing process.

Lesson #6: Designing Is as Much About Social Negotiation as It Is About Creativity

The process of designing involves the creation of visual representations, narratives, fictions, prototypes, and speculative proposals for design solutions, which are used to facilitate communication among participants.[33] Sociologist Andrew Feenberg (1991; 1995) describes technological designs as "negotiated achievements."[34] He notes that the rationality of a particular design solution—the "rightness" of a design—is an outcome of social interactions; designing a solution is fundamentally a process of meaning-making and negotiation. Because designing involves human actors who represent distinct stakes in and influence over the designing process and its outcomes, designers perform valuable cultural work when they negotiate shared understandings and meanings among participants, who come from different disciplinary backgrounds, hold divergent assumptions and values, and have particular investments in the innovation process. By engaging in these social activities, designers participate in the work of technocultural reproduction.[35]

Lesson #7: Designing Is a Process Where the Matter
of the World Becomes Meaningful

Designers are instrumental in the process whereby the materiality of the world becomes meaningful both technologically and culturally.[36] Participants in the designing process are never merely passive receivers of pre-conceived meanings; they are better understood to be active co-producers of the meanings of technology-under-development. These meanings are mediated through the production of objects that can be material as well as digital, representational as well as gestural, and theoretical as well as physical. Engineering design researcher, Louis Bucciarelli (1994) describes design as the place where two worlds collide—the object-world and the world of interests of the design participants.[37] Objects too participate in the designing process by evoking knowledge, stimulating discussion, and manifesting the matter of the world. In engaging with objects, human participants create provisional understandings that are communicated in story form. Objects must be continually reproduced as meaningful entities and participants throughout the designing process. Through the co-creation of objects, a set of shared social understandings emerges about the designing process itself. The collaborative creation of objects is thus fundamental to the process of technological innovation, and to the exercise of the technological imagination.

Lesson #8: Technological Innovation Is Inherently Multidisciplinary

To effectively create innovative technologies, designers must actively seek to identify the multiple contexts within which technologies take shape and have effects (Slack, 1989). This involves a consideration of how all participants in a technocultural formation—the designers, the users, and the generations yet to be born—are implicated in the materialization and the dematerialization of the technology-under-development. The range of expertise required for successful innovation not only includes a deep understanding of technical principles and protocols, but also an incisive knowledge about the psychological, social, political, and institutional contexts that make the innovation meaningful, relevant, and effective. For this reason, technological innovation requires the formation of creative and productive relationships among humanists, artists, engineers, and technologists—each of whom has something necessary to contribute to, and learn from, the experience of collaborative multidisciplinary technology development. Where artists and humanists stand to gain insights about the process of technological reproduction, engineers and technologists are exposed to the systematic methods of interpretation and analysis.

Lesson #9: Technological Innovation Offers the Possibility
of Doing Things Differently

During the designing process, there are many moments when the meanings of a technology-under-development are under construction. Although these moments may be fleeting, each moment of reproduction offers an opportunity to change the way in which technologies are developed, deployed, implemented, and discarded; it also offers opportunities to do something that hasn't been done before, and to create something unique and untried. These are the possibilities that animate the technological imagination.

Before I turn to the tenth lesson (on page 25), let me discuss another aspect of technocultural innovation that focuses on the praxis of designing culture. While the first nine lessons focused on the theoretical and conceptual facets of technocultural innovation, the following section abstracts a set of techniques whereby these theoretical insights are enacted and practiced. This methodological approach blends insights from multiple design disciplines with critical techniques of cultural interpretation that are central to the humanities and interpretive sciences.

The Praxis of Designing Culture

To engage in the practices of creating innovation, designers must employ techniques for elucidating the meanings that cohere within a particular technocultural formation, because these elements will inevitably become part of any resulting assemblage. This is where humanistic methods of interpretation—known as hermeneutics—can be most productively employed in the service of technocultural innovation. Hermeneutics is a field of philosophy and linguistic theory that provides a systematic framework for interpreting meaning.[38] I assert, as do other design researchers, that hermeneutic methods offer useful and important techniques for the purpose of creating innovative technologies.[39]

I have had several opportunities to employ hermeneutic methods in the process of designing new technologies by participating in the projects described in this book. Based on these experiences, I have abstracted a list of key steps that constitute a framework I refer to as "hermeneutic reverse engineering."[40] This framework combines insights from interpretive theory with standard designing practices used by engineers, computer scientists, and creative tinkerers. Reverse engineering is a conventional approach to the design of a new technology. It includes a set of techniques for analyzing an existing technology to determine its constitutive parts and pieces and the interdependencies among functional components. By working backwards from the construction of a functioning technology, a designer gains useful information for the creation of a novel technological instance. In the application of hermeneutic reverse engineering, what is reverse-engineered are the elements that contribute to the meaning of a given technocultural formation.

The protocols of hermeneutic reverse engineering identify both a set of research practices and a design methodology. It includes a set of basic steps for the creation of a cultural analysis, undertaken as the first phase of any technological design project. As the anthropologist Clifford Geertz (1973) aptly noted, the apprehension of culture is a daunting project. What is needed, he argued, is a set of methods to cut the "project down to size." To this end, Geertz proposed the method of "thick description" as a procedure for discovering "the frames of meaning within which people live their lives."[41] Geertz (following Max Weber) defines culture as "webs of significance" (5). The practices of cultural analysis, following Geertz, involve the explication of these webs through the use of basic techniques of description, analysis, and elucidation. To describe something adequately requires the use of specialized vocabulary and knowledge of diverse cultural vernaculars.[42] The step of *analysis* can involve formal methods of linguistic and grammatical parsing, or the decoding of visual symbols or representations. This is the stage where the full range of methods of textual and literacy criticism come into play.[43] The step of *elucidation*—of interpretation—involves the creation of an account of the way in which meaning coheres through the association among various signifying elements. Just as the practices of reverse engineering focus on identifying constitutive components of a functioning technology or system, these steps identify the main elements of signification that invest a situation, object, or technocultural assemblage with meaning. The ultimate aim though is not to stop at this stage of interpretation, but to bring these interpretive insights forward into the practice of technological design and development. Signifying elements are essential resources for technological innovation. The systematic analysis of meaning-making is repeated throughout the subsequent stages, such as rapid prototyping, user testing, and in-situ assessment.

The methods of hermeneutic reverse engineering aren't radical in and of themselves; in fact, they resonate strongly with the aims of user-centered design, participatory design, and "thoughtful design" (Löwgren and Stolterman, 2004: 2)—approaches that I refer to as "design for culture."[44] This approach directs technological innovators to consider such non-technological factors as the social values held by various classes, genders, races, and ethnic communities, as well as the levels of literacy (technological, visual, and traditional) among intended users. To employ the perspective I outline here is not only to consider the role of users who contribute vital insights and directions to the project of technology development, but also to consider a range of other factors that impact the design of the technology-under-development. Where the initial steps—*description; analysis; interpretation*—focus on identifying the semiotics, semantics, or genres of technological objects, subsequent stages focus critical attention on the broader contexts within which an innovative technology will circulate. These broader contexts—what are referred to as the "social" and "cultural" contexts of a particular innovation—are not pre-existing situations or milieus. A context is, according to this perspective, an ensemble of elements. The assemblage that is a context is constituted through the connections or articulations among elements. The final step in this approach is one that is often omitted due to time constraints, intellectual fatigue, or forgetfulness. It is, however, a critically significant step for the purposes of imagining the long-range consequences of a proposed techno-cultural innovation. This is the step that directs designers' attention back to the project at hand: to *reflect* on and *critique* the overall effort in terms of initial objectives, designing process, and broader cultural implications.

The reflexive rehearsal of the designing efforts and outputs create the conditions for transformed understandings and transformative praxis.

My objective in describing this methodological framework is to assert the importance of the role of meaning in the creation of technocultural innovation. When applied to the project of creating technologies, the deployment of this methodological framework offers a set of techniques for 1) identifying the meanings and assumptions that already structure the scene of technological innovation, 2) isolating key signifying elements that influence the technology-under-development, and 3) providing a sense of the possibilities for rearticulating (or reassembling) different meanings for the technology-under-development. The process of technological innovation involves complex social negotiations through which meanings as well as the matter of the world are created, invoked, constituted, and made intelligible by design participants: it is a place where discourse and materiality meet, where the limits of each are constituted, tested, refined, expanded, and reified. As such, it is the place where the technological imagination is most fully engaged in the praxis of technocultural reproduction.

The Organization of This Transmediated Book

To elaborate the ways in which cultural considerations contribute to the design of new technologies, each of the first three chapters focuses on examples of the exercise of the technological imagination that resulted in novel interactive digital experiences. These examples allow me to illustrate specific instances of the use of methods of hermeneutic reverse engineering. The fourth chapter takes a slightly divergent approach: it is a consideration of the work involved in shifting paradigms for the purposes of educating and inspiring culturally attuned technological imaginations. Considered together, the chapters describe technological imaginations engaged in the creative process of designing culture. The contexts of innovation discussed in these chapters include an international political forum, the professional industrial research center, the science-technology museum, and the university. In the scope of this project, these places serve as privileged sites of technocultural reproduction. The theoretical resources invoked in these chapters employ a wide variety of scholarly disciplines, drawing on cultural theory, technoscience studies, engineering

The Iterative Steps of Hermeneutic Reverse Engineering

Observation and description: Often taken-for-granted, this step involves practices that constitute the elements of signification.

Analysis: The step of identifying the arrangement among signifying elements whereby a unity is produced.

Interpretation: The creation of a provisional account of how the elements signify. This step might involve the creation of semiotic analyses of product semantics of similar technologies, the aesthetic characteristics of a communicative genre, the application of a particular interpretive framework (for example feminist, Marxist, post-colonialist), or a functional analysis of a working system. This is an iterative step that continues by drawing more lines of significance.

Articulation: Identifies the relevant elements or contexts that contribute to the intelligibility of the technology-under-development. This involves determining how elements cohere as a unity and how elements are linked to one another.

Rearticulation: This begins the process of rearranging elements through which meaning is reconstituted when elements are combined in novel ways.

Prototype: This stage utilizes the full range of prototyping methods: paper, toy, digital, video, sketches, mime, gestures, and improvisation, to name a few. Prototyping is a physical technique of rearticulation. Prototypes manifest possibilities through the unique use of materials or invention of expressive modalities. Rapid prototyping creates alternative rearticulations quickly and plentifully. Prototyping is an embodied dialogue between people and materials.

Assessment: This stage includes the use of methods of evaluation to determine the effectiveness of a particular interim design effort.

Iteration: These steps are repeated until a social consensus is negotiated, or until a set of constraints imposes an end to the designing process.

Production: Sometimes the production and the designing processes are thoroughly merged. In other cases, the production of the design requires manufacturing capabilities beyond the resources of the initial designers. It is always the case, however, that production will necessarily initiate additional (iterative) designing efforts to accommodate the constraints of fabrication, duplication, distribution, consumption, packaging, and disposal.

Reflection: This step documents, and in some cases actually creates, the rationality of the designing process and outcomes.

Critique: This is an uncommon final step that turns a critical gaze back onto the designing process itself in order to ask questions about the consequences of the practices, outcomes, and long-range implications.

design research, feminist philosophy, information design, new media theory, museum studies, and educational theory. This book thus moves across institutional contexts, scholarly domains, historical references, temporal frameworks, and discursive registers. This is an apt manifestation of the technological imagination at work.

Chapter 1, "Gendering the Technological Imagination" illuminates the broader political purpose of the entire project of this book: not only to think with more complexity about the nature of the technological imagination, but also to explore how this imagination might influence the development of technologies that serve more democratic social objectives. This chapter unpacks the relationship between gender and the technological imagination by examining some of the myths that persist about women and technological innovation. I rely on insights provided by feminist epistemology to elaborate the nature of agency that unfolds during the process of developing technological applications. To illustrate how the methods of hermeneutic reverse engineering are deployed in practice, and to elaborate a reproductive theory of technology, I describe the development of an interactive multimedia documentary that was created for the NGO Forum held in China in 1995. (The NGO Forum was held in conjunction with the 4th U.N. World Conference on Women.) To create the documentary, we (the producers) began with an investigation of the meanings that were already in circulation about the relationship between women and digital technologies. Through our iterative designing practices we attempted to rearticulate different meanings for a set of technologies, casting them as tools for feminist cultural activism. The multimedia documentary, called *Women of the World Talk Back*, served as a particular type of boundary-object that enabled the creation of several cultural constructs, including a set of identities for the designers and the audience members, as well as a set of counter narratives about the implications of the hardware and software we employed. I describe how my account of the creation of a digital application for a specific historical event results in the renarrativization of a set of experiences, memories, and practices to reflect on how the meaning of the project was literally performed in different contexts for different audiences.

Chapter 2, "The Performance of Innovation" describes a set of practices whereby the future was imagined and performed within the institutional context of a professional research center. The focus of this chapter is an interactive museum exhibit called XFR: *Experiments in the Future of Reading* created by the group RED (Research in Experimental Documents), a research-design team that worked at Xerox Palo Alto Research Center (PARC) in the late 1990s. In offering a textual account of the unfolding of a project of technological innovation, I describe instances when hermeneutics were explicitly used in the designing process. To create the exhibit, RED transformed a host of nascent research efforts into a set of unique reading devices, speculating on how the experience of reading might change in the digital future. This resulted in new understandings about the nature of reading and authoring in a digital age. The ensuing experiments addressed the dynamic relationships among bodies, technologies, words, images, and the construction of meaning within the institutional context of the science-technology center. The reading devices are described as examples of evocative knowledge objects (EKOs), which are defined as objects comprising sedimented layers of signifying elements, ranging from the semiotic to the material. The knowledge evoked by the objects is manifested through the interaction between and among readers, content, signifying elements, and through material objects. The reach of these innovative technologies extends from the personal to the social; they were instrumental as props for the performance of identities (for the designers), and for the creation of meaning (for the visitors and other participants); moreover, these technologies served as speculative probes into the cultural realms of reading and authoring, revealing how the process of technocultural innovation both replicates and revises the foundation of meaning-making in the future. The new reading devices developed by RED took the form of new media genres, of new authoring environments, or new forms of the book. All of these experiments in the future of reading rested on recalibrating the context of technology development from exploring one set of possibilities —rationalized within a corporate research context—to considering another set that focused on the technocultural possibilities of innovative devices.

Chapter 3, "Public Interactives and the Design of Technological Literacies" begins by elaborating the broader institutional context of the XFR exhibit by discussing the work of the science-technology center in creating the conditions for the performance of technological innovation. By virtue of the way in which it organizes the presentation of technological knowledge and situates its audiences as the public subjects of science, the science-technology center may be considered a cultural technology in its own right.

Over the past century, the scope of the technocultural work of the museum has evolved from an early focus on the taxonomic collections of the natural world to more recent demonstrations and deployments of technological novelties. I offer a genealogical account of the development of interactive exhibits that considers the early influence of the founding of the Exploratorium in San Francisco, and the industry sponsored information exhibits created by Ray and Charles Eames in the 1960s. While neither of the Eameses ever worked directly for the Exploratorium, its founder, Frank Oppenheimer, shared a basic philosophy with them, which asserted the importance of using art to communicate scientific principles to the general public. Ray and Charles Eames brought this artistic sensibility to their work as the designers of several exhibits, most notably *Mathematica: A World of Numbers and Beyond*, created for IBM and installed in the California Museum of Science and Industry in 1961. This background illuminates some of the historical influences for the design of one of the specific XFR exhibits, *The Reading Wall*. Just as in the Eameses' *Mathematica* exhibit, XFR included the creation of a wall for the presentation of a complex cultural history of important knowledge-making practices. Further, just as with the Eameses' exhibit, writing the reading for *The Reading Wall* involved the development of specific techniques of information design and textual architecture. From a consideration of genre to the symbolic use of dynamic animation for text and images, the creation of this interactive experience engaged the technological imagination in the practices of digital meaning-making. The practices of authoring and designing were completely merged, producing a poetics of interactivity, shaped as much by the affordances of the new device as it was by the histories of reading and writing that served as the content for the digital application. As the author/designer of the interactive digital document, I explicitly considered the technological and reading literacies of the intended audience. I reflect on how these literacies were treated as a design resource. The point is to provide a specific example of the way in which innovations always draw on technocultural understandings and literacies, even as they reconfigure these in novel form. While the knowledge may be transformed in the process, the resulting innovation always reproduces technoculture in some form—as frameworks of understanding, as literacies, and as systems of value and meaning.

Chapter 4, "Designing Learning: The University as a Site of Technocultural Innovation" reflects on the paradigm shifts going on at the edges of formal educational institutions, which are using digital technologies creatively to transform learning within the university. These edge projects involve a range of innovations coming out of the digital humanities that take shape as new pedagogical protocols, curricular offerings, and genres of digital scholarship. As John Seely Brown (2005) famously asserts: "to transform the core, start at the edge."[45] Brown understands that these edge-projects hold great potential to transform the university into a twenty-first-century learning environment. The projects discussed in this chapter lead me to reflect on how the digital humanities contribute to technocultural innovation. I attempt to rearticulate the current interest in technological innovation prevalent at many large research universities to ongoing work in the digital humanities in order to outline how a truly interdisciplinary approach to innovation might seek not only the creation of new intellectual property but also to contribute meaningfully to the transformation of culture more broadly conceived.

This chapter argues that it is no longer tenable to cordon off the study of technology and innovation from the study of culture.[46] Every discipline within the contemporary university has been transformed through the widespread dissemination of new technologies. In some cases, technology is an object of study, as in the digital humanities, communication studies, and legal fields. For other disciplines, technologies have enabled the creation of entire new domains of scholarship and research, as in humanities computing, the natural sciences, engineering sciences, medical sciences, and cinema. In this sense, technology must be considered a post-disciplinary topic. It no longer properly belongs to the analytical and academic work of the special few (the engineers or the scientists) if indeed it ever did. Every discipline within the university has something meaningful to contribute to the understanding and creation of new technologies. With a slightly different flavor, we've been arguing this topic—in the name of "interdisciplinarity"—for more than twenty years. I remain steadfast in my belief that we must incubate research that fosters collaborations among participants from diverse disciplines, for the purposes of designing the technocultures of the future. This chapter includes a discussion of the role of disciplinary-identified collaborators in producing technological innovations and the ethical practices that should guide such multidisciplinary efforts. I conclude the chapter by reflecting on some of the more promising ideas and practices that have emerged in discussions about learning in a digital age such as the open education resource movement and the role of tinkering in knowledge production. I end by speculating about a new learning formation that would combine social networking applications and community make-spaces, designed to foster the cultivation of the technological imagination.

In the concluding chapter, "The Work of a Book in a Digital Age," I invite my readers to meditate on the print book as a technocultural form with specific communicative and expressive affordances: it is well suited to the project of theoretical elaboration, historical reflection, and detailed analysis; it can travel where its author cannot; its level of information compression and expansion is significant; and it enables the expression of ideas in ways very different from other media forms, such as PowerPoint presentations, websites, and DVDs. It is not, however, well suited to every scholarly task of a digital age. To illustrate the limits of what can be expressed in print, I describe the creation of a digital learning object whose design was inspired by a critical, close reading of a semantic mapping application. Describing the dynamic process of meaning making pushes the expressive capabilities of the static book form.

The object that is identified by the title of this book, *Designing Culture*, is only part of a project that from the beginning was conceptualized as a transmedia work of scholarship.[47] In designing the various vectors of this transmedia project, I tried to match the communicative affordances of diverse media with the rhetorical purpose of each element of the project. For this reason, the project includes additional materials that cannot be accessed in print form. For example, packaged with this book is a DVD of the *Women of the World Talk Back* multimedia documentary (discussed at length in chapter 1). Although it was first produced more than a decade ago, it has never circulated in any form, other than as part of presentations by individual members of the design team. In a reversal of roles, the print book becomes a dissemination channel for a digital artifact.

Other parts of the transmedia book, *Designing Culture*, are available on the website designingculture.net. The site is a portal to other works of digital scholarship created as part of the *Designing Culture* project. Although it includes archival video footage of the XFR exhibits, it should not be considered a simple resource site for the print publication. The website does work that the book cannot. For example, in the section that provides access to video clips of the XFR exhibits in action, an application called

"What would McLuhan Say?" provides simple commentaries on the XFR exhibits based on McLuhan's tetradic framework of analysis. The application also allows readers to annotate the cultural meanings of the exhibits. This application enacts one of the central claims of the cultural analysis of the XFR exhibit: that there are multiple meanings possible for any of the XFR interactives. In the print book, I elaborated one set of meanings; the video footage offers another set. To follow through on the practices of hermeneutic reverse engineering, the final gesture of analysis of the XFR exhibit is to turn a critical gaze back onto the individual interactions to ask (as McLuhan suggests), what are the longer-range technocultural implications of these innovations? The website provides a mechanism for opening up the process of critical reflection to the reader; neither myself nor McLuhan has the last word.

Other scholarly materials available on the website include animations of interactive wall books that I created for the original XFR Reading Walls, and for interactive wall exhibits built for museums in Mexico and Singapore. Another section of the website includes a series of interactive maps of technoculture, including an interactive application called "Learning to Love the Questions" that produces questions about the cultural implications of emerging technologies. I offer this application as an example of a learning object that learns through its use by other people. Another section provides links to short video primers that illustrate key concepts about designing culture and contemporary technoculture. In the concluding chapter, I describe the rationale for the use of particular formats for the dissemination of various parts of the *Designing Culture* project.

The materials of this transmedia book project include artifacts of several collaboratively produced multimedia projects I've been involved in as a designer or developer during the past decade. I include these projects not because they have enduring cultural value on their own—although some of them have been the focus of other people's research and analyses—but because they allow me to elaborate the many contexts that gave rise to the development and implementation of innovative technologies.[48] Because I was deeply involved in these collaborative projects, I am able to describe how theory and practice not only informed each other, but also how they diverged at critical junctures.[49] In creating accounts of these projects for the print book, I elaborate explicit moments when cultural theory guided the exercise of the technological imagination. I also recount those moments when theoretical possibilities were shut down—due to constraints imposed by time, ignorance, fatigue, or a lack of imagination. The production of the book project has been a necessary part of my designing practice, for which the final act is to review and reflect the theoretical insights accumulated through the designing process.

Most tellingly, it was through these experiences of making technologies that my sense of the horizon, and the importance of cultural theory, shifted and deepened. For me, the activities that give rise to the creation of new technologies also serve as the means by which new *theoretical* insights are crafted and manifested. The scope of my intellectual work as a humanist was refashioned through my collaborations with colleagues from other disciplines and other professions. As I learned more about the practices of engineering and information design by watching my collaborators, I also saw them work through cultural considerations and related theoretical questions. In the process of making things together, we engaged in sustained discussions about the meaning of what were making. Through those discussions a shared set of understandings emerged, requiring everyone to learn new concepts and new vocabulary. Those shared understandings serve as the foundation for an approach to technological innovation that takes culture seriously, both for the purposes of creating new technologies and new cultural possibilities. Although the activities I refer to throughout the book were personally transformative, I actually don't discuss this level of effects, rather I deploy the biographical as a resource for the formulation of a set of insights about the praxis of designing technocultures of the future. The post-hoc accounts created for this book enabled another set of understandings to emerge about the nature of technology development that were related to, but not the same as, those that held sway during the designing activities. The chapters oscillate between recollections from long-ago moments of technological practice, and insights created through the acts of remembering.

The blind spots of this book are many no doubt. For example, it does not discuss the rise of innovation as a historically specific cultural logic; it does not consider the organization of a particular industry of design; it does not examine the economic aspects of different kinds of technological innovation. What it does do is describe the nature of the technological imagination as it manifested in specific instances of technocultural innovation, which include rituals of communication, new technologies, new media genres, and new pedagogical practices. It seeks to show how innovation must be understood as a complex set of activities, through which individuals create technologies and social relations: in collaboration with others; with the material world; with old technologies; and with phantasms of the future. Perhaps this is why there is so much contemporary interest in innovation and technology development by governments, professional innovators, and amateur do-it-yourselfers: we understand that this is, fundamentally, the process whereby our worlds and our selves are created. Technological innovation creates the conditions of possibility for the unfolding process of becoming human.

This leads me to a final lesson about Technocultural Innovation:

Lesson #10: Failure Is Productive

What I do not elaborate in great detail in this book is the instructive role of failure in these accounts of the process of designing culture. As one might imagine, failure happened often, in many ways, and in many modes. Sometimes the failure was personally embarrassing: as when I failed to correct a racist implication of one of the stories in the XFR exhibit. In other cases the failures were deeply unsettling: as when our entire research group was laid off from Xerox PARC. But over time, encountering failure in its many guises actually became part of every design process. Failure happens more frequently and decidedly than success. I regard this insight from the vantage point of someone who still believes that everyday culture is a zone of struggle and contestation, where failure is but one name for the texture of that struggle. This is to say, while it will never be pleasant, failure is productive. It is a rich resource for the performance of creativity, the design of innovation, and the reproduction of technoculture, and it stands as one of the abiding lessons of designing culture.

one

Gendering the Technological Imagination

In 2005 when Lawrence Summers, who was then president of Harvard University, hypothesized that women's lack of "intrinsic aptitude" was a plausible explanation for the imbalance in the numbers of men and women in high-level positions in science and mathematics professions, he demonstrated not only a peculiar disregard for the sensibilities of his audience (he was speaking at an invitation only conference on women and minorities in the science and engineering workforces), but also a rather simple-minded analysis of a complex social, economic, and technocultural situation.[1] While Summers asserted at the beginning of his speech that he was going to posit three possible hypotheses for the imbalance, by the end of his presentation it was clear that he favored two explanations: that women don't aspire to high-powered jobs (such as those in science and engineering); and that they lack intrinsic aptitude to do these jobs. In short, he put the blame on women for their lack of participation within these professions. In contrast, feminist researchers collectively demonstrate that such a seemingly simple question as why the profession of engineering remains male-dominated in the United States is actually much more complicated to parse, let alone answer.

When focusing on the issue of head count, it is important to tease out matters of history, opportunity, and preference from matters of discrimination and biological sex differences.[2] Well before we agree that lack of "intrinsic aptitude" is a reasonable cause, we might want to consider the contribution of other factors, including social factors, such as

- the demographic distribution of faculty who teach in engineering programs (Hall and Sandler, 1982);
- the biological reproductive practices of women and men at different ages (Landau, 1991);
- the differing opportunities and life responsibilities taken on by men and women with professional engineering credentials (Rosenfeld, 1984);
- the availability of mentors and female-friendly guides (Rosser, 1990);
- gendered socialization patterns (Cockburn, 1985).

Add to these a variety of institutional factors, such as

- the financial remuneration of engineering faculty at all levels (Fogg, 2000);
- the classroom experiences of female students within engineering programs (Hall and Sandler, 1982);
- the institutional practices and policies that guide professional development in academic programs in engineering and sciences (Matyas and Dix, 1992).

Further, add in several technocultural factors, such as

- the historical creation of the professional engineer as a heroic man (Marvin, 1988);
- mass media representations of women and men in relation to technology (Balsamo, 2000a);
- the gendered narratives that circulate in engineering, science, and mathematics textbooks (Rosser, 1990).

To expand on one line of analysis, a feminist investigator might begin by interrogating the question itself: What is the timeframe of this question? How many women were eligible to be hired as professional scientists and engineers that year or in the immediately preceding years? How long have these professional options been available to them? How do women's aspirations, tastes, and preferences for particular careers manifest as, and within, actual employment situations? For example, during the late 1990s (the years preceding Summers's frame of reference), the growth of women-owned companies increased significantly: according to one source, the number of women-owned firms in the United States increased at twice the rate of all firms (14 versus 7 percent) in the six-year period of 1998–2003.[3] This provides a slightly different context for the interpretation of the numbers of women in engineering positions. When we think about the expanding range of choices women now have for employment and possible career paths, the numbers may say more about the desirability (or lack thereof) of engineering jobs compared to others. Feminist research into these questions rests on the assumption that some women want to pursue careers in these professions, while others—even those with the appropriate academic credentials—don't. Research in this direction would investigate how women's choices are realized, thwarted, or transformed through the process of professional employment. My point is that even as Summers claimed that his comments were intended to be provocative, by asserting that "you have to be careful in attributing everything to socialization," he failed to demonstrate a nuanced understanding, either of the question or the possible contributing conditions. In lieu of presenting a more complex account that correctly would have challenged the single-cause analysis, which attributes the imbalance solely to differential socialization patterns, he retreated to a more polemical explanation, locating the cause in women's innate inadequacies.

To be fair to Summers, the persistent gender imbalance, in terms of raw numbers, remains an exceedingly difficult phenomenon to understand, let alone to change. Many academic administrators across the United States have been proactive in seeking strategies to enroll more women in science, technology, engineering, and mathematics (STEM) programs. The National Science Foundation (NSF) initiated its first programs to encourage the participation of women in STEM research in 1991; by the time of Summers's remarks (2005), it is reasonable to expect that these program investments would have yielded increases in the percentages of women employed in engineering and science professions.[4] During the same time, deans and educators were wringing their hands trying to figure out how to get more women, as well as people from racial and ethic minorities, enrolled in STEM programs, and industries were spending considerable effort to attract women as customers, audiences, consumers, and clients of technological goods and services. During the 1990s, several technology makers and retailers shifted considerable marketing resources to focus on the female customer. The electronics industry giant Samsung figured out that the female consumer controls more than fifty percent of domestic electronics purchases. Other players jumped in to address this buying power: Best Buy formulated the "Jill Initiative" to enable the transformation of the working suburban mom into a big-time electronics buyer. The computer company Dell responded by offering device jackets in different colors.[5] Several of the rollicking start-up companies of the 1990s focused their business plans on women as the target consumer for new technological goods and services; two of the more noteworthy included Purple Moon—led by Brenda Laurel—a company that built games for girls and was eventually acquired by Mattel, Inc.; and Her Interactive, Inc., an interactive entertainment company targeting girls of all ages.[6] As efforts designed to address the gender imbalance in technology activities, almost all of these focus attention on the absent, under-consuming, under-producing, abstract female subject. The explanations for her absence vary: some continue to argue that, due to biological factors, women are ill-suited to the demands of technological professions; others assert that it's a consequence of poor socialization (mostly on the part of girls and women; sometimes they remember also to pay attention to the behavior of boys and men). Some posit that technologies don't have enough style. For the most part, though, the discussion fixates on the simple count of female bodies: if we can just get more women into contact with technology, the argument goes, all sorts of good things will happen.

Profit motive aside, the most difficult thing to note about these approaches is that they are not entirely misguided in their intended objectives. It would be interesting—and fair, in a democratic sense—to have more girls and women involved in technology use, development, and research. But their mere presence is not necessarily going to transform the technologies they experience: there is no guarantee that women will do things differently in their engagement with technologies, as consumers, players, or designers. Rather, this belief betrays a biological essentialism that contradicts the accumulated insight of twenty-five years of feminist theory, that gender is a social and cultural enactment. Moreover, this approach, when it is invoked as a way of transforming technology to be more empowering or democratic, ignores the fact that technologies are not mere tools of human agents. As I suggested in the introduction, technologies are not merely objects: they are best understood as assemblages of people, materialities, practices, and possibilities. To transform them requires the employment of a framework that can identify the complex interactions among all these elements. For feminist teachers and scholars, one of the most vexing questions concerns the appropriate posture to assume on the topic of technoculture writ large: how can we support democratic efforts to increase the participation of women, and other underrepresented agents, in the process of technological development, but at the same time avoid a naïve belief in biological, racial, or sexual essentialism?

The Technological Imagination: A Gendered Makeover

As a way to begin to address this question, I turn to a consideration of the technological imagination. As I described in the introduction, this is a mindset and a creative practice of those who analyze, design, and develop technologies. It is an expressive capacity to use what is at hand to create something else. This is a quality of mind that grasps the doubled-nature of technology: as determining and determined, as both autonomous and subservient to human goals. It understands the consequence of technocultural productions and creations from multiple perspectives. It enables a person to understand the broader set of forces that shape the development of new technologies and take account of how these forces might be modified or transformed. More critically, it enables a person to see how emerging technologies get won over to particular ideologies and systems of value, when they could be defined otherwise. Developing this imagination is a necessary step in shifting our collective world-view such that we can evaluate more clearly the path we're on and, more importantly, act ethically in developing the foundation of future technocultures.

As I have argued elsewhere (Balsamo, 2000a), feminists need reliable maps and innovative tools to navigate the technocultural terrain. It is especially important that these maps and tools remain attendant to the dual aims of feminist technoscience studies: to be analytically critical of the social and political consequences of the deployment of scientific knowledge, along with the technological logics and practices that emerge within scientific and technological institutions; and to be steadfastly supportive of, and encouraging to, the women who choose to pursue careers in these fields. The maps we create must be able to guide travelers through rapidly changing landscapes, identify rocky roads and smoother trails, and provide pointers toward destination sites of inspiration. More importantly, we need to provide women guidance in how to do things differently within this landscape. While I am keenly aware that this terrain is uneven and difficult for even the savviest traveler, let alone for those who have been actively discouraged and inadequately trained to use tools and methods, I am also firmly convinced that this territory is exactly where feminists need to venture. I invoke the metaphor of colonizing a terrain consciously and with more than a bit of irony. This territory is far from virgin land; it is, and has always been, populated by geniuses, hero-inventors, renegade hackers, and libertarian technologists. The assumed gender identity of these native inhabitants is male. Feminists know that women too have lived within this territory as geniuses, inventors, hackers, and technologists, but that they have often been invisible as members of the indigenous population. When surveying this territory, most people simply don't see the women who have been there, and are still there, creating significant inventions and innovations.

The first step in gendering the technological imagination is taken in recognizing the persistence of a dominant myth of gender and technology. This myth assigns different roles and values to men's and women's engagement with technology: men are traditionally identified as the idealized and most important agents of technological development, while women are cast as either unfit, uninterested, or incapable. In broad terms, it has been the class of white men who have enjoyed the benefits of formal institutional recognition as agents of the technological imagination. As Autumn Stanley has amply documented, women of all races and ethnicities have been systematically and overtly written out of the historical record of technology development since the mythical beginning.[7]

In an interesting twist of logic, white men who are heralded as hero technologists are subtly degendered: the product of their imaginations is rarely considered to be the expression of a gendered, racialized, and class-based subjectivity or body. Gender, as many feminists have documented, has historically been an attribute of women's work, subjectivity, and bodies.[8] One of the consequences of the degendering of men is that the technological imagination is considered to be without gender. This, of course, is not the case. Women do not bring gender to the technological imagination. Moreover, technology is not a new interest of women: they have always been involved in technocultural innovation, even when institutionally and legally prohibited from being recognized as such.[9] The technological imagination has always been gendered, which is not to say that gender has always been recognized or fully explored as a source of imaginative inspiration.[10]

The next step in gendering the technological imagination is to focus on how things are done differently with technologies, especially as these involve relations with other human beings. The process of doing things differently may be the work of women, but not the expression of essential feminine insight; it may seek different horizons, but not necessarily better ones; it may manifest different values, but not different outcomes. The gendered transformation of the technological imagination is not solely a matter of theory, but a matter of praxis. As much as we try, we will never be able to know in advance how this imagination will be changed by the participation of women (or anyone else, for that matter); its transformation will be evident in what gets enacted.

This is why I am so interested in the notion of designing in its verb form. Designing is a key process of technocultural innovation. It names the practices through which the technological imagination manifests most clearly in the negotiations among people who share an explicit objective of creating new technologies. To say that a given design is a consequence of social negotiations does not mean that technical principles or the material world are irrelevant. The matter of the world too is materialized through the practices of designing. As feminist philosopher and physicist Karen Barad (2003) asserts, "matter does matter." This is not only because the basic building blocks of any technology—what we casually refer to as raw materials—have properties that are non-negotiable, for example they transform at certain temperatures or show stress under certain conditions. Matter matters because the world is always already a plentitude. For any given technology, agency is manifested unevenly by the people who create the device, program it, engineer it, manufacture it, buy it, use it, abuse it, and eventually dispose of it. But agency—defined pragmatically as the ability to affect the technological outcome—is not an exclusive privilege of human beings. In the process of designing, the matter of the world also manifests agency.

While Barad's focus is not specifically on the site of designing, I borrow insights from her work to describe the nature of agency that constitutes designing practice. Before I turn to the implications of her thinking for a consideration of designing practice, let me outline some of her key theoretical moves. Drawing on an epistemology developed by physicist Niels Bohr, Barad elaborates a framework for understanding the nature of agency, materiality, and posthuman performativity that she calls "agential realism." This framework resists the traditional realist ontology that posits an essential distinction between subjects and objects (the material world). Her approach, in contrast to traditional realist ontology, argues that neither subjects nor materiality preexist the interactions that constitute them. Barad (1998: 96) coins the term "intra-action" to "signify the inseparability of 'objects' and 'agencies of observation.'" All distinctions, including those of human, non-human, matter, and materiality are constituted through specific intra-actions. There is no prior distinction between the object that is observed to "be an object" and the activity of observing: intra-actions are primary phenomena. According to Barad, it is through intra-acting that agency manifests, not as property bestowed upon subjects or inherent in their nature, but rather agency materializes through intra-actions that constitute boundaries, demarcations, and distinctions among elements of phenomena. Intra-actions are iterative; they build on one another. She argues (2003: 815) that "it is through specific agenic intra-actions that . . . particular embodied concepts become meaningful," and further that "the material and the discursive are mutually implicated in the dynamics of intra-activity" (822), and "outside of particular agenic intra-actions, 'words,' and 'things' are indeterminate" (820). It is through specific agenic intra-actions that the distinction between words and matter is constituted and, presumably, continually reproduced through subsequent intra-actions. At base, she asserts, "matter is always already an ongoing historicity," and "meaning is . . . an ongoing performance of the world in its differential intelligibility" (821), but she also insists more than once that "no priority is given to either materiality or discursivity" (825). Matter matters because it "plays an active role in its iterative materialization" (826). It is not the passive natural world that is brought into being through cultural practices. In this, Barad firmly refutes the nature/culture dualism that would posit the prior existence of one or the other: both nature and culture are constituted through agenic intra-actions. She suggests that technologies materialize through the "intra-actions of a multitude of practices."[11]

Inspired by Barad's work, I want to think again about the practices of designing. In her terms, designing is the name for one set of practices whereby the world is dynamically reconfigured by specific acts (what Barad calls "intra-actions") through which boundaries are constituted and enacted. A boundary is a distinction that sets one concept apart from another. Textually boundaries are represented by the / in the couplets, actors/world and materiality/discourse. Through intra-actions, boundaries are constituted that mark certain things as "human factors," other things as "elements of materiality," other things as "characteristics of the apparatus," and yet other things as "social influences." It is through intra-actions that important designations are established, those then serve as the foundation for more complex constructions. Devices and apparatuses, as Barad points out, always come to us as already sedimented layers of intra-actions, which means that they are already marked with an intended purpose, a set of meanings, and an already specified relationship to the material world. Although she deploys a different discourse, I consider Barad's insights to be compatible with the framework that I elaborated in the introductory chapter. Using her term, I understand "intra-actions" to constitute elements that are articulated with one another to form assemblages.

The practices of designing constitute a specific set of intra-actions that make the technologies intelligible. To push this a bit further, the practices of designing literally make the material world intelligible. Intra-actions are iterative: the boundaries, demarcations, and marks that constitute elements of basic phenomena are constantly in the process of reformulation. Understanding the iterative nature of intra-actions supports the fact that technologies do not get set in place once and only once, but that the arrangements among elements must be reproduced over time and place. Just as "matter does not exist outside of time, history, or culture" (Barad, 1998: 109), so too is this true for technologies: they are always in the process of materializing through intra-actions. More to the point of this chapter, every intra-action that constitutes a technology offers an opportunity to do things differently. Intra-actions may be strongly constrained by sedimented layers of previous intra-actions, but they are not strictly determined by those previous intra-actions. It is these moments of possibility that need to be explored and exploited for the purposes of designing technoculture differently.

Participants who engage in the set of practices and social negotiations that constitute the designing process constantly move between former understandings and new insights. Participants' presuppositions about their understanding of the design task, the material world, the influences of other participants, and indeed even of their own identities as designers, are continually revisited and revised in the process of continued interactions with other participants, creative tools, raw materials, and institutional forms—all in the aim of designing something new. Designers bring many presuppositions (the build-up of previous intra-actions) to the design situation, which manifest as historically and culturally specific assumptions and beliefs. Understanding that presuppositions are an inevitable element of the designing scene sets the stage for a methodical interrogation of these layers of knowing and belief. The aim is not necessarily to discard prior understandings, beliefs, meanings, interpretations, or attributions, but to understand how they are constituted and how they might be creatively reconfigured in the service of technological innovation. This also sets the stage for identifying other ways of knowing and new contexts that may contribute inspiration and imaginative resources to the designing process. This provides an opening for considering the creative role of gender in the exercise of the technological imagination, one that avoids falling into biologically essentialist claims that women will naturally design technologies differently than men.

By modeling and improvising in a social setting, participation in collaborative acts of designing new technologies enables people to learn both practices and habits of mind from other collaborators. Furthermore, collaborations that involve people with expertise in different domains provide a more diverse set of practices and frameworks to draw on in a creative endeavor. If indeed the genesis of creativity is the "escape from one range of assumptions to another"—as architectural-design theorists William Mitchell, Allen Inouye, and Marjory Blumenthal (2003) suggest—then the inclusion of people with different backgrounds and varied expertise on a collaborative design team is a critically important source of creative thinking. Diversity among design participants is generative, not because of some innate biological or ethnic quality, but because people embody different sets of assumptions. Sometimes these assumptions are shaped by background; sometimes they are shaped by domain expertise.[12] This argument supports the call not only for the creation of multidisciplinary design teams (that include artist-practitioners, humanists, along with technology experts such as computer scientists and engineers), but also for those diverse in culture, gender, ethnicity, and race. In this sense, designers manifest creativity, not only by mediating between culture writ large and the immediate social setting of the design team, but also by negotiating and apprehending the sets of assumptions held by individual collaborators.

Just as all good designing work includes the careful consideration of materials, conventions, technical codes, and audience expectations, so too it includes a consideration of the layers of meaning that are already invested in the technology-under-development. These layers of meaning include the beliefs and ways of knowing that designers already embody, and the meanings that circulate about particular types of technology, aesthetics, value, and affordances. To gender the technological imagination is to acknowledge that all participants bring gendered, racial, and class-based assumptions to the designing process. These assumptions contribute to the creation of meaning for a technology-under-development. Acknowledging different sets of assumptions enables designers to identify the many contexts within which technologies become meaningful, and then more fully assess how these various contexts might contribute or constrain the meaning (and the deployment, and success, and social value) of the technology-under-development. At a base level, this approach demonstrates how culture is not only an inevitable part of the designing process, but also an important, under-utilized creative resource in the process of technocultural innovation. It suggests ways that design participants can identify and understand the technocultural meanings that not only influence the technology-under-development, but also the participants themselves.[13] These insights, drawing on work in feminist epistemology, illuminate the nature of agency that manifests in the practices of designing new technologies.

Women Making Multimedia: Women of the World Talk Back
(written with Mary Hocks)

Informed by a shared background in feminist cultural studies, my colleague Mary Hocks and I conceptualized a multifaceted project of feminist technocultural activism that would explore the dynamics of gendering the technological imagination. During the mid-1990s, both Mary and I were working in academic programs that were equipped with rich technological resources.[14] We discussed several ideas for using those resources specifically in the interest of educating and engaging female students in the use of new digital technologies. We both held an explicit pedagogical objective to involve our selves and our students in the design and critique of new media. Thus, we brought to this project a shared interest in the design and analysis of new media, as well as a sense of the pedagogical potential of these emerging media forms for the purpose of doing things differently with a set of new media-making tools.

An invitation to attend the 1995 NGO Forum held in conjunction with the United Nations Fourth World Conference on Women in Beijing, China provided the opportunity to put our ideas into practice.[15] We constituted a delegation of participants from Georgia Institute of Technology. The 1995 UN Conference brought together heads of state and government officials to debate and draft a *Platform For Action* that would reinforce the resolutions outlined during the 1985 Third World Conference on Women, held in Nairobi. The Beijing conference was organized to exert pressure on global governments to enact the objectives and policies adopted at the Nairobi conference. As members of an officially registered NGO delegation, we had lobbying privileges that enabled us to meet with members of the U.S. delegation at Beijing. We focused our lobbying efforts on two areas of critical concern outlined in the *Draft Platform for Action*: women and the media; and the education and training of women in science and technology.[16] We recognized that our participation in the Forum would present us with a rare opportunity to enter into discussions, on a global level, concerning the education of women in science and technology, as well as their training in mass media. Indeed, we had the opportunity to lobby several members of the official U.S. delegation directly, including Donna Shalala, Veronica Biggens, and Elizabeth Coleman.[17] We presented them with a position paper on the topic of "Education of Women in Science and Technology." We circulated a letter among the delegates that strongly urged them to support an expanded definition of the term "literacy" to include both scientific and technological literacy. Moreover, we encouraged them to support policy statements that outlined the importance of the media as a powerful socialization device, one that shapes the expectations and treatment of women worldwide.

In addition to our lobbying efforts, we created an interactive multimedia application called *Women of the World Talk Back*. We explicitly drew insights from feminist cultural theory to create the visual language and interactive poetics of the digital experience, and it was addressed to the international feminist audiences who would also be attending the NGO Forum. With it, we explored the possibilities of using what were then new digital technologies to facilitate cross-cultural dialogue. We drew inspiration from women's material culture, such that the symbols, colors, and textures—together with the design of the content and the structure of the video narratives—were imagined through different global perspectives. The application included videotaped statements, by international spokespersons, on the global situation of women; it also featured interviews with Forum and UN organizers, as well as with other activists from various global women's organizations such as Women in Development and OXFAM International.

The interactive multimedia piece was created using then state-of-the-art authoring programs (Macromedia Director), graphic design programs (Photoshop), and CD-ROM mastering programs. The first version ran on a desktop Apple Macintosh system. Originally, we conceived *Women of the World Talk Back* as a video-based CD-ROM interactive experience. In early 1995 the World Wide Web was still a relatively new medium, with limited bandwidth for the distribution of digital video. While we have since watched with interest the growth of feminist resources on the web, when we began the project there were few websites or CD-ROM titles that specifically addressed feminist concerns. Having said that, a couple of notable exceptions stand out: Christine Tamblyn's CD-ROM (1993), "She Loves It, She Loves It Not: Women and Technology," that explored a feminist's ambivalence about technology; Brenda Laurel's early work at Purple Moon that produced the first non-Barbie-based games for girls; and Lynn Hershman's video project called *Lorna*.[18] Although we did not conceptualize our project as a work of art, but as a matter of communicative praxis, we were inspired by a range of important art and technology experiments created by artists such as Viebeke Sorensen, Barbara Kruger, Judy Malloy, Laurie Anderson, and Trinh Min-Ha.[19]

The basic organizing framework for the multimedia piece started with the conception of its communicative aims: it was designed as a ritualized form of a digital communication where we would, in effect, issue an invocation that in turn would invite a response from other NGO participants.[20] The framework for the project drew on media theorist James Carey's elaboration of a ritual model of communication that proposes that communicative acts are directed toward the representation of shared beliefs across time and space.[21] In contrast to a telephony model that posits communication as the transmission or transportation of information from an active sender to a passive receiver, a ritual-based model of communication focuses on the solemn performance of community, communion, and connection through the acts of invocation and response. The interactive piece was designed as a call-and-response ritual. As the title implies, through the mediation of this interactive application, we issued an invitation to other NGO Forum participants to talk back to the global leaders featured in the video pieces. In the process of eliciting these responses, we hoped to engage in conversations with other Forum attendees about the most pressing issues facing women across the globe. In this way, the *Women of the World Talk Back* was intended to establish connections with other people within a well-defined social and political context. We aimed to create a communication experience that brought people together to discuss conference themes. By explicitly rejecting the sender-receiver model of communication, we sought to amplify the meaning of the personal computer, not simply as the technological platform for the presentation of our multimedia creation, but more importantly as a technocultural stage that enabled international dialogues.

The narratives that we crafted from video interviews put in circulation a set of insights about the global situation of women.[22] These narratives took shape as four short *Video Dialogues* that addressed the basic questions and topics of the UN conference: 1) What Do Women Want?; 2) Access to Education; 3) Economic Opportunities; 4) Empowerment. Running two to three minutes in duration, each *Video Dialogue* follows the genre conventions of a public service announcement, using short takes of close-up shots of people making emphatic statements (sound bites). For example, the *Video Dialogue* called "Access to Education" offers a concise narrative statement about the importance of the education of the girl-child across broad cultural contexts, ending with a call for a change in curriculum at all levels.[23] The videos were explicitly edited to include multiple voices and to represent differences in perspectives between developing and developed countries. For example, although several participants were based in New York (at the UN), we made spare use of US nationals. Efforts were made to include the insights of women situated in different national contexts. In the end, however, these videos included statements from seasoned international spokespeople. The tone of their language and choice of vocabulary reflect their shared experiences as participants in global political conversations.

The project was well received during the NGO Forum and afterwards. Not only did we actively engage in many conversations with the women from around the world, we were also able to video-record a dozen or so talk back statements. It was through these conversations that we gained insights about the global situation of women and technology. We met dozens of NGO participants through the mediation of this multimedia application. As such, it served as an evocative knowledge object that enabled us to talk with people about their specific objectives in participating in the Forum. We were especially interested in hearing about how women across the globe are using the media to serve their activist aims, enhancing the quality of life for women and their families. We talked informally with publishers about women's newsletters from Haiti, artists from Mexico, and television producers from India. We learned that women around the globe are keenly interested in using technology and media—everything from video to print—to educate themselves and their communities about important concerns ranging from political rights to basic health issues.

While there remains a striking global imbalance in the distribution and access to new communication technologies, such as fax machines, video players, computers, and network availability, there is also an increasing interest among women, from all parts of the world, in the use of new information technologies for grassroots organizing and educational efforts. For example, we met one woman from Tanzania who produces educational television programs for women. She wanted to know if we planned to distribute the application in video form so that she could run it on her television station. Other women with access to computer networks encouraged us to develop a website based on the project. Even though we discussed issues of distribution and access to the project quite extensively, both before and after the Forum, we didn't really know how we were going to distribute the application after we returned. The original project was event specific: it was designed to facilitate our conversations with other Forum participants. We imagined using it in our classes as a piece of feminist educational material that could enable us to explicate a theoretically informed feminist designing practice. But after our conversations with several women at the Forum, we began to think about how we might make the application available to other people. This raised questions about what audience we imagined for the project. The question of audience sent us back to consider the foundational purpose of the entire project, including its scope and design. The shift in our notion of audience led us to reconsider the visual rhetoric of the interface and the inclusion of additional materials. Thinking about new and broader audiences helped us define the kinds of feminist interventions possible in various forms of digital media.[24] In this way, our objectives were revised as the project was enacted. Where the initial intended audience was the people we would meet at the NGO Forum, we expanded our conception of audience to include scholars and teachers in Women's Studies, as well as new media producers interested in alternative design paradigms and the creation of activist media projects. After the conference, *Women of the World Talk Back* was redesigned as a multimedia documentary, a genre of new media that has as its primary purpose the archival recording of a series of historically specific experiences. Thus the project now includes the material we gathered while in China—in the form of a documentary video on the NGO Forum—and a module about the controversies and difficulties leading up to the Forum. The most recent version incorporates the talk back statements from people we interviewed at the Forum, the visual and audio material documenting the participation of members of the Georgia Tech delegation, and the white paper on the education of women in science and technology that we used as the basis for our lobbying efforts with members of the official U.S. delegation to the UN Conference.

In the intervening years, between the historical moment of the project's creation (1995) and the publication of this book (2011), which provides the occasion for reflection on the lessons learned, both Mary and I developed presentations (most often delivered separately) about the experience of attending the NGO Forum and of designing the *Women of the World Talk Back* multimedia documentary. My presentations often focused on elaborating how feminist cultural theory informed the design of the project. An early objective was to encourage gender studies students to imagine the social and political possibilities of new media and to inspire them to learn how to design and develop new media applications. I argued then, as I do now, that technology must be more fully integrated within women's studies curricula, as an object of theoretical analysis, as a topic of critical investigation, and as a platform for creative and political praxis. I also hoped to suggest to other multimedia developers, who have the privilege of access and creative skills, to imagine how their resources might be deployed in the service of creating culturally responsible media experiences.

When we began the project, I had just completed a work of feminist cultural criticism that explored the gendered implications of a range of biologically reproductive technologies (Balsamo, 1996). The *Women of the World Talk Back* project was an early attempt to investigate the cultural processes of digital and technological, rather than biological and corporeal, reproduction. As many feminist critics suggested, these technologies accumulate meanings that are often antithetical to feminist values and objectives. Our goal was to explore how these digital technologies could be used in the service of feminist political activism. Indeed, we began the designing process by investigating the meanings, circulating in the early 1990s, of the class of devices and applications broadly identified as information technologies. In reflecting now on the meaning of the application, I understand that it enabled us to explore the possibilities of rearticulating the meaning of a set of emerging technologies for the purposes of creating a work of feminist media activism. As I outlined in the Introduction, part of every designing process involves the rearticulation of a new meaning for the technology-under-development. Designing always requires the creation of an understanding of previous articulations—identifying the signifying elements that provide meaning for a known technology—in the service of creating something new. Rearticulation involves a recombinant logic where signifying elements are integrated to create new meanings. The practices of rearticulation make possibilities materialize, and in so doing the ensemble of meanings of a technology is inevitably reconfigured. Both Mary and I intentionally wanted to do things differently with the technologies to which we had access. We drew on feminist theory to help us imagine not only what to do differently in our designing process, but also how to do things differently. Reflecting on our design process, we might now describe our actions of rearticulation in Karen Barad's terms as "agenic intra-actions" (Barad, 2003). In this sense, practices of designing draw on and call forth situated knowledges—Donna Haraway's (1988) term for the inevitably partial knowledge of humans in interaction with the world and each other, that can contribute insight into, but never exhaust, the multiplicity of the material world. Haraway (1991: 187) explores the problem of "how to have *simultaneously* an account of radical historical contingency for all knowledge claims and knowing subjects, a critical practice for recognizing our own 'semiotic technologies' for making meanings, *and* a nononsense commitment to faithful accounts of a 'real' world, one that can be partially shared and friendly to earth-wide projects of finite freedom, adequate material abundance, modest meaning in suffering, and limited happiness." Sandra Harding's (1991: 138) notion of "strong objectivity" is important here as well, as when she argues that instead of renouncing the possibility of objectivity, feminists must be more rigorously objective in being able to account for how scientists' background beliefs, values, and assumptions influence their practice of science. The foundational philosophical project for all three feminist thinkers (Barad, Haraway, Harding) is similar: to create an account of technological practice that acknowledges both the contingency of knowledge and the matter of the real world without resorting either to a positivism that forecloses agency and transformation, or to a constructivism that implodes as relativism and ends up overprivileging language and culture. Understanding the epistemological structure of the practice of designing is another important step in gendering the technological imagination.

In designing the *Women of the World Talk Back* application with the intent of facilitating dialogue and exchange among people, but not as a vehicle for the circulation of a message from a sender to a passive receiver, we considered the communicative consequences of our designing practice. Based on an analysis of the meanings of information technologies that circulated at the time, we identified several key elements that we explicitly reconfigured in this project: 1) the use of an alternative model of communication as a framework for the information architecture of the application (as ritual instead of telephony); 2) the use of women's material culture as an aesthetic resource; 3) the circulation of educational instead of commercial narratives; and 4) the creation of participatory subject positions for users. For the most part, we believe we were successful in these more delimited efforts. But when we turned our attention to the use of the web as an infrastructure for the dissemination of digital information, we realized the limitations of our efforts to rearticulate the broader technocultural formation.

By the early spring of 1995, we began to get a sense of the emerging power of the web as a platform for global real-time communication. In the process of preparing to send seven people and $25,000 worth of equipment to China, we learned firsthand how important the web could be in facilitating international communication. For example, early that summer websites started updating travel information on a regular basis, which made the then-typical static text-based and image-based information sites more useful for time-sensitive activities. In early June 1995, the Feminist Majority website began posting daily updates about visa processing delays: here we learned where to apply for our visas such that they would be processed in a timely fashion.[25] As a consequence, we sent our delegates' passports to Houston, Texas, instead of Chicago, New York, or San Francisco for processing. Some of our Atlanta colleagues—including a couple of people who worked at the Carter Center—who weren't as well informed experienced significant delays in getting their visas approved. By the time we returned from China in September 1995, the web had exploded as a communication platform; where early in 1995 it was still an emerging media form, in the space of six months it had transformed into the dominant media form for the dissemination of digital information. As we considered our options for disseminating the application, we realized that it was too video-heavy for the technological infrastructure of the newly emerging World Wide Web. Server access, modem speed, and modes of connectivity would not allow us to circulate the amount of digital video included in the application. In short order, we found ourselves caught in between emerging technocultural moments: in the space of six months the day of the CD ROM had passed, and the web had emerged as the preferred mode of digital information circulation. Although we created an early web essay about the project, it never circulated in its full multimedia and interactive form— until its publication as part of this transmedia book project.

Assembling the Story, Disassembling the Project

These next paragraphs explore another dimension of the assemblage that is known as the *Women of the World Talk Back* project. Because the project, and indeed all the elements involved with it, is inherently multiple, the stories that can be told are many. Where the previous stories relied on realistic tropes, the one that follows is braced by theoretical work borrowed from technoscience studies.

The *Women of the World Talk Back* "project" was an extended series of moments that began in the late months of 1994 and extended until today; it involved a host of practices—communicative, graphic, transactional—whereby people, devices, objects, and events accumulated layers of meaning as they were assembled (articulated) as part of the interactive multimedia application called *Women of the World Talk Back*. Most of the elements in this assemblage were already constituted to have an identity: all the elements, including those that go by the proper names of Anne and Mary, were already ensembles of bodies, subject positions, capabilities, and code, among other things. The previous section unfolded the contours of one narrative about these elements. Although it didn't follow a strict chronology, it did suggest a factual account of the creation of a digital project, and the situations in which that digital application served as a boundary-object for the purposes of constituting a set of identities for a group of people. Lucy Suchman (2005: 379) calls these types of boundary-objects "affiliative objects" because they mediate relationships among people and things.[26] As an affiliative object, the *Women of the World Talk Back* application was an active participant in the creation of identities, bonds, dispositions, emotions, hopes, and frustrations. In this sense, the constitution of this affiliative object was, as Suchman trenchantly posits, a "strategic resource in the alignment of professional identities and organizational positionings" (379). In our case, the documentary qua affiliative object was implicated in the construction of identities for Anne and Mary as feminist media activists. These identities were forged through our articulatory practices, whereby we used new technologies to circulate feminist political insights. During the time of the NGO Forum, each of us belonged to multiple organizations—some formal, some ad hoc. In a theoretical sense, the documentary served as a resource to align these identities—as teachers within particular educational institutions, as feminists with specific political investments, and as participants in an international debate about the importance of educating women in science and technology.

If poststructuralist theory propagated the insight that we needed to decenter the subject and subjectivity as the locus of self-present rational knowledge, the companion move suggested by technoscience studies, especially actor-network theory, asserts that the object too must be radically decentered as the privileged locus of coherence in accounts of technology development and deployment. Thus it is important to remember in this set of accounts that the digital application was never a singular thing with set boundaries or well-defined edges. It was always, and still is, an unfolding set of possibilities, animated in the intra-actions that include human fingers striking keys, middleware reading machine code, machine code acting on lines of zeros and ones, materials conducting energy in the form of heat, and so on. The technological object in this sense is more accurately constituted as multiplicity, or as John Law contends, as "more than one, but less than many."[27] To destabilize the *Women of the World Talk Back* as a *project* is to assert that it was an enactment of a thousand encounters that don't naturally cohere except through one of our storytelling performances. It's not that the thousand encounters were wildly random and unconnected; they were, in a theoretical sense, best understood as intentional acts of boundary-making that served to manifest the project-ness of the *Women of the World Talk Back* efforts.

Even though I served as project manager for the effort, at no point was I an omniscient participant who knew completely what the project should be, could be, or would turn out to be. The notes I made during the time we spent collectively working to create the application now serve as traces of a process of thinking intentionally about design, travel, and feminist global activism. Like breadcrumbs laid down over a decade ago, they are useful now in the act of remembering those moments before, during, and after the days of the NGO Forum. These notes, however, capture neither the reality of the designing process, nor the lived experience of participating in the Forum. They are memory-triggers that help me recreate an account that is neither fiction nor history, or maybe both fiction and history. And like all narrative accounts, this one too is partial, purposeful, and thoroughly personal in voice and judgment.

Designing Feminist Futures: "The Time is Now for Us"

In preparation for our participation in the NGO Forum, I had the opportunity to interview Patsy Robertson, a senior media advisor for the United Nations who served as the chief spokeswoman for the fourth UN Conference. At one point I asked if there were interventions (outlined in the Draft Platform for Action) that should be put off until foundational work has been accomplished? I was referring specifically to U.S.-based concerns inserted into the platform that argued for increased access to technology and support for the education of women in science and technology. She replied quickly and forcefully: *"The time is now for us."*[28] Her words stuck with me in the intervening years, as I've had the occasion to reflect on the experiences involved in building the multimedia application and participating in the 1995 NGO Forum. One of the consequences is that I've tried to think differently about my own feminist interventions. More poetically, I wonder: *How NOW?*

What I've realized is that despite its Dr. Seussian semantics, the question, "How Now?" is more complex than it first appears. Invoking both the concepts of practice and time, this sound bite has sent me back to revisit foundational feminist work in an effort to unpack the compressed meaning of this small phrase. "How?" is a question that women have wrestled with since long before the term *feminist* came into vogue. "How?" is the basic question that guided thousands of female innovators, inventors, scientists, and philosophers. As feminist historians and technoscience critics understand quite well, the right to ask this question, and the right to explore its answers has been a privilege often denied to women. We also know it is a question that women live with every day, at every moment: How do I do this? How do I get there from here? How did this happen? In its best form, the question "How?" announces the fascination of an engaged mind; in its worst, it is the tragic lament of a knowing victim. In occupying both subject positions simultaneously, and a range of those between, women, throughout history, have demonstrated the many ways in which the question "How?" can be a matter of life and death.

Practice and theory seemed at one point antithetical concepts. In the late 1970s and early 1980s, feminists struggled to elucidate the logic that connected one to the other. Was theory elitist? Shouldn't practice serve as the true horizon of feminist efforts? Was there even such a thing as practice without theory? Showing the influence of these earlier feminist moments, my preoccupation with the question, "How Now?" again raises the issue of the relationship between theory and practice:[29] after theory and criticism, what next? Here, I'm not asking, what is the future of feminist theory and criticism; I'm asking how now do I proceed with my life, my scholarship, and my world-making? How then, for me, are theory and practice related? I believe that the purpose of theory is to inspire us to ask more incisive questions about the phenomena that terrify and fascinate us; the purpose of criticism is to illuminate the complexity of the phenomena in such a way that others are provoked to formulate their own theoretical under-standings, accounts, and questions. The horizon of this iterative ques-tioning and analysis is transformed practice. For me, the aim of feminist technocultural studies is to theorize and critically analyze the situation of gendered subjects—across cultures and across contexts—and to provide insights, if not exactly blueprints, for the transformation of those situations and contexts through intentional practice. We need maps and tools, not simply to theorize with, but also to guide us to act and transform the worlds within which we live.

We work, under the banner of feminism, for the improvement of wom-en's lives. Yet, one of the most provocative lessons I learned, through my participation in the 1995 NGO Forum and Fourth UN World Conference on Women, is that there is no global consensus on what it means to improve women's lives. Other than a wide-scale call to intervene against and cease the violence done to women in every national context, I found no singular feminist answer to the question, "How Now?"

Thus, a provisional response to my question, "How Now?" sends me deeper into the investigation of the dynamics of design. The horizon of this investigation is the illumination of a set of practices whereby the future, as a set of perpetual *nows*, will be realized. I'm interested in the process whereby the future is brought forth out of the present. I don't seek to predict the stories, artifacts, technologies, and power arrangements that emerge from the current moment to form the next current moment. The daily practice I engage in now focuses on the design of technocultural artifacts: my research investigates practices of meaning-making—how the meanings of new technologies are reproduced, structured, manipulated, hijacked, and sometimes contested. My intent is to participate consciously in the act of designing technoculture in ways that are ethically and socially responsible. This, too, is a consequence of gendering the technological imagination.

two

The Performance of Innovation

Do we make the future as we make history? If it is the case that "men make history, but not under conditions of their own making," as Marx so famously asserted, what are the conditions whereby the future is made? The future is always marked as something inherently polymorphous: it is either *The Future*, ominous and bright, somehow holding together as a coherent totality, or it is *futures* in the plural, where the term invokes the fecundity of contradictory possibilities that will unfold simultaneously and inevitably. In either case, the future is the term for the ever receding next that emerges from the now. Our fascination with the future is ancient, our devices for predicting it as varied as ourselves, yet it remains always just out of reach.

The Future begins in the imagination. In this sense, science fiction authors are celebrated architects of the future. Not only is the future a defining trope of the genre, but also such speculations form the archive of our desires about the future: where are those flying cars anyway?[1] Throughout this archive, the literary and technological imaginations fuse to visualize a future where—regardless of the particular bent of the projected social system (utopian or dystopian)—

technology is the only constant. Literary critics understand that the cultural work of science fiction, or "scientification" as Hugo Gernsback first named it in 1926, is as much about the narrativization of the anxieties and preoccupations of the present of the author as it is a speculation of things to come (Ross, 1991).[2] In this sense, every work of science fiction is a work of time-travel, in that it projects a future based on a present that reveals its cultural logic most fully when analyzed historically. Whether it takes shape as the scientific novels of Jules Verne, the art of anticipatory writing of H. G. Wells, or a cyberpunk story about the future fifteen minutes from now, science fiction has long served as a narrative lens through which we can read how the future is produced first in our imaginations, well before it is produced in the laboratories of scientists and engineers, the design studios, or the kitchens and the garages of everyday people.

In a more materialist sense, the design of the future is the work of those professionals who create buildings with symbolic structures and materials consciously chosen to endure.[3] As a special class of futurist, architects have always used innovative technologies in the service of designing the future; in the process, both the future and technology are given shape and meaning.[4] More recently, the professional moniker of the architect has been expanded to refer to new areas of expertise, as in the case of information architect, database architect, and chip architect. These new domains of infrastructure require creative design; once created, they establish the conditions of possibility for future activities. Thus, those who architect the structures of the present, whether digital, virtual, or material, are engaged in the practice of designing our futures.

Predicting the future is an ancient preoccupation, involving richly symbolic practices of divination and mystical projections of significance and relevance. These practices now include the rationalist sciences of market research, risk analysis, and technology forecasting.[5] Forecasting the future for the purposes of ensuring corporate immortality (the real purpose of any corporation) is a robust industry unto itself. The *Institute for the Future*, for example, engages a network of researchers to investigate emerging trends and discontinuities in order to help people make "better, more informed decisions about the future."[6] As the organization's website proclaims, "We provide the foresight to create insights that lead to action"; it seeks to build "the future by understanding it deeply." Strategic-minded business leaders can subscribe to the institute's *Ten-Year Forecast Program* to gain access to reports and analyses of unfolding social and economic trends. *The Technology Horizons Program* offers members an insider's view of emerging innovations coming out of Silicon Valley. While it is unclear whether Silicon Valley will remain the epicenter of global technological innovation in the future, certainly in the past it had been one of the most celebrated places where the future—our present—was first imagined, prototyped, and eventually set in motion.

Inventing the Future In Spite of Itself

Silicon Valley is the name for a mythologized yet real place where the future has been invented, not once, but at least twice in recent history. Silicon Valley, whose proper name is the Santa Clara Valley, begins south of San Francisco, near the town of Burlingame, then extends south along the peninsula to San Jose. In the center of this valley is Palo Alto, the location of David Packard's garage where, in 1939, he and William Hewlett founded their namesake company, and with it the myth that Silicon Valley is the place where the future is created through pregnant moments of technological innovation.[7] In the second invention myth, the technology that signifies the future is the personal computer. By the turn of the millennium, Palo Alto had become the home of numerous start-up companies, venture capital firms, and the NASDAQ stock exchange. More importantly, for the purposes of the history recounted in this chapter, Palo Alto was the place where, in 1970, the Xerox Corporation chose to establish its new research center, called Xerox Palo Alto Research Center (PARC). This is the place where the personal computer was first brought into existence as a working prototype. Although it was, and still is, a very real place, where two hundred researchers work on an assortment of technological and scientific projects, PARC itself has been mythologized as a significant part of Silicon Valley's reinvention of the future.

As the story goes, PARC was—from its beginnings—designed to be the place within the Xerox Corporation where offbeat researchers could incubate blue-sky ideas, without the pressures of demonstrating product marketability; this was one of the reasons it was purposefully located far from Xerox's corporate headquarters in Rochester, New York (Brand, 1972). PARC's research charter, established by its first director, Dr. George Pake, was to create the architecture of information.[8] As history would have it,

1973 was a banner year for PARC, when a group of researchers in its Computer Science Laboratory (CSL) first articulated a vision for the future of human-scale computing. In place of room-size mainframe computers, used primarily for data compilation and calculations, CSL promoted the concept of personal distributed computing, where the size of a computer would be scaled to human (desktop) use, and where machines would be connected to each other to form a communication network—both among machines and among the humans using them. That same year, to demonstrate the feasibility of this vision, a group of CSL researchers constructed the Alto personal computer. Eventually it featured the first example of a What-you-see-is-what-you-get (WYSIWYG) text editor and the first example of a graphical user interface (GUI); it incorporated Doug Englebart's mouse input device, and other novel elements such as a system of commands listed as items on a menu, and applications graphically represented by icons. 1973 was also the year that other PARC researchers developed the first laser printer, registered the patent for the networking system called Ethernet, and created the concept of client/server architecture. Taken together, these innovations marked a shift in thinking about computing, away from the emphasis on centrally located mainframe machines for the purposes of rapid data processing, and toward the creation of a distributed system of networked devices that could be used both for communication purposes and computation. By 1975 there were more than two hundred Altos in use at PARC and throughout Xerox. And yet, despite the functional success of these desktop computers, when the PARC researchers pushed to have Xerox mass produce the Alto III, executives at corporate headquarters said "no thanks."[9]

What happens next in the history of PARC is the stuff whereby the myth takes flight. As recounted in books such as *Fumbling the Future: How Xerox Invented, then Ignored the First Personal Computer*, the story involves larger-than-life personalities and spectacular corporate missteps (Smith and Alexander, 1988). It recounts how the corporation failed to embrace many of the key technologies of the computer age: when Goliath (Xerox) stumbled, the small Davids of the Valley were able to triumph by using PARC technologies as the basis for the creation of the new companies that eventually became pillars of the digital age. For example, Bob Metcalfe, the PARC researcher who invented the networking protocol, Ethernet, left PARC to establish the 3Com Corporation in 1979. Soon after, in 1982, John

Warnock and Charles Geschke, researchers at PARC in the 1970s, left to found the Adobe Corporation, furthering their previous work on the development of a portable document format (pdf) protocol. Among the most apocryphal stories is one that recounts how Steve Jobs created Apple Corporation's first mass-produced personal computer in 1983, inspired by a demonstration of Smalltalk, the first object-oriented programming language created at PARC in the 1970s. Apparently, Apple's first personal computer, the LISA, incorporated several elements that had been developed by PARC researchers in the 1970s, such as the GUI, drop-down menus, and a hierarchical file system with folders. The fact that many key technologies first created at PARC ultimately served as the enabling technologies that launched other corporations, now considered industry giants, contributes to the myth of PARC as the place of revolutionary technological innovation.

Several theories circulate to explain why the Xerox Corporation failed to profit from the the future invented at PARC. Some analysts posit that it was a consequence of Xerox's reliance on a business model, based on toner sales and pages copied, that didn't translate into the digital realm (Hamel, 2000). Others suggest that it was a consequence of a failure of imagination on the part of corporate officers, who simply couldn't see beyond their current customer base or core technology sales system (Hiltzik, 1999). The persistent imputation that Xerox fumbled the future masks an important part of the reality of the innovation produced at PARC. Xerox, in fact, did profit from certain PARC inventions, most notably the development of red laser printing, which became the basis of a billion-dollar revenue stream by the mid-1980s. Nonetheless, even as recently as 2000, one of the first things a new PARC employee learned was that the ethos of the Center continues to be influenced by the belief that Xerox, the Corporation, sometimes jokingly referred to as "the mothership," has never really grokked the work or the value of PARC research; or so the story goes.[10]

In considering the research conducted at PARC, and how this work contributed to the invention of a range of technologies that became key elements of contemporary digital culture, it is difficult to separate fact from legend, politics from mythology, and innovation from marketing rhetoric. In the 1970s, PARC employed a group of computer scientists who prototyped many of the major components of the technological infrastructure of the digital age. It also was the first to employ non-computer scientists—

psychologists, linguists, anthropologists, and eventually humanists—in the creative enterprise of imagining the future of computing. In this, PARC was the site of significant innovation, both in idea creation and multidisciplinary technology development. How do these facts get turned into legend?

Lucy Suchman, a research scientist and anthropologist who worked at PARC from 1980–2000, investigates how the legend of PARC, as a center for innovation, was actively created through the work practices of organizational participants, both within and across organizational boundaries.[11] Suchman offers a chronicle of PARC research, depicting it as a set of social and material practices that had as outcomes both the manifestation of new ideas and the performance of a particular identity of the research lab. As Suchman puts it, PARC is a place where the everyday work practices of scientists, engineers, managers, and corporate decision-makers, as well as a set of organizational events and logics, and a research program focused on technological innovation, all intersected and unfolded to produce significant research and development. The work of PARC involved the social and material practices of real people producing and performing science and innovation.

Inspired by Suchman's project, this chapter contributes an episodic account of how the work-practices of a collaborative research group sometimes purposefully (re)-produced the identity of PARC as a center of innovation. The focus of this chapter is on the design practices of a research group that I was a part of called RED: Research on Experimental Documents, which worked at PARC from 1999–2001. It includes reference to singular biographies, the creation of identities, and rhetorical strategies, as well as engagement with a range of boundary-objects that were integral to the group's research-design effort. As historian Carolyn Steedman (1987: 6) reminds us, the challenge here, as with all reflective cultural analysis, is to remember that "personal interpretations of past time—the stories that people tell themselves in order to explain how they got to the place they currently inhabit—are often in deep and ambiguous conflict with official interpretive devices of culture."[12] In the case of PARC, the official "interpretive devices of culture" that compulsively rehearse its legendary status, in lieu of a consideration of the actual work-practices of situated actors and agents, cannot be simply reproduced as narratives of truth. What I offer here is a provisional and partial narrative of the way in which RED participated in the performance of the future in its work at Xerox PARC.

RED@PARC: Research in Experimental Documents

In 1997, Rich Gold, a researcher and middle manager at Xerox PARC, formed a group called RED: *Research on Experimental Documents.* To fully elaborate the work of RED@PARC requires a short detour through Gold's biography, because it includes a reckoning of his efforts at transforming the relationship between the Xerox Corporation and its famous research center such that, in the future, the *future* wouldn't be fumbled so dramatically again.[13] Gold joined the PARC staff in 1991 as a researcher in the area of ubiquitous computing, where he worked closely with PARC's Chief Technology Officer, Mark Weiser, and PARC's celebrated Director—and Chief Scientist of Xerox—John Seely Brown.[14] Brown encouraged Gold to become a corporate provocateur, cultural mediator, and institutional visionary, and to act as a catalyst for creative thinking and practice.[15] Gold's first effort to intervene in the organizational culture at PARC was manifested in the creation of the PARC Artist-in-Residence (PAIR) program that put avant-garde media artists together with PARC research scientists, based on shared interests in technology.[16] Gold believed that the involvement of artists in the activities of the research center would inspire the technologists to adopt new modes of seeing and to think about new contexts for their research. In turn, the artists gained access to embryonic technologies not yet available to a wider public. Of course PARC researchers had engaged in aesthetic and artistic efforts prior to the institutionalization of the PAIR program, and some of these had involved artists collaborating with researchers, while others were carried out by the researchers alone. It wasn't until Rich Gold inaugurated the PAIR program, however, that these efforts were formally organized and recognized as a valuable aspect of the work of the Center. The list of artists who participated in the PAIR program is impressive, as is the list of researchers with whom they collaborated.[17] This program existed for 10 years at PARC and was emulated by other organizations, both corporate and governmental.[18] Gold's explorations of the boundary conditions that separate art from science and technology served as the basis of what he often referred to as corporate performance art.[19]

In the mid-1990s Gold sought to create a new kind of research group at PARC.[20] Drawing on the successes as well as the difficulties he experienced in creating PAIR, he believed that a research center such as PARC could not only serve as an institution of technological innovation, but also as a stage

My cartoon matrix of creative hats.

1. Rich Gold's sketch of the four creative disciplines. (Rich Gold, *The Plentitude*, 2007)

for the enactment of alternative research practices.[21] In creating RED, Gold purposefully recruited PARC researchers who had backgrounds in art, science, design, engineering, or several of these fields.[22] From the beginning, the identity of RED embodied the insights and expertise of these four domains (see figure 1). To justify the existence of RED, Gold often referred to a popular PARC saying: "the best way to predict the future is to build it." He asserted that the future is created within the four creative disciplines of art, science, design, and engineering. Each of these disciplines is in the business of creating the new; each has protocols for the creation of new knowledge, forms of expression, and material artifacts; each has rules for recognizing and evaluating something as new; and each implicitly draws inspiration from the other. According to Gold, truly innovative research must combine insights from all four disciplines; therefore, the way to create the future at PARC, Gold asserted, would be through the constitution of a group that manifested the insights of these four disciplines.[23]

Once formed, the group took on the commitment to enact collaborative cross-disciplinary research, and eventually created an explicit research charter: "To explore and develop *new media genres* through the design of *new document forms* while employing *innovative research methods*." At the broadest level, RED's focus on the design and prototyping of new media genres was consistent with the aims of Xerox—to be a leader in the development of digital documents. Built into RED's charter was an implicit assertion that the function of the group was unique within the Xerox universe. RED was to be to PARC what PARC was to Xerox: it was a group that was created (according to Gold) to keep PARC's head above water. RED manifested the multidisciplinary range that was the hallmark of PARC's research staff. The boundaries of RED's research were defined by its charter, rather than by a domain of technological production, and included an explicit commitment to innovating new design-based research methods.[24] This had both positive and, as the group learned over time, negative consequences. Participants in RED enjoyed many of the same privileges as those participating in other PARC labs, who were not, for the most part, expected to get involved in the process of new product development. Thus, RED enjoyed the freedom to construct future technology scenarios that were not beholden to the logics or economics of mass production. For example, instead of working on new document forms that were smaller and faster—the qualities driving technology research in Silicon Valley at the time—RED could do exactly the opposite, designing document forms that were bigger and more massive than typical consumer commodities. This approach prompted RED to elaborate their research framework as an example of "speculative design research" (Balsamo, et al., 2000). The license to speculate was an enabling condition for much of the work of RED.

The Performance and Exhibition of Research

In 1998, representatives from the San Jose Museum of Technological Innovation approached PARC with the invitation to showcase some of the work done by participants in the PAIR program. The Tech Museum had just opened a new space called the Center of the Edge Gallery, which was specifically designed to showcase innovative technologies coming out of Silicon Valley. Because few of the PAIR collaborations resulted in the kind of art/technology demonstrations that could be displayed in a gallery space, Rich Gold (as the PAIR coordinator) proposed an alternative plan. He convinced both PARC management and the decision-makers at Xerox corporate headquarters that this invitation represented a perfect opportunity for RED to demonstrate its value to PARC and Xerox as a particular kind of research-design group. The idea was that RED would coordinate the production of a theme-based museum exhibit, based on collaborations with other PARC researchers, to create new demonstrations of emerging technologies; these would, as the Tech Museum wanted, highlight the innovation going on in Silicon Valley. Because the invitation came from the Tech Museum, a high-profile cultural institution that had recently opened in Silicon Valley, to rave reviews, Gold was able to secure significant funding, from a marketing division of Xerox, for the creation of the exhibit.[25]

The timeframe for the project was delimited: there would be approximately 18 months between the day the invitation was first tendered and the opening day of the exhibit. During this time, RED worked exclusively on the design and fabrication of exhibit materials; most other research projects were suspended. What was being designed were not only the material aspects of the exhibit and interactives, but also the group's understanding of the design challenge itself. RED's interest in the Tech Museum's invitation was due not primarily to the desire for getting involved in the business of museum exhibit design, but to the need of an appropriate setting for the group's research interests. Having said that, RED was keenly aware that the museum setting imposed additional constraints on the group's research and design efforts.[26] For example, the pieces of the exhibit had to be both safe and in compliance with the requirements of the Americans with Disabilities Act (ADA), as well as reliable and easily maintained by the museum's technical staff. Thus, the nature of the original invitation had a strongly determining effect on what eventually got designed and built. Anything that was installed in the museum had to be robust enough to endure six months of use by as many as 2000 visitors daily, which had been a conservative estimate. Moreover, anything to be installed in the Center of the Edge Gallery had to signify innovation; the resulting installation had to prop up not one, but two institutional identities: that of the Tech Museum as the premier cultural institution, having a privileged relationship to innovations coming out of Silicon Valley, and that of PARC as a center of innovation, not just in the 1970s—as the legend would have it— but also at the turn of the new millennium. Given that RED's research charter also trumpeted a commitment to the production of new media genres, and innovative research methods, the project was, from the beginning, framed within a particular narrative—that of a story, announcing the future through the staging of innovative technologies.

To address the Tech Museum's invitation, RED explored the question of what signified innovation at PARC. RED wanted to communicate something about the general nature of research as method, prototype, demonstration, and always in-process of unfolding and of becoming. RED discussed the semiotics of research at PARC. At the time (1999), a popular PARC tagline stated that it was a place that studied everything from "atoms to culture." This tagline was typically used to publicize the multidisciplinary approach of PARC research, the range of which spanned from the microscopic to the macro-social. As is obvious, this is a broad range, and extremely difficult to signify through a collection of objects; it encompasses the theoretical, conceptual, and entirely fictional. As a first step in creating the installation, the members of RED visited the five labs at PARC, both to see who was giving good demo and to conduct a creative inventory of PARC research. At the time, physicists were participating in blue laser research; anthropologists were studying work place behaviors; new devices, such as electronic paper and MEMS robots, were being prototyped; and new document applications, such as hypertext annotation programs, were being developed.[27] The initial creative inventory yielded more than 40 projects that would eventually be considered for the creation of the museum installation.

Over time, the question was refined: what signifies research to a public within a specific institutional space? Through its initial analysis of the science/technology center (as a particular type of museum) RED learned that visitors come to these places expecting to see something new, to be challenged, and to participate in real-time interactions with technology. The two previous installations hosted by the Tech Museum provided divergent examples of how to stage research for public audiences.[28] The first exhibit, by Interval Research Center, focused on art and technology works, not on demonstrations of innovation per se.[29] The second exhibit, by AT&T, offered a walk-through interactive commercial. The story of innovation was subsumed to the promotion of new AT&T services and applications. In reviewing the structure of these two exhibits, RED realized the importance of creating an overall narrative for the PARC installation, and this became the focus of early designing efforts. In creating a story of PARC that would serve as the narrative framework for the creation of the Tech Museum installation, RED was engaging in a practice of technology-transfer where the meaning of a technology (or set of technologies) is narrativized for a particular audience, one that comes already prepared to make connections between the current moment and the future-on-display in various interactives.[30] In creating the devices and interactive experiences that would constitute the exhibit, RED was also designing the social and technocultural contexts within which the audience would experience them.

An Example of Hermeneutic Reverse Engineering

The development of the museum installation was informed by a sustained collaborative investigation of the history of reading, which in turn inspired RED to formulate several critiques about the influence of new technologies on the practices of reading, writing, and meaning-making.[31] The first critique challenged the assertion that all media would converge onto a singular technological platform. In Silicon Valley in 1999, the religion of convergence was at a fever pitch: people were wildly promoting the notion of a single reading device for the future, when all media interaction would take place on a PDA (personal digital assistant) or a mobile phone.[32] RED offered an alternative scenario, one marked by an extravagant proliferation of devices, the emergence of many new reading situations, and the creation of a spectrum of new media genres. RED's second critique addressed the future of both textuality and books: as the group studied the history of reading, it became clear that there was nothing to suggest that text—or print-based books—would disappear in the future.[33] Although they realized that the production of print-based books would change, through the use of new digital technologies, RED believed that text, and indeed alphabetic literacy (at least in the U.S. context), would remain a critically important medium of communication. For this reason, RED decided to focus on the role of text in the creation of new reading devices and experiences.

In their designing practice, RED drew on theories of media and techniques of cultural analysis, especially via the work by Marshall McLuhan and Roland Barthes. As I described in the introduction, I refer to this design methodology as "hermeneutic reverse engineering." In the context of RED's research and designing practice, the deployment of this approach involved an explicit consideration of how the meanings of reading in a digital age are constructed. To elaborate these meanings, RED created several two-by-two matrices, which mapped the connotations of various

Table 1. Permutations of the logics of reading.

PUBLIC Reading by a collective group	PRIVATE Reading by an embodied individual
SYNCHRONOUS Reading within the same time	ASYNCHRONOUS Reading out-of-time

aspects of reading. These matrices resembled Greimasian squares, named for A. J. Greimas (1976), as a methodology for mapping the semiotic oppositions among pairs of terms. This exercise began by positing a simple opposition of two activities, reading in "public" and reading in "private" (see table 1).

The set of terms was expanded to include a temporal dimension to elaborate the description of diverse reading situations: reading synchronously and asynchronously. The resulting semiotic map of four logically possible reading situations manifested a set of abstract ideas about text-based reading. This enabled the group to create a shared set of understandings for subsequent discussions. Based on this elaboration of four different reading situations, RED identified a characteristic form of reading that exemplified the qualities of each scene (see table 2). This level of semiotic analysis focused attention on the socio-technological forms of reading devices. For example, to illustrate the notion of private synchronic reading, "children's books read aloud" implies both a social situation—between adult and child—and a particular technological form: the printed children's book.

Table 2. Ideal types of different logics of reading.

PUBLIC: synchronous PowerPoint presentations	PRIVATE: synchronous Children's books read aloud
PUBLIC: asynchronous Billboards and monuments	PRIVATE: asynchronous Novels and bound books

Table 3. Distribution of XFR exhibits as experiments in different logics of reading.

PUBLIC: People	PRIVATE: People
The Reading Wall	Listen Readers
Tilty Tables	Fluid Reader
Hyperbolic Comics	Speeder Reader
Walk-in Comix	

PUBLIC: Machines	PRIVATE: Machines
Reading Eye Dog	Glyph-O-Scope

Even if they weren't as logically rigorous as a true Greimasian square might imply, these formulations helped RED think through the overarching structure of the entire collection of interactives, and helped to clarify the range of reading devices that would fill out the story of the exhibit.[34] The mapping exercise led to various experiments in creating squares of signification that would suggest new combinations of categories to describe reading situations. In table 3, the PUBLIC/PRIVATE binary is combined with a new opposition between two types of reading agents, PEOPLE/MACHINES. The terms listed in each quadrant were the names of individual interactives that were being developed at the time.

These mapping exercises provided the group with a shared vocabulary and sense of a typology of reading situations, affordances, and participants. A discussion about McLuhan's theory of media helped to contextualize the technocultural work of proposed interactives. As the designing process unfolded, and the interactives were prototyped for demonstration during charettes, it became clear that each interactive was going to involve the reconfiguration of human sense ratios (of the visual and the aural, of the tactile and the visual, for example). We began to understand the interactives as probes into a range of new technocultural possibilities. I considered the two-by-two matrices as cognitive maps of the expanse of McLuhan's Gutenberg Galaxy.[35]

The creation of these representational materials, such as the two-by-two matrices, interim working titles, small chap books, models, prototypes, and other physical assemblages, were critically important in the iterative design of the exhibit's overarching narrative. Although it is common for design researchers to acknowledge the important role of representations in designing practice, the meaning of "representations" often slides into the purely symbolic, as if these stand in for something else that is already ontologically stable: an idea; a set of materials; or a directive. The nature of the objects that were compulsively manufactured by RED, in the course of designing the museum exhibit, were hybrid material-discursive ensembles. They were not simply visual or tactile maps of ideas already formed, but more like a language, used to make ideas cohere in material form. The objects may be considered a manifestation of RED's representational and articulatory practices, but as computational philosopher Brian Cantwell Smith clarifies, they were not simply the missives of RED's already constituted designerly intentionality. Material objects, according to Smith, are "culturally, historically, and socially plural—and yet not just the products of the imagination or intentional whim of a person, society, or community either, but made of the stuff of the world, as resistant and wily and obstreperous as the rest of us" (1996: 363).[36] Smith asserts that all reality is the middle ground where subjects and objects co-present to each other: objects present themselves; subjects register objects as objects.

Let me try to unpack this assertion. As ways of reifying design thinking, material objects should be understood as artificially fixed traces of the oscillation between moments of enactment. Some objects were representational, such as the foam-core model that presented the exhibit at a 1:10 scale; other objects were poetic enunciations, expressed through the aesthetics of typography, paper texture, and textual layout; none of these objects simply re-presented ideas: they were the matter through which ideas were shaped and put into circulation. In the process, relations among members of RED, and the identities of all participants, also materialized. For example, Steve Harrison, the RED member who created the foam-core model, didn't build it because he was the designated architect of the exhibit: in building the model he manifested his identity as architect. Through the obsessive iteration of object making, the discourse of the exhibition, including its key narrative elements, plots, look and feel, scope, theories, and identities of its designers/authors, was constituted.

When RED turned its attention more specifically to the design of the overall look and feel of the exhibit, an important aspect of the project was clarified, and with it the eventual title of the installation. As part of the process of developing an environmental treatment that would provide the

2. The layout and lighting of the *XFR* exhibit was designed to evoke a feeling of a research lab at night. (Photo by Deanna Hovath/Xerox PARC)

appropriate context for the collection of interactives, RED studied popular cultural representations of laboratories.[37] From a collection of photographs, which was intended to provide inspiration for the symbolic treatment of the installation's environment, came the rather simple idea that the new exhibit would be designed to evoke the look and feel of a laboratory at night: it would make use of glowing instruments, pools of light, tangles of wires, and bits and pieces of exposed metal infrastructure (see figure 2). The individual interactives would be staged as research in progress—where it would appear that the researchers had left their demos running for the enjoyment of late-night lab visitors. While in hindsight this may seem like a rather obvious decision, it was certainly not obvious during the designing process; getting hijacked by the obvious in contradiction to the clever is one of the delights of designing. With this look and feel established, other decisions, such as the building materials, were easier to make. For example, most of the interactives were constructed out of a modular metal building system called "80/20," whose product semantics connote industrial, high-tech qualities: structural materials are made out of smooth brushed aluminum, which offers clean lines with no ornamentation.[38]

The mise-en-scene of the exhibit included an element that is a stock setting in popular cultural representations of the laboratory—the lab bench. This design decision conformed to an expectation we believed visitors would bring to the exhibit. The creation of the lab bench as part of the exhibit's material design language offered a stage for displaying several kinds of interactives. Placing them on a lab bench helped create narrative coherence among the interactives, even though they were quite distinct from one another. Thus, the form factor of the lab bench served as a narrative frame that communicated—from a distance—something about the intended meaning of the interactive experience. In keeping with RED's methods of genre-based design, other elements of the mise-en-scene of the lab were identified as key to the narrative coherence of the exhibit: low-level task lighting suggested the mystery of a lab after dark; pegboard behind the explanatory signs was used to convey the appearance of bulletin boards; aligning interactives off-axis from one another was meant to connote the mild chaos of a tinkerer's space.

Where RED deliberately worked against visitor expectations, and against the genre conventions of typical museum technology exhibits, was in the use and design of the interface for each of the interactives. In the process of exploring the logics and affordances of possible modes of interactivity, the group discussed the device-based technological literacy that could be expected of Tech Museum visitors. Several research projects at PARC were exploring alternative interface designs, and RED wanted to explore modes of interactivity that used familiar bodily gestures.[39] For these reasons, several of the XFR interactives incorporated game-interface devices, such as a joystick or a steering wheel, while others relied on the naturalized hand gestures of finger touching and page turning. Others required full body movement: to tilt a tabletop, or move a display along a wall. This commitment challenged RED to develop modes of engagement that quickly and simply engaged visitors, without the help of extensive instruction.

The iterative design of the overall mise-en-scene enabled the group to finally agree on the title of the exhibit: *XFR: eXperiments in the Future of Reading* (see figure 3). The title helped RED in its authoring efforts across the board, from developing the overarching narrative, to creating content for individual interactives, to suggesting the appropriate mode of address on signage. The team of artists, designers, and fabricators who would collaborate in building the actual exhibit was subsequently finalized.[40] Five

3. *XFR* at the Center of the Edge Gallery in the San Jose Museum of Technological Innovation. (Photo by Deanna Horvath/Xerox PARC)

months before opening day, XFR was documented in a laser-cut booklet, produced by RED, which listed the speculative reading interactives that would be part of the final museum installation. The entire exhibit consisted of 11 distinct speculative reading experiments and a 500-square-foot Book Artists' Studio.[41] The XFR exhibit was installed in the Center of the Edge Gallery at the Tech Museum of Innovation, located in San Jose, from March through September, 2000; from January through December, 2001, it toured science/technology centers throughout the United States. During its tour, more than 4 million people visited the science/technology centers where XFR was installed. In March, 2002, XFR returned to Palo Alto in crates and boxes. By that time, RED was no longer working at PARC: the exhibit had transformed from an active research project into an archival collection of research devices, building materials, fabrication tools, representational detritus, and permanently unfinished designs.

We are taught, very subtly, how to read deeply. When presented with a paper-based book, literate people in the twenty-first century begin to apprehend meaning by the very act of recognizing the book's form. A reader knows what to do with such an artifact, how to open it, handle the pages, and find its content.[42] In fact, mass culture is predicated on this kind of unconscious consumption of semantic complexity. We are not often encouraged to reflect on how meaning is constructed through the semiotic accretion of symbolic forms, visual effects, and medium-specific conventions. RED's understanding of deep reading drew implicitly on work by sociologist Michel de Certeau, who elaborated the many ways in which reading has long been misunderstood as a passive act of consumption. As de Certeau (1984: 167) asserted, the mythology of "informing through books" relied on the assumption that the reading public is "more or less resistant" and "imprinted by and like the text which is imposed on it." This mythology invests the capacity of creativity onto the figure of the technicians and producers, where the "only initiative takes place in the technical laboratories." He further elaborates:

> What needs to be put in question is unfortunately not this division of labor (it is only too real), but the assimilation of reading to passivity. In fact, to read is to wander through an imposed system (that of the text, analogous to the constructed order of a city or of a supermarket). Recent analyses show that "every reading modifies its object," that (as Borges already pointed out) "one literature differs from another less by its text than by the way in which it is read," and that a system of verbal or iconic signs is a reservoir of forms, to which the reader must give meaning . . . The reader takes neither the position of the author, nor an author's position. He invents in text something different from what [was] "intended." He detaches them from their lost or accessory origin. He combines their fragments and creates something un-known in the space organized by their capacity for allowing an indefinite plurality of meanings. (169)

Reading, as de Certeau (172) so beautifully describes it, is the meeting of a reader and the "poetic operations (the practitioner's constructions) of a text." This theoretical framework subtly shaped the development of the reading experiences made manifest in each XFR interactive.

Through the iterative process of designing various XFR interactives, a broad thesis took shape on the changing nature of reading and writing in the digital age. Gold identified this as the *Deep Reading/Total Writing* thesis; subsequently it served as one of the guiding narratives for the creation of the exhibit. The act of deep reading involves forming an understanding of all aspects of a mediated presentation, including the words, font, color, graphics, animation, scale, social context, and medium.

The act of total writing creates a deep reading experience, in which the author is understood as the creator of a multi-layered system of meaning, where each component of the symbolic presentation is understood to be potentially authored in some way. The exhibit created for the Tech museum was conceptualized as a deep reading/total writing experiment, where the researchers—in this case, RED members working collaboratively in small teams—authored not only the content, but also the entire interactive reading experience, including the technology, medium, presentation, and social context of reception. The XFR interactives were designed to make unconscious deep-reading habits more conscious, by making the layers of meaning more obvious. The strategy was to provoke reflection through the act of defamiliarization. In confronting an unfamiliar interface or mode of interactivity, readers (we believed) would be prompted to actively search for meaning, in an attempt to figure out how it is that this thing with text (and sometimes images) makes sense. In those brief moments before recognition—of this that is unfamiliar as an example of that which I know—unfolds the possibilities of engagement.

In discussions about the theoretical status of the XFR interactives, Gold described them as "evocative knowledge objects" (EKOs). As such, these interactives create the conditions for the evocation of knowledge that manifests in the interaction between and among readers, content, layers of meaning, and devices. This was the grain of meaning implied by the doubled nature of RED's design experimentation in total authoring/deep reading. For Rich Gold, total authoring referred to the way each signifying layer of the interactive was actively designed. The meaningfulness of the interactive was built through an accretion of signifying layers, which included elements ranging from the macro to the micro: social context, symbolism, and materiality of built form, texture of materials, weight and mass, lighting, signage, mode of interactivity, digital display, genre, narrative structure, use of language, vocabulary, relationship of text to image, fonts, colors, layout, temporality of display, dynamics of animation, quality of the sound, and even grain of voice. Even this long list of signifying layers does not exhaust the meaningful aspects of the XFR interactives; we know that a designer's intent is no guarantee that the meaning projected onto the interactives (or even built into them) is the meaning that other people apprehend. As EKOs, the interactives served as a fulcrum for the meeting between reader and designer. Whereas the consequence of that meeting was ideally the evocation of knowledge, the meanings evoked could not be determined in advance by reference to designerly intent, no matter how fully RED rationalized the activity of total authoring.

Indeed, the XFR interactives evoked an abundance of meaning, both for those visitors/readers who encountered them in the context of the Tech Museum, and for those involved in designing them. Each RED member invested meaning in the interactives in various ways: as engineers; as researchers; as designers; as artists; as scientists; as fabricators; and as authors. In turn, the interactives were implicated in the constitution of designers' identities and capabilities.

In chapter 3, I describe how this played out for me individually in creating the application for the *The Reading Wall*. In designing this interactive, a flock of identities was constituted for me: as researcher; historian; designer; and digital author. In the process, my capabilities—to author, design, research, or create a history—were manifested to me, and presumably to my colleagues, through my encounters with the digital application that I was developing. My interactions were always built on past experiences, even when I was doing something new; bodily habits were invoked; knowledge that I hadn't consciously remembered was evoked; emotions were provoked.[43] *The Reading Wall*, as a socio-technological and cultural object, was not just some thing that I experienced in its many stages of becoming: it was deeply involved in the constitution of my sense of self— both during the XFR designing process and since then.

As a category of material artifacts, the XFR interactives are usefully understood as socio-technocultural assemblages in that their meaningfulness manifests through the interaction between a reader/user, a designer/ author, as well as through mechanical, computational, and digital parts and pieces: it is difficult to find the right word to describe their object status. By the time the exhibit was installed, each separate piece had its own proper name; moreover, the collection of things had several identifying monikers. The overall exhibit comprised several elements that were referred to in different ways: as a collection of speculative reading devices; a set of reading experiments; a collection of technological artifacts; a portfolio of designed pieces; and as EKOs. In their most generic form, I have referred to them as *interactives*, to keep the focus on the mediating effects of their design and use.[44] Their shifting categorization was a consequence of the many ways in which the elements could be described, explained, and analyzed.

Each of the XFR interactives can be isolated as a singular element of the overall exhibit, with a proper name and a list of technological components. And yet, in light of the discussion above, it is more accurate to describe each interactive as a plurality.[45] This kind of description is not easily accommodated by the conventions of a print book. While I can create textual descriptions of technical specifications, or offer images of the built form of each device, I cannot show the dynamic interplay between users, device, and content, which structures the meaning-making activity of each object. Print is an inadequate medium for conveying the multiple meanings of each interactive. To allow for the creation of multiple meanings, I created entries for each interactive on the *Designing Culture* website that includes short video clips, technical specifications, and a set of McLuhanesque interpretations. What follows here in the print book is a set of thumbnail sketches, providing brief descriptions of each interactive. The decision to include this material in the print book was based on an appreciation of the unique affordances of print to serve as an archival medium of historical efforts. So even as I rely on a digital website to accommodate the plurality of meanings that coalesce around each interactive, I (like many others) am skeptical about the effectiveness of digital media as a repository for archival material (Waters and Garrett, 1996). Putting aside worries about the longevity of information stored in various modes, the print medium also

THE PEACE TABLE

PEACE

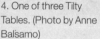

English · Klingon · French · Pig-Latin · Spanish
Thai · Swahili · Tongan · Norwegian
Vietnamese · Blackfoot · Burmese · Esperanto · Hindi
Persian · Russian
Chinese · Zulu
Portugese · Farsi
Eskimo · Indonesian · Lithuanian · Malay · Dutch
Mongolian · Greek · Hippie · German
Japanese · Bosnian · Cherokee · Hebrew · Arabic

4. One of three Tilty Tables. (Photo by Anne Balsamo)

provides an opportunity to describe the nature of the experiments that guided the research and design of each interactive. To this end, the next section provides a description of the category of experiments that were part of the research program made manifest by the XFR exhibit.

Experiments in Scale

During the late 1990s, media pundits were convinced that the future of reading would be dominated by the use of hand-held reading devices. RED was interested in desgining reading devices that involved the entirety of the reader's body, not just the hand and eye. Two XFR interactives explored the nature of reading at different scales. The first, *The Tilty Tables*, presented multiple ways to read large documents. This tangible surface interface device was used to display three different types of spatialized documents. To read using a Tilty Table, a reader tilted the table in various directions. One of the Tilty Tables displayed a document called the "Napkin Draw-ings"; if printed, the "Napkin Drawing" document would have measured 30 feet by 30 feet. A second Tilty Table called the "Peace Table" allowed readers to roll a virtual ball around a projected surface (see figure 4). When the ball rolled over the name of one of the languages displayed on the

5. The title panels of *Walk-In Comix*. (Photo by Anne Balsamo)

tabletop, the word for "peace" in that language appeared in the center of the table. A third Tilty Table called "Twisted Tales" presented flows of text drawn from a database of folklore stories from different countries.

The second interactive, *Walk-In Comix*, was the largest experiment in terms of physical size. It presented a room-sized graphic novel called *Slip to Text*, which told the story of five teenagers who become lost in a world of text; each teenager contributes something important to the task of deciphering a way out of the textual world (see figure 5). The design and presentation of the story borrowed from the conventions of sequential graphic novels. The physical walls of the room reproduced narrative panels. A sub-text was printed on panels laid out on the floor. Visitors read the story by walking through the architectural space. Peepholes drew visitors in close to read the stories behind the walls, and embedded ambient sound amplified the experience of an embodied immersive reading experience.

Experiments in Augmented Books

Two of the XFR interactives explored how the experience of book reading might change in the future, as a consequence of digital augmentation.[46] These experiments represented investigations of the limit-conditions of the category of book-ness: what makes a book, a book? One experiment explored the use of audio as illustration for children's books. *Listen Readers* encouraged the exploration of the nature of multi-modal reading while preserving the tactile pleasure of the paper-based book form (see figure 6). This interactive combined two immersive experiences: reading a beautifully illustrated children's book, and hearing a rich ambient soundscape, while seated in a large, overstuffed chair. Just as a reader's hand makes a story unfold by turning the pages of a typical book, in these books the reader's gestures controlled the audio presentation. In this case, the intent was to preserve the notion of the book as a pleasurable tactile object.

A second experiment deconstructed the notion of the book into its elemental foundation: the word. *Speeder Reader* used familiar videogame interface devices—steering wheel, stick shift, and gas pedal—to enable readers to drive through a story that was presented one word at a time (see figure 7). A view plate showed a "word-ometer," and above that, where the windshield would normally be, was a window where single words flashed one after another. By pressing the floor pedal, the reader increased or decreased the velocity of the presentation of the words. Because standard punctuation marks rely on the space of a page to make sense, new kinds of punctuation were designed that worked with the dynamic form of text presentation. For example, instead of using indented spaces to signal the beginning of new paragraphs or sections of the story, *Speeder Reader* used long pauses to signify topic changes.

Experiments in History and Present

Two of the exhibits explored the implications of epigraphic reading in a digital age. In anticipation of truly ubiquitous computing environments, these interactives examined how physical walls can serve as communicative interfaces when augmented with digital capabilities. Walls have long been significant cultural mechanisms: they display histories, establish borders, and serve as the infrastructure of community and cultural identity. *The Reading Wall* presented the history of reading, writing, and communication in two modes: as a static printed timeline and as interactive digital episodes (see figure 8). The physical form of the exhibit consisted of three sixteen-foot-long wall segments. Mounted on each wall was a forty-two-inch plasma display, which could be slid along a track on the wall. The plasma displays presented episodes from the dynamic interactive application called "The

6. Visitors using *Listen Readers*. (Photo by Anne Balsamo)

7. A young man uses *Speeder Reader*. (Photo by Anne Balsamo)

History of Reading." Each wall-segment displayed 12 episodes, with 36 episodes covering the key moments in the histories of reading and writing, from the use of pictograms to the consideration of literacy in a digital age.

The interactive called *What Haven't You Read Lately?* (WHYRL?) presented images of text in diverse landscapes from various parts of the world (see figure 9). When a viewer approached the wall-sized screen, textual captions and questions appeared on the images, which provided a poetic meditation on the contextual nature of reading. The point of the exhibit was to draw people's attention to what happens when confronted with

8. A visitor reads an episode in the "History of Reading." (Photo by Anne Balsamo)

9. A visitor triggers questions about text in the landscape on the exhibit *What Haven't You Read Lately?* (Photo by Anne Balsamo)

unfamiliar text, in languages we don't understand; we can decode meaning by reading the relationship between text and landscape.

Experiments in New Media Genres

RED speculated that the evolution of a new genre could be cultivated by the conscious design of a hybrid media form, emerging through the playful combining of elements from familiar and conventional semantic systems. In the recombinant process, the conventions of the genre are reproduced, even as they are slightly reconfigured. Many of the XFR interactives were the results of thought experiments in the hybridization and combinatory logics of multi-modal media. *Hyperbolic Comics* used the "Hyperbolic

Tree" application developed by Inxight Software, Inc. as a graphic authoring environment. A hyperbolic space is a two-dimensional space for representing the structural relationship among connected elements, such as the linkages of pages on a website. Its story, "Henry's World," combined the graphic conventions of comic book storytelling, the non-linear narrative structure of hypertexts, and the navigational mode of spatialized digital browsing in hyperbolic space (see figure 10). This interactive allowed readers to explore the many dimensions of Henry's world: his dreams; school; friends; and family.

Fluid Fiction presented a new narrative form: the interactive nested short story. In its compressed form, the story, *Harry the Ape*, consisted of 30 lines of text; next to specific words in the story were small red triangles that indicated a hyperlink. As a reader followed various links, the words of the sentence would dynamically expand to reveal new sentence endings, hidden jokes, or entertaining tangents (see figure 11). In fluidly opening the space of the basic short story, the interactive mimicked the way a good storyteller embellishes a tale, based on the interests and reactions of the audience.

Experiments in the Art of the Book

The largest area of the XFR exhibit was wildly interactive in the most human of ways: it involved eight Bay Area book artists working in a studio installed at the Tech Museum, as part of the XFR show (see figure 12). The eight artists—the last group designated as PAIR artists—included Michael Bartalos, Joceyln Bergen, Kathleen Burch, Ann Chamberlain, Julie Chen, Charles Hobson, Brian Janusiak, and Steve Woodall.[47] Each artist spent three weeks working in the state-of-the-art digital studio. During this time, they interacted with museum visitors and docents, gave impromptu lessons on book making, and produced stunning works of art.[48] Along with traditional book making tools, the *Book Artist's Studio* was equipped with color printers and copiers, digital software applications, and a laser-cutter. Each artist produced a version of a book that could be made from a single sheet of paper. These one-sheet books created the occasion for interactions between book artists and members of the museum public. The book artists engaged with these technologies for the purposes of demonstrating the creative possibilities of using new digital techniques in the creation of a traditional art form.

10. The map of "Henry's World" displayed on *Hyperbolic Comics*. (Photo by Anne Balsamo)

HARRY THE APE

Once upon a time there was a Universe, dark and big with only a sugar dusting of stars spread unevenly through the bleakness. Around one lonesome star a handful of planets circled in an endless, (well to be perfectly honest, not really endless because gravity will slowly pull the planets into the star where they will burn up in a big puff of smoke), elliptical (well to be perfectly honest not really elliptical because everything in the Universe-including other planets, comets, the occasional meteor, black holes and even creatures with telekinetic as well as hyper-mental, super-brainiac, remote kinesis, electro-static, super-coolant, super-fly powers, envision, enlightenment and even double-hyper-karate powers can move the planets off their normal paths. The universe, it turns out, is filled with such powers.) dance. On one of these planets there was a jungle, lush and green, filled with all manner of plant and animal. One of these animals was Harry the Ape whose long red fur fluttered in the wind and gleamed in the morning sun. Harry was such a big ape that he didn't notice that on his foot lived a small brown, blue-eyed mouse, buried in his big toe's fur. The Mouse's name was Mary and Mary lived by eating the food that Harry dropped. Mary particularly loved the banana peels which often fell like slimy, stringy rain. In Mary's brown fur there lived a small, quiet, spider by the name of Sam. Sam loved to eat the lice that lived in Mary's fur. Munch, munch, munch. In Sam the Spider's stomach lived an amoebae named Anne along with her whole squirmy family. The amoebas lived on small portions of the lice that Sam ate. Anne the Amoebae had never met Harry the Ape, but wherever Harry went, Anne went too. And they all spun around in the Universe, which was dark and very, very big.

11. A screen shot of *Fluid Fiction* that shows embedded fluid annotations.

12. The *Book Artist's Studio* as installed at the San Jose Museum of Technological Innovation. (Photo by Anne Balsamo)

Experiments in Machine Reading

From early on RED wanted to explore the implications of the development of reading machines, both those that could be helpful in processing the glut of information people encounter every day, and those that read behind the backs of people: bar code scanners; RFID readers; and new cryptographic technologies. For more than a decade, PARC researchers had been working on the creation of a digital watermarking system called *DataGlyphs*, which involves a technique for embedding digital information in ordinary-looking images. Using a special printing algorithm, grayscale images are created using slash marks (data-glyphs) instead of dots. The data-glyphs are oriented in one of two directions, as a fore-slash (/) or a back-slash (\). The binary orientation of the slash can be decoded using a specially equipped camera. The Glyph-O-Scope built for XFR resembled a large microscope that functioned like a secret decoder ring, which could read messages hidden in what appeared to be ordinary images on paper postcards (see figure 13). When the postcard images that comprised data-glyphs were viewed through the scope, hidden information, in the form of images and text, was superimposed on the image of the paper postcard.

13. A family uses the *Glyph-O-Scope*. (Photo by Anne Balsamo)

Embedding information into what appear to be simple images raises the question of what it means when machines can read things that people cannot.

The Evolution of a Dog

The creation of the *Reading Eye Dog* interactive began with a cultural objective: RED wanted to include an experiment in machine-assisted language translation.[49] An early idea for the translation station was based on the children's game *Telephone*, in which one person starts a chain of communication by uttering a sentence or phrase to another person, that person repeats the sentence to yet another, and so on. The enjoyment of the game turns on the way the original utterance is mangled through the exchanges between messengers. An early conception for a translation machine interactive tried to model the *Telephone* game (see figure 14). In this version, the visitor would input a sentence or phrase. The sentence would then be sequentially inputted into several language translation applications, one after the other. After the chain of translations, the sentence would be spoken aloud for the visitor to hear. After lengthy discussion about the functionality of machine translation applications, RED decided not to pursue this idea for the interactive. The reasoning was that such translation applications produce imperfect results. Many mistakes would have been made as the original sentence was handed off from one translation application to another. Given that it was likely that many visitors to the Tech Museum would have been native English speakers, we presumed that the typical visitor would have inputted a sentence in English; the translation application would then process this sentence through other languages and finally output it in English. We believed that this would have provided the occasion for the reproduction of prejudicial projections about the supremacy of English in comparison to other languages. The punch line of the interactive experience would have been always at the expense of non-English translations.

The design team continued to push on the notion of a helpful reading machine, to come up with the concept of a personal translation companion (see figure 15). This concept eventually got reworked into the notion of a personal reading companion. The designing process was mediated and punctuated by the production and iteration of Banny Banerjee's evocative design sketches. These sketches figured prominently as objects-to-think-with, which played a significant role in the physical construction of the built piece.

As the group worked on the semiotics of the notion of a personal reading companion, the sketches became helpful articulatory objects, through which a set of design commitments became reified. At one point, the sketches suggested a humanoid figure as the form factor of the personal reading companion (see figure 16). In the process, other members of RED continued working on the underlying applications that would be used in the interactive. In discussing the functionality of optical character recognition (OCR) and speech-to-text applications, we realized that these applications were still imperfect. Any reading that would be accomplished by this interactive would still be rife with mistakes, due to imprecise lighting conditions, smudged text, unrecognizable words, and random processing errors. RED decided not to pursue a humanoid figure as the form factor for the interactive, because we knew that Tech Museum visitors would already be familiar with Hollywood conventions of talking humanoid robots. When compared to the robot C-3PO, who has perfect diction and a crisp British accent, we realized that any humanoid reading machine we would build would appear less than believable. We then turned our attention to working on a helpful non-human reading companion (see figure 17).

14. Rich Gold's early sketches for translation station.

15. Banny Banerjee's early sketches for a translation machine.

Every year in August, PARC employees are allowed to bring their dogs to work. It was shortly after this annual event that the design team decided that the form factor of the personal reading companion was going to resemble a dog (see figures 18 and 19). Whether a matter of coincidence or the influence of the dogs' visit to the research center, the decision resolved one of the most vexing design issues, that the underlying applications

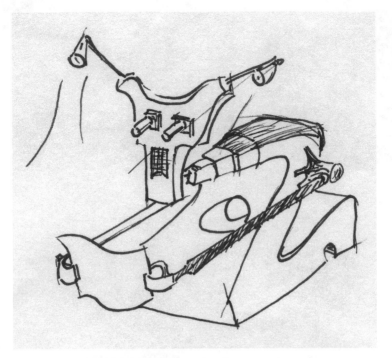

16. Banny Banerjee's sketches for a personal reading companion.

17. Banny Banerjee's sketches for a personal reading companion.

made many mistakes: common words were sometimes mispronounced if the lighting or source print image was faint. The helpful machine was going to stumble at times. Using the dog form encouraged people to forgive the errors made by the device. Rather than interact with a very dumb humanoid robot, the experience was one of interacting with a very smart dog. RED: *Reading Eye Dog* very quickly became the mascot for the exhibit (see figure 20).

RED: *Reading Eye Dog* could read a range of material: books, newspapers, and brochures. Video cameras mounted behind the lenses of eyeglasses captured a digital image of material on a reading stand. This image was then inputted into an OCR application, which parsed the image into text, words, and images. The output of the OCR application was submitted to a speech synthesizing application. The entire process from image capture to speech synthesis took 15 seconds. The stages of image and speech processing were displayed on screens mounted on the front and back of the robot. The synthetic voice used was modified to include dog-like utterances. When the OCR or speech synthesis application didn't recognize a word, the synthesized voice was programmed to say the word "arf" or "woof." In this way, the performance of the synthesized voice output was aligned with the built form of the interactive dog.

The Reading Body

Let me reflect on the lessons learned about reading through the process of creating these interactives, and then watching how people read with them.[50] Broadly construed, the XFR exhibit focused on the dynamic relationship between bodies, technologies, words, images, and the construction of meaning within a particular social context: the science / technology museum. The XFR interactives demonstrated divergent kinds of reading. The WHYRL? experiment, for example, provided a critical reading experience, where readers were invited to engage the meta-critique provoked by the annotations that accompanied the images of text in the landscape. RED: *Reading Eye Dog* presented yet another kind of reading, created through the simulation of a vocalization of written text. *The Reading Wall* specifically explored issues related to modes of public reading. The *Listen Readers* and *Walk-In Comix* were designed as stages for social reading experiences.

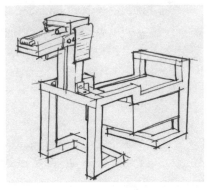

18. The *Reading Eye Dog* comes into focus. (Sketches by Banny Banerjee).

19. The First CAD of the *Reading Eye Dog*. (CAD by Banny Banerjee).

20. *RED: Reading Eye Dog.* (Photo by Deanna Horvath/Xerox PARC).

Because they were installed in a museum and not an art gallery, each interactive was designed to withstand the use and abuse of large numbers of people of different ages. All the interactives represent a core commitment to the materiality of reading: to be used with hands, feet, and bodily weight. In focusing on the body of the reader, these interactives probed another dimension of the future of reading: the role of the body in the practice of meaning-making. Throughout the history of reading, the body has assumed distinct roles: as a vocalization instrument (before the development of silent reading); as a performance instrument (where the text was literally enacted by the gestures and flourishes of a reader's body); as a temple of quiescence (when the body was disciplined to remain still and the eye mobilized); and more recently, as an interface device where the reader's body assumes a posture that supports the productive activity of hand and eye. Throughout the XFR exhibit, the reader's body was provoked to engage the speculative reading devices in multiple ways, with hands, eyes, and ears, as well as by bending, reaching, lifting, walking, poking, touching, and pointing. The reader's body enacted a variety of reading postures and gestures; all these embodied activities contribute to the act of meaning-making. This led to the understanding that there is no singular future of reading, only futures that will unfold through the intra-actions among readers, books, texts, and objects.

The RED Shift

In the process of creating the exhibit, RED refined its understanding of its own research methods.[51] The members of RED brought diverse design experiences to the project: architectural; sound; product; information; lighting; interfaces; and toy. Even as RED's methods were deeply informed by other disciplines, over time the group began to codify an account of its own research practices. This discursive construction of the definition of RED's research methodology was documented in various monographs, and performed using various objects of that research.[52] At the broadest level, RED understood that its methodology—as a system of practices that manifests a particular epistemological coherence—was an example of speculative design research. Unlike typical descriptions of engineering design methods, which identify the domains of design according to instrumentality, such as "design *for* manufacturability," or "design *for* sustainability," RED's research focused on the practices of design itself. Underlying RED's methodology was a shared, but largely unstated belief that design—the group's ostensible domain of study—was a deeply social act, involving distributed practices of meaning-making.[53] In particular, RED focused its research efforts on an infrastructural element of meaning: the role of genre.

Genre is a construct that emerges through distributed social practices of meaning-making. A genre is a second-order semiotic device that organizes meaning in a particular way. Both authors and readers must recognize the conventions of a genre for it to be meaningful. Single instances of expression that manifest genre characteristics only make sense within a context of multiple instances. As RED understood all too well, to take on the project of designing a new genre was to take on an unusual research agenda. As a work of speculative design research, the construction of a new genre involves developing a mode of expression or a new medium for a social situation that does not yet exist, where neither authors nor readers recognize the genre conventions in play. While we know that new genres can develop very rapidly (the homepage, for example), the elements that give rise to a genre (such as the capabilities of authoring tools, the semiotics of the design language, the affordances of the medium, the sensibilities of the reader or audience member) are difficult to specify in advance. This complex dynamic was at the center of RED's research charter. It took on a dual project: 1) to investigate the conditions whereby new genres come into existence; and 2) to create (and design) the first instances of plausible new (media) genres. RED's research on the design of new genres took shape as physical speculations about plausible futures. These weren't simply hypotheses about a set of theoretical possibilities that might give rise to new reading experiences, but rather exhibits that manifested several instances of those reading experiences.[54] RED understood that the real proof of the success of its research efforts would happen over time, as other people engaged and transformed those first instances into multiple manifestations of a new genre.[55]

RED was especially interested in the possibility that one could track the evolution, or "genre-fication," of a new device or media form. Given that RED was creating the first instance of several interactive experiences, and with them instances of new media genres, the group was poised to watch how a single instance might be replicated or reproduced by other designers, such that it evolved into a genre.[56] At one point, the distinction between "genre-fication" and commoditization was discussed explicitly. While RED hoped that it was possible that some of the interactives would eventually be duplicated as research devices for other experimental situations, they never intended that the interactives would be turned into marketable products or consumer devices. In some cases, RED worked explicitly against the logics of marketability. This is not to say that there wasn't branding happening throughout the exhibit—a title banner bearing the Xerox corporate logo framed the entire installation, for example—but the interactives weren't originally designed as marketable commodities. In fact, RED consciously explored ways to violate certain conventions of typical consumer interface design—banishing keyboards and mice, for example. In creating unconventional modes of interactivity, RED had to be less radical in the creation of content. This is one of the reasons many of the interactives draw on the genre conventions of comics. In authoring the stories and content for the interactives, RED employed a level of vocabulary that was not at all radical in its use of theory.[57] The problem with purposefully violating conventions, even in the service of creating new ones, is that one runs the risk of making something that is incomprehensible to one's intended audience. Designer theorists call this the "paradox of design" (Krippendorf, 1995: 156; Dorst, 2006: 14). In this sense, the experiments of XFR were also investigations into the boundary between novelty and incomprehensibility.

The process whereby a set of research practices were codified as a methodology was the outcome of an iterative designing process, during which plausible theoretical explanations were hacked, recombined, and reworked. As cultural theorist Stuart Hall once remarked, if we have long understood that reality is socially constructed, we must also appreciate the extent to which it is narratively constructed as well; the creation of RED's account of its research methodology was a sustained example in the narrative construction of reality.[58] This reality was shifting, partial, and continually refined; in the process certain versions took flight.[59] The narrative construction of reality unfolded through the embodied actions of using language, writing, making marks on paper, sending emails, circulating paper, making drafts, listening, ventriloquizing, miming, and gesturing. These expressive gestures did not simply represent phases of the design process, they were the means by which individual RED members made sense of the research process, their identities, and the objectives of the design project.

At one point, RED member Matt Gorbet proposed the concept of the RED *Shift*, in order to describe the overall research philosophy enacted throughout the XFR project.[60] He described it to me as "an interdisciplinary practice, by which technology that is in development or designed for a given purpose is coerced into performing a new function, usually to some expressive or artistic end." For example, to create the interactive, *Hyber-*

bolic Comics, RED borrowed the Hyperbolic Tree technology from Inxight Software, Inc. and with the developer's permission détourned it to serve another purpose: that of a graphic authoring environment, resulting in the interactive application called "Henry's World."[61] Subjecting Inxight's technology-under-development to the RED *Shift* served to push the limits of thinking about technology in terms of its functionality, its limit-conditions, and its usefulness for other cultural purposes. In some cases it led to the creation of new intellectual property; in others the pay-off was in making an undervalued technology more visible and present for multiple audiences, both inside and outside Xerox.[62] The predominant texture of the RED *Shift* was cultural: the technologies used for each interactive were recontextualized as expressive technocultural elements: as illustrations of new media genres, new reading experiences, and new authoring environments. As described in the previous section, there were several experimental vectors guiding the designing effort for each interactive that investigated distinct aspects of the nature of reading: the scale of the reading experience; the dynamic nature of augmented books; and the nature of machine reading. All of these experiments rested on shifting the context of technology development from exploring one set of possibilities—rationalized within a corporate research context—to considering another set, focused on the technocultural possibilities of these emerging technologies.

Probably the greatest payoff of the use of the RED *Shift* technique was how it also shifted RED's understanding about the nature of technology itself. RED began to think of technology as a medium of expression that could be authored and sculpted in creative ways, using a range of styles. In searching to understand how an embryonic technology could be shifted, RED had the opportunity to investigate the manner in which technologies get narrativized, fixed to serve particular purposes such that other possibilities of use are foreclosed. The RED *Shift* was often first manifested in the creation of prototypes and demonstrations of designs in progress during RED's group meetings, or as part of charettes. At these moments, the meaning of the RED *Shift* was performed in the way that technologies were combined and operated as prototypes of interactives.[63] A full complement of theatrical techniques was employed in these performances. In the beginning stages of the designing process, the interactives were more conceptual than technological: foam-core mock-ups, common item stand-ins, and fanciful approximations were used in demos to convey the embryonic idea for a particular interactive. These props were narrativized with standard performative gestures, commonly recognized as hand-waving and poetic misdirection. Irrational descriptions were routine parts of the improvisation of technology demonstrations, as exemplified when the demo-maestro (the person demonstrating a new technology) came to a technical function that hadn't been fully worked out, boldly claiming with a wave of the hand, "and then something magical happens." It wasn't only during the design charettes or the group demonstrations of prototypes that the work of the RED *Shift* was performed, however: it happened during the installation, the many guided tours, and RED's performative PowerPoint presentations. It was through these iterative performances of narrative incantations that the RED *Shift* was enacted such that RED's members and audiences came to believe the prototypes were real. To stretch an insight from cultural theorist, Michel de Certeau (1984: 186), "These narrations have the twofold and strange power of transforming seeing into believing, and of fabricating realities out of appearances."[64] Key to the cultural work performed by these narratives is the practice of citation. Fundamentally, citation is a process of establishing credibility through reference to others who have already been invested with reality-status. In the cultural arena of the technology demo, the practice of citation sometimes involves the strategic invocation of technical principles or the work of other researchers, but more typically it is enacted by the materialization of a device prototype. In this way, a technology-under-development participates in a complex legitimation dance: it is simultaneously a performance of a fiction and the material referent of its own reality status.

Technological Fictions of What Came to Be

During my time with RED, I labored as a designer and project manager, digital author, theorist, writer, cheerleader, spokeswoman, consultant, resident techno-humanist, feminist, and tour-guide.[65] But this chapter is not a chronicle of my singular experiences working at PARC. Instead it is better understood as an incomplete narrative of the work of RED at Xerox PARC, authored by me, specifically as part of this transmedia book project. It is over-determined by my experiences and interpretations: that is inescapable. It is a work of technocultural fiction, as much as of institutional history. It is reliable, reflective, and plausible. It is incomplete, partial, and contestable. What else could it be?

Of particular interest to me, for my purposes here, is Lucy Suchman's discussion of the theoretical position of the organizational subject, who might—as I hoped to do in this chapter—want to create a theoretically informed account of the experiences of working as a researcher at PARC. As Suchman (2007) notes, recent developments in theorizing the subject in science studies, cultural anthropology, and feminist theory question the premise of the self-standing individual as the location of agency.[66] More- over, as John Law suggests, any accounting of experience by a subject, decentered or not, must also be understood as a particular narrative con- struction through which the coherence of the experience is performed. In the process of constructing a post-hoc narrative of a research project that unfolded at Xerox PARC during the late 1990s, I had to construct a subject position from which to author this account.

Let me describe some of the complexities of this task. One of my objectives for this chapter was to present a report of the work of a group of people, employed at PARC, who developed a set of new reading devices as part of their collaborative research efforts. I was hired to contribute a particular set of skills and scholarly expertise to this group; I went to PARC to engage in the group's collaborative research activities. I did *not* go to PARC to study this group as an ethnographer or even as a cul- tural critic. Upon joining the group, I learned that they had already made a commitment to study their own research practices; this commitment was built into their research charter. So even before I landed, my sta- tus as a self-standing subject was already destabilized.[67] As a new resi- dent within the industry research center, I was joining the group as an outsider who, by virtue of institutional pronouncements and economic transactions, would become an insider—engaged in a collaborative pro- cess of reflexively creating a story about the group's research practices, through the fictional stance of an imagined outsider. Inside, outside, imag- ined, performed, enacted, the boundaries that constituted my identity at PARC were always already in flux. As an individual (with a particular biography of sedimented experiences, cohering for me as my biography and my self) I continued to explore theoretical questions that had been part of my scholarly practice for more than a decade. At the same time,

I was a part of a multiplicitous subject—the collaborative group known as RED—which was the collective agent responsible for the design and production of a set of new technologies. RED was in turn one of the institutional units within the entity known as PARC. The cast of characters in this story multiply quickly: RED (a collective subject); I (the fictional moniker of Anne-the-author); named characters (the members of RED and others); and nameless others (organizational functionaries and corporate ideal-types).[68]

To address the broader aims of this transmedia book project, I wanted to recount the efforts of RED to create new research on the future of reading. The question I wrestled with concerned how I might speak about this research. I don't write *as* a subject position; I enact subject positions through my writing. Neither the constitution not the shifts of my subjectivity were the focal point of my research or designing activities. While I have several research notebooks filled with meeting notes, design annotations, to-do lists, diagrams, sketches, and other traces of my engagement with colleagues, these notebooks only remind me of the order of events and discussions, not of the changes in subjective understandings of myself-in-relation to colleagues, to co-participants, or to the technological materials I tinkered with in the course of this project; yet, in turning my attention to recounting the work of RED over a three-year period, all I have to draw on is a subjective set of understandings about what the group was doing at any given time. While the aim of this chapter was not to privilege a biographical portrait of myself as a multiply constituted subject within the social networks at PARC, I inevitably construct accounts of a shifting set of understandings, subject positions, affiliations, and world-making that are deeply influenced by my personal recollections. Although the creation of this narrative was not the original focus of my research effort, or RED's, it is now its inescapable conclusion.

As the noted sociologist of technology Bruno Latour asserts, "By definition, a technological project is a fiction, since at the outset it does not exist, and there is no way it can exist yet because it is in the project phase."[69] He goes on to elaborate: the observer of technologies under development

is free to study engineers who are creating fictions, since fiction, the production of a state of technology from five to fifty years in the future . . . is part of their [the engineers'] job. They invent a means of transportation that does not exist, paper passengers, opportunities that have to be created, places that have to be designed (often from scratch), component industries, technological revolutions. They're novelists. With just one difference: their project—which is at first indistinguishable from a novel—will gradually veer in one direction or another. Either it will remain a project in the file drawers . . . or else it will be transformed into an object. In the beginning, there is no distinction between projects and objects. The two circulate from office to office in the form of paper, plans, departmental memos, speeches, scale models, and occasional synopses . . . the observer of technologies has to be very careful not to differentiate too hastily between signs and things, between projects and objects, between fiction and reality, between a novel about feelings and what is inscribed in the nature of things. (1996: 24)

Indeed, what I recounted here is the unfolding of a technocutural project that eventually veered toward becoming a set of objects. The shelf life of the objects varied: some objects only existed for a short period of time (March through September of 2000); many are now (2010) gathering dust in crates in Menlo Park; hundreds of artifacts are scattered as personal computer files, snatches of code, reworked digital applications, file folders of papers, patents, personal memories, and theoretical insights. Others are still in working order in labs and showrooms. The purpose of this chapter was to offer a textual account of a project of technocultural innovation as it moved through stages of becoming, on its way to its current status as part of an archive of a real place known as PARC. While the research was engaged in the technological performance of the future, it is now only accessible as a historical chronicle of a set of work practices that have long since been concluded.

three

Public Interactives and the
Design of Technological Literacies

Although there are many places where people can and do learn about new technologies—formally in schools and other educational institutions, informally though the popular culture of science fiction, through social networks, websites, and even advertisements —the contemporary science/technology museum is one of the few institutions that has built into its mission the objective to communicate science and technological knowledge to the public. These museums and centers are ensembles of devices, demonstrations, practices, buildings, educational programs, and professional identities. Social anthropologist Sharon Macdonald refers to them as "cultural technologies," because they arrange culture in particular ways: they stage opportunities for informal science learning, and in the process they constitute the publics for science; they craft mission statements that specify their role as interlocutors, mediating between the science of the laboratory and a science for the people; and they develop exhibits that validate certain topics as properly scientific, and which nominate new technologies as innovative and newsworthy.[1] These institutions perform important cultural work, as stages for the enactment of myths and truths about what counts as science, as technology, and as knowledge. This chapter considers how these institutions serve as sites of technology transfer, where the knowledge produced in the lab is communicated and performed for the public through special exhibits, hands-on experiences, and interactive spectacles. I revisit some of the key shifts in the way that science/technology museums have performed their cultural work over the past century. I am particularly interested in tracing a genealogy of a designerly approach to museum exhibit production, a development that involved the work of famous designers, such as Charles and Ray Eames, and well-known science centers like the Exploratorium in San Francisco. This historical discussion provides a context for the elaboration of the designing process involved in creating one of the XFR exhibits called *The Reading Wall*. I delve into this process in order to elaborate the role played by museum exhibit designers in creating works of knowledge-transfer between the lab and members of the museum-going public. In doing this articulatory labor they serve as cultural mediators, drawing on current literacies of technology as a design resource to create exhibits that will shape the technological literacies of the future.

Just as the institutional form of the science museum has changed throughout history, so too has the scope of its cultural work (Macdonald, 1998).[2] These shifts reflect the museum's changing role in the constitution of scientific knowledge, in the creation of identities of nation, citizens, the public, and in modes of representing science (for example, as embedded within a historically specific location, or as a set of universal principles). The earliest precursors to the genre of science museum include cabinets of curiosities during the early sixteenth century. As many have pointed out, these collections did not simply reflect what was already constituted as scientific knowledge, they participated in the consolidation of a cultural identity for the practice of science. Over time the initial often fanciful nature of the collection of curiosities was rationalized to instantiate taxonomic orderings of the natural world. By the eighteenth century, collections were in the process of becoming institutionalized as places where people, mostly elites, could witness the ordering of the natural world; from this ordering was derived a whole range of scientific facts, which in turn vested a certain set of practices and practitioners with the power to produce truth.

If those early collections—of curiosities and subsequently of ordered taxonomies of the natural world—were deeply implicated in the constitution of a cultural identity for science, the development of industrial and technology museums in the late nineteenth century were equally implicated in the early formations of nationalism throughout the developed world. As Macdonald writes: "By the early decades of the twentieth century, most of the first wave of nation-states could boast not only a national museum, but national museums of both natural history and of science and technology . . . [alongside] national museums of art and other subjects" (1998: 10). The identity of the public of the museum also shifted. Whereas the early cabinets and displays of collections indexing the natural world were designed for the edification of elites and fellow (scientific) collectors, the displays of natural history and industrial national wonders were directed to the mass public, who were cast in a particular relationship to the nation-state and to one another (as members of particular classes, races, and genders). According to cultural historian Tony Bennett (1995: 46), these public museums operated differently from their predecessors, describing them as "an apparatus whose orientation is primarily governmental. As such, it is concerned not only to impress the visitor with a message of power, but also to induct her or him into new forms of programming the self aimed at producing new types of conduct and self-shaping."[3]

By the middle of the twentieth century, the project of the science museum, and its related institutions, the industrial museum and the science center, shifted again to take up a role as a cultural mediator of scientific knowledge, responsible for demystifying the nature of science for the general public. Macdonald characterizes these broad changes in the cultural purpose of museums as functioning as technologies of truth, of the nation-state, and of representation. Macdonald's primary purpose in tracing the implications of this set of historic changes is to discuss transformations in modes of display. As she rightly points out, such transformations were part of broader epistemic shifts concerning the ways of apprehending subjects, objects, and the world. By tracing the changes over several centuries of the form of the science museum, as well as the modes of display enacted by these museums, we can note how the pedagogical strategies of these institutions also changed. Beginning with the 1893 World's Columbian Exposition in Chicago, science and technology-based exhibitions shifted focus almost exclusively to the machines of the industrial age: engines, automobiles, scientific instruments, and calculating devices. Where earlier industrial museums relied on collections of artifacts as the basis for exhibitions that itemized the order of the natural world, later museums staged exhibits as testimonies to the wonders of the industrial age. The stories told about these artifacts trumpeted the role of technology as the engine of progress. For example, in 1933 the Museum of Science and Industry opened in Chicago in conjunction with the city's Century of Progress Exposition. Not only did the Museum of Science and Industry display an impressive range of new technologies, including a working coalmine, it also functioned to narrativize the technologies that were already part of Chicago's industrial landscape.[4] As Bennett (1995: 77) maintains: "Museums of science and technology, heirs to the rhetoric of progress developed in national and international exhibitions, completed the evolutionary picture in representing the history of industry and manufacture as a series of progressive innovations leading up to the contemporary triumphs of industrial capitalism." The exhibits within these museums featured the scientific and technological products that made progress possible. This was a tautological argument, of course, because progress was already defined, both as developments in science and as the accumulation of technological marvels. Nonetheless, the key pedagogical strategy enacted by these exhibits was of demonstration and guided tours. Through the organized layout of exhibits within the museum space, visitors followed prefigured paths of travel for which a particular narrative unfolded concerning the meaning of the objects and artifacts on display.[5] This was an explicit pedagogical strategy: museum visitors were to be educated via their movements through museum spaces. Having organized the story of the objects in this way, the museum served as a narrative apparatus, which also called forth the performative participation of the museum visitor in making the story manifest. "Organized walking" is Bennett's term for the mental and corporeal performance of meaning-making, whereby the museum visitor not only learns the story of progress, but also constitutes herself as a subject of progress through the act of witnessing the scientific and technological marvels on display.

By enabling museum visitors to see into these featured objects of science and technology, later modes of display pushed the logic of witnessing further. The aesthetics of the visible inspired the design and development of such exhibits as the visible car, the visible heart, and of course, the visible human, where some portion of the internal organization of the object is revealed by having been encased in glass. These exhibits were both occasioned by, and implicated in, the reproduction of an episteme of the visual: where revealing and seeing became the enabling conditions for the production of new knowledge and understanding.[6] While the cultural fascination with visualism animated the development of science throughout the nineteenth century, as well as served as an enabling condition for the historical emergence of cinema, it also influenced the development of a new paradigm of exhibition and display for science and technology museums. The proliferation of exhibits of visuality—for example, the walk-through heart in the Museum of Science and Industry in Chicago—also marked an evolutionary moment in the pedagogy of science/technology museums. Where earlier the layout of objects within a museum's collection functioned as stops on an organized tour, through which the visitor (as *flâneur*) was to learn the story of these objects as structured by the tour path, the see-through exhibits were designed to perform their own stories by revealing their inner workings to a voyeuristic public. The objects themselves became performers in the circulation of new narratives and mythologies: "Stories and messages, rather than taxonomies, then, are the museums' new fictions" (MacDonald and Silverstone, 1990: 177). This shift, from presenting taxonomies of the natural world to propagating stories about the cultural role of science and technology, as well as the relationship of the visitor to particular objects, marks another key moment in the transformation of the cultural work of the science/technology center—as it became a key site for the reproduction of cultural narratives about science and technology for the general public. Central to this shift was a change in the identity of the visitor as well, who now was positioned as a voyeur and co-participant of the fictions on offer.

By the late 1950s the focus of science exhibitions shifted from a fascination with the visible products of science to an investigation of the processes of science (Arnold, 1996; MacDonald, 1998). Coterminous with this shift, science museums began to include exhibits designed to provide opportunities for visitors to participate in the process of acquiring scientific understanding. The pedagogical mission was less focused on providing context for understanding spectacular machines and visible objects, but more on providing an elaboration of underlying scientific principles. Central to this broad shift was the development of science centers as a new institutional space for the provision of informal science education for the general public. Whereas earlier industrial museums represented the nature of science as a collection of specific technologies, contextualized within the history of a particular nation or contributing to a particular zeitgeist (of progress for example), the modern science center was created to enlighten, educate, and inspire the museum-going public about the creative practices of scientific and technological innovation, which were freed from historical and cultural contexts altogether.[7] This pedagogical impulse was grounded in a set of democratic ideals: the processes of scientific understanding and technological invention would be open to all students, regardless of national identity or class. Exhibits, therefore, were divested of matters of national identity or ideological program in favor of appealing to the natural curiosity and native intelligence that visitors embodied, and which served as the foundation of everyday knowledge-making practices.

Probably the most well-known, and indeed the earliest, example of a science center that exemplified this approach is the Exploratorium in San Francisco, which was created explicitly to address and enhance the public's understanding of science. In 1968, founder Frank Oppenheimer (1968: 1) offered a "poem" for the new organization of a science museum that could fulfill the pressing need to create an environment where "people can become familiar with the details of science and technology and begin to gain some understanding by controlling and watching the behavior of laboratory apparatuses and machinery." "The whole point of the Exploratorium," Oppenheimer (Hein, 1986: xv) explained, "is to make it possible for people to believe they can understand the world around them." This represents an explicit shift in pedagogical strategy, away from merely walking the guided tour and toward the control and manipulation of laboratory apparatuses. This was the beginning of a hands-on approach to the demonstration of science and technology for the purpose of engaging the public's curiosity about the way things work.

Oppenheimer believed that the way to get people excited to learn about science and technology was to involve a "glorious mix of disciplines" in the design of a new museum of science.[8] For Oppenheimer, the glorious mix must involve scientists as well as artists, technologists as well as designers. As sociologist Andrew Barry (2001: 103) notes: "blurring the boundaries of art and science was an important part of the Exploratorium's pedagogic strategy, for by doing so it was hoped that the centre's visitors might begin to understand that science was a *creative* activity." Indeed, for more than three decades, artists-in-residence have co-designed and collaborated on the creation of interactive exhibits for the Exploratorium. These exhibits have been well received by the Exploratorium's visitors and widely duplicated for other museums.[9] The aesthetic character of these exhibits has varied: some, such as those by Ned Kahn or Bill Bell, were realized in more conventionally aesthetic forms—by the use of beautiful materials such as wood and polished molded plastic, for example—while others were created from common at-hand materials, evincing what might be considered an anti- (designerly) aesthetic, having used, for example, rough wood and exposed connectors. Many artist-created exhibits deliberately avoided any specific invocation of underlying scientific principles, which created a tension with Oppenheimer's original ideals. For example, one piece from the famous *Seeing the Light* exhibit created at the Exploratorium demonstrates a simple visual phenomenon: created by renowned exhibit artist Bob Miller, "Christmas Tree Balls" consists of an array of silver ornaments sandwiched between two pieces of Plexiglas, held in a wooden frame. The piece works by offering the visitor the opportunity to meditate on the subtle differences of multiplied curved reflections. A peephole in the side of the case allows visitors to see that this really is just a collection of Christmas tree balls. The exhibit does manifest Oppenheimer's original instruction, to create exhibits that would provoke a visitor to notice phenomena that are often taken for granted, but its staging within the *Seeing the Light* exhibit did not include any explanatory signage about the underlying nature of the visual effect. At best, these artist-created exhibits could be understood as provoking a state of defamiliarization—a well-worn pedagogical gesture of twentieth-century art—and thereby enacting a strategy for engaging laypeople (the non-scientists) in a necessary pre-rational step of scientific discovery. At worst, a pronounced tension is produced, between Oppenheimer's pedagogical mission—to educate visitors about the processes of science—and his resolute commitment to the necessary collaboration between art and science, which has the purpose of communicating the creative essence of scientific practice to a lay audience.[10]

When it opened in 1969, the Exploratorium was the first of its kind. Since then its influence has spread to other science and technology museums throughout the world. Some of these have explicitly tried to mediate the tension between the commitment to public pedagogy and the important role of non-instrumental art to communicate the creativity of science.

One of the most successful is the New York Hall of Science (NYHOS), which actually now owns and displays the original Exploratorium *Seeing the Light* exhibit. Over the past ten years, the NYHOS has collected some of the most significant art-science/technology exhibits created in the United States during the past half century.[11] In 2006, the NYHOS added significantly to its collection when it permanently installed the interactive exhibition *Mathematica: A World of Numbers and Beyond*, first created by Charles and Ray Eames in 1961 for the Los Angeles Museum of Science and Industry. This exhibit is described as the "ancestor of many contemporary science exhibitions, predating the participatory displays that were pioneered by the Exploratorium" in the 1970s (Rothstein 2004: E1).[12] If one of the marks of the paradigm-shifting influence of the Exploratorium was the recognition of the importance of having artists collaborate on the creation of hands-on exhibits and demonstrations, then the far-reaching significance of the *Mathematica* exhibit was its designerly sensibility, brought to bear on the public communication of scientific and technological information. One of the consequences of these paradigm-shifting experiments is that, in the intervening three decades, the exhibit designer has come to replace the museum curator as the key architect for the cultural work of the science/technology center.[13]

Another Vector of the Eames Design Legacy

As an iconic pair of mid-century designers, Charles and Ray Eames contributed much to the look and feel of postwar America; but far beyond merely defining the "way that America sits down," they were actively involved in creating the field of information design through film productions, presentations, and public exhibitions that focused on elaborating the functionality of new devices—the Polaroid Land Camera, for example—and on the underlying science of natural phenomena.[14] Make no mistake: Charles and Ray Eames embodied a host of cultural contradictions. They were designers who maintained an abiding commitment to the social mission of "good design"; they believed that design could improve society; they also saw themselves as visual communicators who actively supported efforts to educate the public about scientific and technological principles; yet their design work was commissioned by some of the most powerful multinational entities of the postwar era, including IBM, Westinghouse, Columbia Broadcasting System, the Rand Foundation, and several units of the U.S. Government, such as the State Department and the U.S. Information Agency (Lipstadt, 1997).[15] Charles and Ray Eames believed that education was not just the province of schools and universities, but that it was something businesses needed to invest in—not simply because of some vague notion of social good, but because such investments developed important qualities in the desired consumer base for these businesses. They extolled the virtues of computers as problem-solving machines and were keen to cast these new technologies as life-enhancing for people around the globe (Albrecht, 1997: 38). They argued successfully that this interest overlapped significantly with the business of IBM, for example. During their lifelong collaboration with the computer company, they produced dozens of films, presentations, and exhibitions for the company, which were designed to visually communicate scientific principles to lay audiences. Produced in 1961 for a new wing of the California Museum of Science and Industry, and underwritten by IBM, *Mathematica: The World of Numbers and Beyond* was the Eameses' first major public exhibit. As related by Demetrios (2001: 181), they had ambitious objectives for this exhibit: "The education goals of *Mathematica*, though quite valuable, were not its only ends. Charles and Ray saw the idea of it and other projects as the potential beginning of a new value system for society at large. Charles put the challenge of the exhibition this way: 'One of the great secrets of science is the genuine fun and pleasure that scientists get out of it. One of the purposes of this exhibition is to let the cat out of the bag.'"[16] As such, the exhibit was designed to communicate the history and breadth of mathematics to a general public, an act that would also introduce this same public to the basis of both computational logic and the wonders of the computer, and equally importantly, to the creative process of science itself.

As a mixed media spectacle involving the use of images, text, graphics, simulations, illustration, and gaming, the *Mathematica* exhibit impresses viewers even today, and it has stood the test of time for more than 50 years. The Eameses articulated the goal for the exhibit: "It should be of interest to a bright student and not embarrass the most knowledgeable mathematician" (Demetrios, 2001: 180).[17] Although they asserted that the pleasure of the exhibit should come from the science, not from the "wrapper the designer put around it," they deployed innovative craftwork in the creation of exhibit models and interactives (181). Construction methods were of the highest quality, as were the materials: models were built out of rosewood, oak, and brass, while fine hand drawings and illustrations were included among the explanatory texts. They described the exhibit as being the result of a deep conversation between art, science, and technology.

The pedagogical modes of *Mathematica* involve text and image presentations, physical demonstrations of mathematical phenomena, mixed media collage assemblies, and interactive illustrations.[18] The entire exhibit communicates a clear message from fifty feet away; at the same time it rewards the reader who spends time close-up with the textual and image saturated surfaces. From this glut of information Charles and Ray Eames created a topically organized exhibit that included six interactive units: "celestial machines"; "the moebius band"; "probability"; "topology"; "minimal surfaces"; "projective geometry"; and "multiplication." The modes of interactivity vary. For example, in the "probability" unit, when the visitor presses a large button, 30,000 plastic balls fall through an array of steel pins until they randomly land at the bottom of the exhibit. As they fall, a particular pattern plays out: the formation of a bell curve. This happens every time even though there is an indefinite number of paths that any ball can take from opening to landing. The interactive is framed by a quotation from Sir Francis Galton (who first formulated the concept of the bell curve): "The theory of probability is nothing more than good sense confirmed by calculation."[19]

At the New York Hall of Science, where the exhibit is currently installed, the entire exhibit is architecturally contained between two walls: *The Image Wall* and *The History Wall*. *The Image Wall* displays visual materials and objects annotated according to their mathematical importance. The mixed media of this wall includes a real starfish, an image of R. Buckminster Fuller's geodesic dome, diagrams, and two-dimensional models mounted directly onto the wall. A forty-foot long, eight-foot tall timeline called "The Men of Modern Mathematics" runs along the other wall, depicting the history of the development of mathematics from 1000 CE to the present (1960s).[20] *The History Wall* demonstrates the mastery of its creators as information designers, and manifests the art of information design before it was even recognized as such. The wall includes a conventionally designed timeline that divides its span into centuries; key events in the history of mathematics are marked by typographic flourishes. Layered on top of the graphic design is another trajectory of historical elements: the biographies of the (so-called) great men who contributed important mathematical ideas. The interactivity of *The History Wall* is highly conventional —viewers apprehend it by standing close and reading from left to right, top to bottom; but in terms of its use of the semiotics of spatial organization and layout, its implied movement, choice of font, scale, and layering of types of information, these walls are a testament to the information design artistry of Charles and Ray Eames.

The Reading Wall: Writing the Reading on the Wall

When asked about the social nature of designing (in a videotaped interview) Charles Eames (1972) replied that creativity is not a solo activity: "One must always acknowledge those who have gone before." Indeed, this is one of the reasons for my explication of the Eameses' work in interactive exhibit design. Their *Mathematica* exhibit was both a direct and indirect influence on the design of the *Experiments in the Future of Reading* (XFR) exhibit that I described in the previous chapter. Their attention to detail inspired the designers of the XFR exhibit (the members of RED and collaborative fabricators) to pay close attention to the quality of materials and the craftsmanship of the individual elements; this was evident in everything from the choice of materials for the form factor of each XFR interactive to the information design of the digital material presented as part of each experience.[21] More directly, one of the signature interactives of the XFR exhibit, *The Reading Wall* (and its digital application called "Episodes in the History of Reading"), was designed in conscious dialogue with the *Mathematica* exhibit. Just as the Eameses' *History Wall* presented the history of mathematics as a spectacle of visuality rather than a collection of facts for mastery, the XFR *Reading Wall* was designed as a layered presentation of visual material that evoked relationships among the multiple strands of the cultural histories of reading and writing. Unlike *The History Wall*, the narrative presented on *The Reading Wall* did not reproduce history as the sole work of men of genius. *The Reading Wall* explicitly drew on multiple sources about the development of practices of reading in different cultures, the materialities of writing, and the social institutions of literacy. In weaving together diverse narratives, the digital application created as part of this interactive wall exhibit was designed to complicate the notion of a singular master narrative of the historical development of reading, writing, and communication forms.

Traditionally walls have played an important role in the reproduction of cultural memory and history. Throughout history, writings on walls, whether carved, painted, or sculpted, in the form of glyphs, cuneiform, Roman lettering, or bas relief images, have depicted accounts of significant cultural events: great battles; great tragedies; great victories; and the reign of great rulers. Wall inscriptions often commemorate the events that comprise the history of a culture. They were used for different purposes: to preserve memories in the face of a culture's defeat; to trumpet the conquests of an army; to prop up the morale of a beleaguered society; to assuage the ego of an impotent ruler. It is also the case, however, that inscribed walls were used pedagogically. New members of a culture—children, foreigners, captives, slaves, and prisoners of war—were brought into understandings about that culture by having the walls read to them. Through a combination of oral and written practices, the history of a culture was—and in many cases still is—reproduced from generation to generation via the mediation of epigraphic writing. This cultural history of a communication form motivated the decision to design *The Reading Wall* as a monument to the history of reading.[22]

The Reading Wall interactive communicated its messages in several ways.[23] It comprised three separate sixteen-foot long walls that stood ten feet high (see figure 21). Each sixteen-foot wall included a printed graphic that displayed information about the history of reading and writing in the form of generic timeline elements (dates, locations, key events), noteworthy quotations, and a long graphic ribbon that repeated the phrase "reading is always changing" in the five most commonly spoken languages of San Jose, California (the location of the Tech Museum): English, Spanish, Tagalog, Vietnamese, and Chinese. Each wall segment included a printed background that employed the typographic conventions of a generic timeline to communicate the key events of part of that history (see figure 22). The title of the overall piece was displayed over the three wall segments: The first segment—on the far left of the exhibit—displayed the beginning of the title: "Episodes In"; the second displayed the middle part of the title: "The History"; the third—on the far right—displayed the last part of the title: "Of Reading." This layout encouraged a particular reading of the walls: visitors were subtly guided to the far left wall where they would find, not surprisingly, the earliest dates and historical markers. In total, *The Reading Wall* included a forty-eight-foot long timeline covering 25,000 years. Mounted along each wall was a metal track, on which hung a large plasma display in portrait orientation. The display moved along the track. The material that appeared on the plasma screen was cued by its position on the wall. This created a relationship between the digital episodes displayed on the screen and the static printed material displayed on the wall. The animated digital displays also communicated a three-part treatment of the history of reading:

"Part 1 . . . being about the first writing systems, books and libraries."

"Part 2 . . . being about the spread of printing and new reading habits."

"Part 3 . . . being about the rise of mass communication and new reading machines."

In all, the wall segments were designed to communicate in each of three modes: 1) through the built form and its location vis-à-vis the other two walls; 2) through the static timeline information printed on the wall surface; and 3) through the digital material animated on the display. The process of writing the reading on the wall involved methods of iterative information design, where each mode of communication was authored and re-authored many times over.

The timeline is a spatialized genre: mapping temporal markers and events onto space invokes a visual rhetoric that implies causality, progress, and intention. The genre characteristics of the static printed timeline subtly shape the expectations of museum visitors, who not only learn that what they read on these displays counts as history, but also are encouraged to ascribe causal effect to events that are presented in a particular spatial layout. *The Reading Wall* provided multiple spaces of historical representation. The printed timeline offered a diachronic chronicle of the interwoven histories of reading, writing, and communication forms. The screen made available synchronic episodes of particular historical moments that shaped, and were shaped by, other historical events. The design team understood that visitors would embody certain literacies and expectations about the conventional mode of historical presentation. In acknowledging the importance of visitor expectations, but still wanting to rethink the mode of historical display, *The Reading Wall* both reproduced and reconfigured

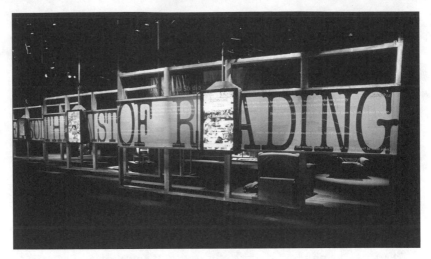

21. *The Reading Wall: Episodes in the History of Reading* as installed at the San Jose Museum of Technological Innovation. (Photo by Anne Balsamo)

22. A close-up of the printed background of *The Reading Wall* shows elements of the conventional typographic design of timelines. (Photo by Anne Balsamo)

the conventions of the static presentation of historical material. The printed background used the typographic conventions of static timeline presentation, while the animated digital material relied on an episodic narrative structure for the presentation of key events in the long, intertwined histories of reading.

Michel de Certeau (1984: 134–36) describes the scriptural economy as involving three elements: 1) the blank page as a space where the writing subject can create her own world; 2) the "production of a system of objects" by the writing subject that make this space meaning-full; and 3) the "transformation of the natural world." All writing, according to de Certeau, has the "goal of social efficacy. It manipulates its exteriority." This is an apt description of the process of authoring/designing for digital environments. The blank page is a space of possibility within which the writing subject can create her own fantastic landscape. The elements of this landscape are semiotic objects: the objects that produce meaning—in combination, juxtaposition, and form, as well as through movement—but in digital environments this landscape is never simply blank, awaiting the semiotic play of a system of objects. This space is already marked by material conditions that are sometimes non-negotiable. That is to say, in a digital authoring environment—where the intent is to author writing to be read from a digital display—the blank page has already been delimited in ways that subtly, but surely, constrain the hand of the digital author. For example, in the case of authoring *The Reading Wall*, the choice of plasma display provided a specific screen resolution that affected the readability of fonts. The number of pixels per inch (ppi) determined whether or not fonts of a certain size were readable. In some cases, certain font styles could not be used because the resolution was too coarse to allow for the easy recognition of spaces between letters. Given that font styles are a common semiotic resource in digital applications—where the symbolism of the font treatment is used to augment the look and feel of a given digital document—by limiting the range of fonts able to be read on the screen, the resolution characteristics of the plasma display clearly impacted the range of possibilities of the digital blank page. If the ultimate goal weren't social transformation and communicatability, then perhaps the readability of fonts would not be an issue; but then, presumably, we wouldn't understand that what was produced and displayed was written or authored in the same sense as de Certeau intends.

The practices of authorship and design merged completely in creating the digital episodes that were displayed on *The Reading Wall*. Created using several digital applications, each application subtly influenced not only the content of the text, but also the possibilities of expression enabled by the different applications.[24] In this case, both the practice and act of authoring extended well beyond the production of textual elements, the selection of a rhetorical style, and the enactment of a voice. Authoring also involved font selection, color choice, the determination of background graphic treatment and layout, the design of effects for the textual elements and images, and the creation of a meaning for the dynamic presentation of those elements. Each authoring practice transformed the digital environment: colored it—divided it into meaningful sections; marked it; and left traces on it—but it also transformed what was, and could be, written. Although the textual elements of *The Reading Wall* were first authored in Microsoft Word, once these elements were imported into Photoshop, the textual elements often had to be rewritten to accommodate font size, leading, kerning, and other typographic considerations. The amount of text that could be presented on the screen was determined by screen resolution and pixel aspect ratio, which often occasioned the substitution of words, the rephrasing of ideas, and the deletion of text in favor of an evocative image. It was never simply the case that the material for *The Reading Wall* was written elsewhere and then transported to a digital application for display on the plasma screen. It was only through the iterative practices of writing and rewriting, designing and redesigning within the constraints of various digital applications, that *The Reading Wall* could be said to have been authored at all.

The creation of the digital wall application involved familiar techniques of content development. RED member Steve Harrison created the initial historical trajectory that listed the key moments visitors would expect to see in a timeline about the history of reading. He realized from the beginning that this project in information design was also a historiographic venture. To get started on the actual authoring process, I conducted an initial creative inventory of historical materials, including timelines, books, and images. As I did, I began to understand that I was not simply producing another historical account, but a different mode of historical inscription (see figure 23). Although I employed standard historiographic methods in the creation of the episodic narrative content, I realized that the

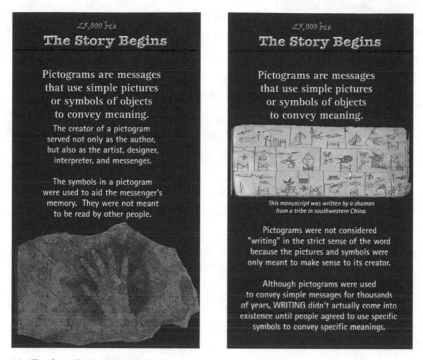

25,000 bce

The Story Begins

Pictograms are messages
that use simple pictures
or symbols of objects
to convey meaning.

The creator of a pictogram
served not only as the author,
but also as the artist, designer,
interpreter, and messenger.

The symbols in a pictogram
were used to aid the messenger's
memory. They were not meant
to be read by other people.

25,000 bce

The Story Begins

Pictograms are messages
that use simple pictures
or symbols of objects
to convey meaning.

*This manuscript was written by a shaman
from a tribe in southwestern China.*

Pictograms were not considered
"writing" in the strict sense of the word
because the pictures and symbols were
only meant to make sense to its creator.

Although pictograms were used
to convey simple messages for thousands
of years, WRITING didn't actually come into
existence until people agreed to use specific
symbols to convey specific meanings.

23. "The Story Begins." Screen shots from two moments of the first episode in *The History of Reading*. (Photo by Anne Balsamo)

output would be something generically different than a typical historical account. To be sure, I wanted the historical dates and references to be verifiable by other scholars. Thus, I consulted multiple academic sources for descriptions of each key moment. I reviewed my selection and narrative treatment of key episodes from multiple perspectives, and conducted additional research when necessary in order to reconcile contradictory claims. Yet, what was eventually authored did not conform to any recognizable genre of historical writing. I needed to learn *how* to write on these walls because the authoring process used to create digital episodes for *The Reading Wall* was thoroughly influenced by technological characteristics of the digital writing surface.

In creating the digital application for *The Reading Wall* I learned two lessons about the process of digital authoring: first, that the material characteristics of the technologies of display significantly influenced what I could do, and second, that the processes of authoring and designing have merged completely. As the primary digital author of *The Reading Wall* material, the history that I was in effect rewriting for this interactive device was shaped by several theoretical commitments. For example, I consciously sought to avoid attributing agency to technological devices so as not to reproduce the technological determinism of the common histories of reading and writing. The digital episodes include references to the materiality of writing surfaces, the rise of specific social and political institutions (such as libraries and mandatory public education), the development of social practices of literacy and censorship, and the cross-cultural innovations that enabled the spread of printing throughout Europe. Simultaneously, I wrestled with the technological influence of a particular form of information display: the static timeline. As I was trying to write a narrative that refused a technological-determinist account of the history of reading and writing, I had to negotiate the very real constraints imposed by the technological form I was designing for.

In itemizing the manner in which the possibilities of the blank page of the digital display were constrained by characteristics of the technological elements, it is apparent that every blank page is in some respects never really blank. The affordances of the medium always subtly shape the landscape of possibilities (in de Certeau's sense).[25] But this does not need to collapse into an argument for the technological determination of a digital writing application; digital environments and applications should be understood as functioning as do different materialities of writing such as stone, papyrus, silk, and paper—by evincing different possibilities, as well as constraints, for expression. For a designer, the objective is to understand the way in which a particular materiality, or in this case digital application, can be modulated effectively for specific communicative purposes. This is not to say that the device is a mere tool in the hands of a designer. Tools do impose constraints. As I argued in the introduction, we need to think in more complex ways about the relationship between technology and culture that avoids getting trapped within debates about lines of determination, as if these debates could definitively settle the essential vectors of influence and control between humans and their devices. It is a more creative enterprise, I argue, to figure out the dynamics of constraint and possibility in the process of trying to make something innovative. This non-linear and highly iterative designing process is apparently quite typical in the creation of interactive exhibits.[26] This was the underlying opportunity that animated the writing for *The Reading Wall*: to investigate how this new hybrid writing surface could be authored in a way that other blank pages could not, and to discover the possibilities for designing a new reading experience using a range of digital technologies, textual design conventions, and animation conventions for dynamic typography.

The Poetics of Interactivity

The Reading Wall presented readers with an unusual hybrid interface, combining the two-dimensional formalism of a book's page with the linear spatiality of a scroll's textual space, and the choreography of cinematic editing with the dynamism of animated text. The rules of information design for this new reading experience were created in the process of authoring the digital application for the interactive wall as a new expressive and physical form.[27] Literary historian and digital information theorist Jerome McGann (2002) elaborates this process by identifying the nature of the parameters of the information design process. McGann asserts that the information designer—the professional graphic semiologist or information architect—has limited parameters to work with: 1) the visible mark, which is defined according to qualities such as size, luminosity, texture, color, shape, and orientation; 2) the space of the page, which is defined according to dimensions of the plane, the environment, or time; and 3) the direction of graphic presentation—from top to bottom and left to right.[28] These parameters identify "how the language of poetic form works" (99). McGann uses the term "textspace" to describe the space of textual possibility: "Movement, textual as well as human, occurs within a fixed space where the relations of things are unimaginably deep and complex. One divides this space in order to mark a way into those complex relations" (99). The process of information design includes not simply the authoring of content but a mapping and fixing of the textspace such that the spatial organization of elements within it (the page, the screen) makes sense and must be understood as contributing to the meaning of the whole reading experience.

As the designer of the dynamic digital application displayed on *The Reading Wall*, let me draw on McGann's insights to elaborate the key design characteristics of the information design of the application. The textspace of *The Reading Wall* combined the bibliographic textuality of a book with the epigraphic spatiality of a wall; as a new hybrid medium of expression, it required the development of a specialized visual language and the creation of new rhetorical codes. Following formal bibliographic conventions, the digital material presented on the screen comprised words, text blocks, punctuation, alignment arrangements, font size, font color, font type, images, graphic elements, background color, and spatial zones of demarcation. These elements conveyed formal typographic and bibliographic meanings. For example, the two-dimensional space was conventionally divided so that material was meant to be read from top to bottom: the episode's time frame and title appeared at the top of the page space; the thesis statement for the episode appeared under the title; words, texts, images, and graphic elements were laid out below. Moreover, the shape of the words denoted emphasis: thesis statements for each episode used a larger font than did explanatory statements; caption statements used a smaller font size. Likewise, there was a standard graphical treatment for all episode titles. This is a typical description of the process of information design, in which the creation of a visual language based on explicit semiotic values enables the consistent and theoretically motivated deployment of the elements.

But because this interactive also enacted a scrolling textual space, the movement of the screen along the wall animated the visual elements presented on each page space such that the fixity of the page space was fleeting. It was also the case that the visual language authored for *The Reading Wall* included specific animation effects: as a reader moved the display the elements of an episode's page space were assembled in a dynamic fashion.[29] These effects were both aesthetic and semiotic. For example, to create a sense of visual parallelism, the dynamic opening and closing of an episode were closely matched. When a reader moved the display to another location, thereby arriving at the space of a new episode, the elements of that episode would be assembled through the reader's movement of the display. The animation effects were then reversed as the reader continued to move through the episode: in essence the elements of the episode were symmetrically disassembled. For example, if an element entered the page space from screen-left, it exited screen-right. If an element came into focus on the page space by growing in size and in intensity, then it exited the page space by shrinking and fading to the background. These techniques extended the formal characteristics of the bibliographic page-space to dynamic motion through an epigraphic textspace.[30]

Reading the Writing on the Wall

Writing surfaces influence the shape of written letters.

The Romans inscribed the walls of their monuments by chiseling letters in stone.

The hardness of the stone and the angular shape of the chisel dictated the shape of the letters.

Writers had to know the craft of stone carving in order to accurately calculate the distance and placement of letters.

The walls in the major cities of the Roman Empire were covered with writing.

Wall writing, such as an inscription on a monument, is called "epigraphic" writing.

24. "Reading the Writing on the Wall." Screen shot of episode eight of *The History of Reading*.

Media artist Margaret Morse (2003: 16) invokes the phrase "poetics of interactivity" to refer to the expressive practices of meaning-making that involve the engagement between humans and machines.[31] In the case of *The Reading Wall*, the interactive poetics were designed to signify something about the nature of reading: of reading both epigraphically and historically. *The Reading Wall* could be read in several ways and at different distances of engagement. The message conveyed at the farthest viewing distance (approximately fifty feet) was that this exhibit would perform important cultural work: the work of monuments. Everything was designed to signify the monumental purpose of the exhibit: the length of the wall segments, as well as the thickness and mass of its steel frame. Given that this was the exhibit that communicated multiple histories of the development of reading, writing, and communication forms—some of the very practices that constitute human culture—and that these histories are widespread and temporally vast, the form factor of this interactive was designed to perform monumentalness (see figure 24).

At a distance of thirty feet, a reader could see the three wall segments located in the center of the XFR exhibit; at this distance, a reader could begin to apprehend a relationship between the walls and the other exhibits that suggested a privileged position for the walls and the material displayed there. The overall layout of the XFR exhibit and the specific position of the three wall segments subtly guided visitors to the left-most wall segment. At a twenty-foot distance from the wall, a reader would see the title displayed across all three wall segments: wall 1: "Episodes In"; wall 2: "The History"; and, wall 3: "Of Reading." From this distance, the reader could begin to apprehend that the three segments were three parts of one narrative about the history of reading. At this same distance, the astute reader would begin to be oriented to the multiple narrative forms presented on *The Reading Wall*. She would see a printed (generic) timeline, and also read the title that announced the availability of episodes in the history of reading. At a ten-foot distance, the reader would see that the displays showed an animated screen saver, providing the title of the particular wall segment as well as an injunction to move the display in one of two directions (back or forth along the wall). At closer range, the semiotics of the timeline would become more evident to the reader as she read dates, textual descriptions, and textual layout arrayed according to generic timeline conventions. The earliest dates appear to the left; simultaneous events are vertically aligned; noteworthy moments or comments are printed in larger, bolder fonts. At arm's length, the viewer was able to read the printed static surface and move the display so as to animate and read the digital writing on the wall.

At an arm's length distance and through the process of moving the display along the wall, the reader encountered another dimension of the poetics of interactivity designed for *The Reading Wall*. This dimension manifests the essence of historical displacement and of the nature of reading itself. At an elemental level, the design of the visual language and the animation of digital elements contributed to the creation of a poetics of interactivity that augmented the overall cultural meaning of *The Reading Wall*. Movement of the display, which happened as the reader used his or her body weight to pull or push the display in one of two directions, animated the text and images of each digital episode: the choreography of the reader's body in contact with the device was designed to constitute a semiosis of reading. Moving from one episode to the next, a reader / device moved both through time and through space. As the reader and the display moved along the wall—in either direction, back or forward—the visual elements of the episodes appeared and disappeared. On the reader's part, the actual reading of historical material (comprising text, words, images, captions, titles, dates) took place in one space, in one temporality. When reading an episode, the reader's present was the stage for the opportunity to apprehend a narrative of the past. As the now of the reader's present gave way to the next moment, and the next episode was assembled, the past (in the form of the episode just read) dissipated: it had no presence on the digital display. As soon as the reader moved, the present changed, and with the movement to the next episode, the phenomenological unfolding yielded a new assembly of text/image elements. Once the reader and display moved, the previous episode disappeared from sight, no longer able to be viewed or experienced through reading in that space, and at that time. This mode of interactivity was designed to evoke a performance of the poetics of history. No one returns to history—its place-ness is ephemeral, accessible only through displaced representations or embodied memories. All that was left in the space of the previously viewed episode were the traces of that historical moment reproduced as a set of marks on the static timeline displayed on the physical part of the wall.

In walking along the wall, oscillating between a reading of the static printed background and a reading of the animated digital foreground, the reader accumulates insight by sampling material from different display spaces. Here we return to one of the key theoretical objectives for the creation of *The Reading Wall*: to contest the assumed passivity of the reader.[32] On this point de Certeau is worth quoting at length:

> In reality, the activity of reading has on the contrary all the characteristics of a silent production: the drift across the page, the metamorphosis of the text effected by the wandering eyes of the reader, the improvisation and expectation of meanings inferred from a few words, leaps over written spaces in an ephemeral dance. But since he is incapable of stockpiling (unless he writes or records), the reader cannot protect himself against the erosion of time (while reading, he forgets himself and he forgets what he has read) unless he buys the object (book, image), which is no more than a substitute (the spoor or promise) of moments 'lost' in reading. He insinuates into another person's text the

ruses of pleasure and appropriation: he poaches on it, is transported into it, and pluralizes himself in it like the internal rumblings of one's body. Ruse, metaphor, arrangement, this production is also an 'invention' of the memory. Words become the outlet or product of silent histories. The readable transforms itself into the memorable . . . the thin film of writing becomes a movement of strata, a play of spaces. A different world (the reader's) slips into the author's place. (1984: xxi)

This quotation from de Certeau should make clear that any account I offer that focuses on the act of writing the reading on the wall is of course an incomplete account of the practice of epigraphic meaning-making: for it only offers a description (post-hoc at that) of a rationalization of the authoring/design of a non-typical reading experience. The meaning of *The Reading Wall* is by no means accounted for by elaborating the steps of its information design, its theoretical preoccupations, or even its poetics. What meaning was read was far more heterogeneous and enigmatic.

As de Certeau elaborates, meaning is also an effect of the negotiation on the part of readers of power dynamics inherent in the social stratification between writers and readers. De Certeau (1984: 172–73) refers to this as the politics of reading: "Reading is thus situated at the point where social stratification (class relationships) and poetic operations (the practitioner's constructions of a text) intersect: a social hierarchization seeks to make the reader conform to the information distributed by an elite (or semi-elite); reading operations manipulate the reader by insinuating their inventiveness into the cracks in a cultural orthodoxy . . . The autonomy of the reader depends on a transformation of the social relationships that over-determine his relation to texts." The cultural orthodoxy invoked by de Certeau refers to what for him is a definitional situation in which elites write and read based on their dialogue with other elites. "*Barthes reads Proust in Stendahal's text*" (174). The intertextual references among literary works are deployed by a writer for the purposes of informing the reader of "what is to be thought" (172).

De Certeau deprivileges the productive acts of the writer to insist on the productive nature of reading. He contradicts any simple-minded notion that casts reading as a passive act when he describes reading as "poaching" and characterizes the everyday practice of reading as fundamentally tactical in nature (1984: 165). Building on this insight, we can understand reading as a practice that is inherently mutable and queer: it is a practice of improvisation performed in negotiation with a set of rules established by others. In the case of *The Reading Wall*, the experience of reading must be considered a complex set of interactions among the reader, the author/designer, and the technological device and interface, each of which plays a role in the creation of meaning.

I describe the process of designing *The Reading Wall*—which included my acts of writing the reading for the walls—as a collaborative exercise of the technological imaginations of those involved in its design. This imagination understands how technologies simultaneously establish rules, constraints, and contexts within which emerge a creative and unpredictable improvisation, expressing something not previously known to any of the participants. In this sense, *The Reading Wall* might be usefully understood as an example of what Katherine Hayles (2002: 25) calls a "technotext," which she elaborates as "a literary work that interrogates the inscription technology that produces it; it mobilizes reflexive loops between its imaginative world and the material apparatus embodying that creation as a physical presence." As was the case with the other XFR exhibits, *The Reading Wall* was authored/designed to encourage visitors to pay attention to the materiality of the reading experience. As Hayles points out, "to change the material artifact is to transform the context and circumstances for interacting with the words, which inevitably changes the meaning of the words as well. This transformation of meaning is especially potent when the words reflexively interact with the inscription technologies that produce them" (23–24). To encourage readers to reflect on the relationship between the experience and materiality of reading, technotexts use defamiliarization as a tactic of literacy training.[33] As a new mode of expression, a technotext is a hybrid technocultural form that draws on conventional literacies, refracting these meaning-making practices through the use of technological applications and devices.

It was inevitable that *The Reading Wall* episodes reproduced elements of cultural orthodoxies because they were informed by European and American scholarship on the history of reading and elaborated in terms of key events in U.S. history. A few years later when I turned my attention to creating a Spanish-language version of *The Reading Wall* called *Deslízate en el Tiempo: Episodios en la Historia de la Comunicación*, for the Papalote Children's Museum in Mexico City—a project where I explicitly tried to

The Deep Reading/Total Authoring Thesis

As discussed earlier in this chapter, during the process of designing the *XFR* exhibit, RED investigated the historical development of science and technology museums to note how the genre conventions of such museums have changed over time. Based on that research, RED identified the salient characteristics of the cultural setting of the Tech museum as a way of understanding the social and symbolic conventions that would most likely influence the meaning of what RED could and would design. The decision to focus on the creation of new reading devices rather than new authoring devices was the result of a prolonged discussion about prevailing conventions of museum exhibit design. In subtle ways this decision was imposed on RED by the context we were designing for—namely the Tech museum. Although the Visitor Guide to the Tech Museum declared, "Be amazed. Do amazing things. And discover the inner innovator in you," there were relatively few opportunities for visitors to engage in truly open-ended creative activities. The hands-on exhibits were constrained in subtle ways so as to prohibit the use of offensive language, for example, or to delimit the amount of time any one visitor spent at any one interactive. From early on in the collaboration, the Tech museum staff expressed concern with the "throughput" of proposed *XFR* interactives—the number of visitors who could use any one interactive at any time. An interactive can "fail" if it is too popular or "sticky" because when visitors spend too much time in any one place the overall flow of traffic through the museum is impeded. These were some of the reasons that justified RED's decision that the *expressive* part of each interactive—the authoring possibilities presented by different devices—would be part of RED's research program, but not part of the interactive experiences offered in the *XFR* exhibit. This was reflected in Rich Gold's assertion that part of RED's research program was exploring the process of "total authoring" whereby the authoring and design functions merge in the creation of new devices and applications. In one sense, to focus on new reading experiences rather than new authoring practices might be seen as falling back onto an old divide that placed a higher value on reading literacy than on writing literacy; yet the communicative strategy manifested in different *XFR* interactives pushed the notion of reading literacy into new directions. Even to take "reading" as the topic for the creation of an entire three thousand square-foot exhibit was a radical gesture within the context of traditional science and technology center exhibits. The Tech museum staff often asserted, "visitors don't read at the Tech Museum"; we would see them slightly shake their heads at our refusal to abandon the "reading changes" topic. We didn't contest the Tech Museum staff's understanding of their visitors' penchant for reading (or not); we knew that this understanding was part of the general belief system of exhibit designers at other hands-on learning centers. Indeed, their reservations were well supported (see, for example, Thomas and Caulton, 1996). RED believed that when presented with new reading devices and unfamiliar reading genres, Tech Museum visitors would be enticed to engage in more sustained reading activities. Our belief was born out in the evidence collected by an independent exhibit evaluator (Meluch, 2000) who observed museum visitors interacting with the *XFR* exhibit pieces. In the initial beta test, as well as in the evaluation of the outside reviewer, visitors took time to read the material presented in various interactives. As the summative evaluation states: "When compared with the exhibit goals stated above, findings in each of the studies reveal a considerable measure of success. The vast majority of visitors felt that they had experienced something new, expressed a very high level enjoyment of this exhibit and satisfaction with it relative to other exhibits at the Tech. They also acknowledged being made aware of a wide variety of new and possible future technologies for reading" (2). The evaluation documented that the average length of time a visitor spent in the *XFR* exhibit was twenty-six minutes and the average time spent at any one interactive was twenty-seven seconds. At a theoretical level, the *XFR* exhibits demonstrated a complex understanding of the notion of the book: as a structured relation among material forms, modes of textuality, genres, literacies, and social conventions. At the level of exhibition messaging, the aim of the installation was to encourage visitors to reflect on how reading might change in the future with the use of new technologies and digital modes of interactive storytelling.

work against an Anglo-centric cultural orthodoxy about the development of communication technologies—I learned that matters of language translation were simple to address in comparison to matters of narrative and literacy.[34] For example, in working with the exhibit development staff at the museum in Mexico City, I was surprised to learn that they were not interested in a narrative account that situated the development of communication technologies in a specific Mexican context. When the staff read the treatment I prepared, which included dates for the wide-scale spread of telephones, television, and the Internet throughout Mexico, they asked that I replace these dates with those that mark the development of these technologies in the United States. Other episodes that invoked specific events in Mexican history were also slightly rewritten to refer to events based in the United States. At first I was perplexed about the reason for these revisions. I wondered if it were due to the fact that these technologies

of communication were not yet widely available to various Mexican populations, especially in the poorer states of Chiapas, Oaxaca, and Tabasco.
When I asked about this, the response surprised and enlightened me. As
one staff member replied, "we want to have the same history as the U.S., we
feel that it is, in many ways, our history as well." The only culturally specific
episode that survived this process of collaborative authorship was one on
the history of wall writing that discussed the significance of Mayan wall
inscriptions. Throughout the collaboration with my Mexican colleagues
we developed shared understandings of the histories of key technologies
in Mexico. Most communication technologies arrived in Mexico through
adoption and adaptation of technologies that were invented elsewhere.
The histories that they wanted displayed on their wall were the histories of
the invention of these technologies. I learned that there are differences
between "cultural orthodoxies" and the diffusion of innovation across geo-
political boundaries. Innovations may get dispersed with a particular ideological wrapper, but that does not necessarily say anything about the way in
which they are received or implemented.[35]

In reflecting on the experiences of authoring/designing applications for
these interactive walls, I came to think differently about the social stratification between author/designer and reader. In subtle distinction to de
Certeau's assertion that social stratification insinuates the reader into the
literary cultural orthodoxy of the author/designer, I understood the process as one of implicating the reader into a particular technology of literacy.
To assert this may be a matter of semantics, as technologies of literacy do
imply cultural orthodoxies. Yet I believe that the focus on the notion of
technologies of literacy offers a more expansive way to think about the
cultural implications of the design of innovative interactive experiences.

Among the elements that make up the nature of the literacy required of
readers of The Reading Wall were those borrowed explicitly from print
technology. This included the formation of words into text blocks, built
out of grammatically correct sentences, and the symbolic use of page space
to communicate a hierarchy of textual elements: the title of the episode
prominently located at the top served to organize all elements that subsequently appeared. In addition to the conventions of information display
borrowed from print, the digital application relied heavily on conventions
of dynamic media to communicate particular narrative ideas. The design
of The Reading Wall presumed that readers were already initiated members

of a technocultural order of the printed book. As the the author/designer of the wall application, I not only relied on readers' technological literacy, but also explicitly used it as a design resource.

In the process of interacting with *The Reading Wall*, readers' technological literacy was exercised and subtly refined. As an evocative knowledge object the interactive was designed to evoke readers' understandings of the semiosis of digital textuality, of the semiotics of material form, and of the epistemological structure of the museum setting. To the extent that these understandings were already part of the core competencies (literacies) of the reader, the interactive experience would make sense. But it is also the case that *The Reading Wall* provided the occasion where nascent competencies could be called forth to be practiced and reinforced. This is an example of how technological engagements with interactive devices perform the technocultural work of shaping future literacies, by building on the meaning-making practices already understood by readers/users. This is the process whereby the literacy of technology becomes a technology of literacy.

The Literacy of Technology/The Technology of Literacy

The term "literacy" refers to a concept that is rhetorically powerful, but difficult to define.[36] In some discussions it identifies an idealized domain of knowledge, while in others it is the name given to a set of cultural practices. It is a common understanding that the primary objective of mandatory education (K–12 in the United States) is to provide literacy to school-age students. Sometimes the discussion of literacy moves away from the discussion of educational curricula, per se, to include questions about the general public and its basic level of knowledge about a particular topic: scientific literacy or geographic literacy, for example. Even the most basic review of the history of the concept demonstrates that its definition is bound by time and culture, insofar as what counts as literacy or illiteracy varies across cultural situations and historical eras. Literacy is now conventionally understood to refer to the acquisition of reading and writing skills, but that wasn't always the case. Early literacy movements in the United States focused more heavily on the teaching of reading skills, to the exclusion of writing skills, and for the past two hundred years even the notion of reading literacy has been defined in reference to a specific technology of communication: the printed text. The ability to read printed material, for example, is taken to be a sign, as well as an objective, of basic literacy programs.

The XFR exhibit enacted a particular stance regarding the notion of technological literacy, which subtly took issue with two popular propositions about the relationship between technology and literacy.[37] Simply put, the two related but opposing propositions claim that either technology erodes traditional literacy or technology can solve the problems of illiteracy. While this is not the place to rehearse the fuller discussions that give rise to these propositions, I want to unpack a few of the implications of these statements, in order to develop a more nuanced consideration of the relationship between technology and literacy, which has implications for the development of a robust technological imagination.

The first proposition, that technology erodes traditional literacy, circulates most frequently as a caricature of the discussion about the implications of the spreading use of computer technologies and digital environments, particularly as both tools and sites for writing and reading. The term "technology" in the first proposition generally means computers and digital applications.[38] The term "traditional literacy" means typographic reading and writing skills. This proposition holds that the use of computers in the classroom erodes traditional text-based competencies of narrative construction, rhetorical expression, and critical analysis, because these competencies are no longer taught, valued, or practiced in a disciplined manner.[39] This position often asserts that the computer distracts from basic literacy education by becoming the overwhelming focus of classroom practice. When this proposition mistakenly sets up an opposition between technology and literacy, it masks the fact that all literacies have a technological material basis. Writing, of course is a technology; so too is the page, the book, and the alphabet. Print encompasses multiple technologies. Framed by the invocation of a crisis in literacy, the second proposition fixes the cause of the crisis on specific technologies that, in addition to computers and digital applications, may also include television, video games, computer games, and even new library services.[40] In the best cases, the invocation of a crisis in literacy is a rhetorical move, designed to provoke serious discussion about a topic that is often overlooked and devalued. This move is unnecessary really: literacy is a foundational cultural consideration. Literacy is important, period. We do not need to invoke the urgency of a crisis in order to justify the investigation of the effectiveness of literacy programs or the discussion of new approaches to literacy and pedagogy. As Jonathan Taylor writes in his editor's column for the inaugural issue of the online *Journal of Technology and Literacy*:

> We are in the midst of a literacy crisis. How often has that phrase been repeated? How many people accept this statement unconditionally?
>
> The literacy crisis in America, and in many countries, is not so much that kids or adults can't read; while there are literacy gaps that need attention, the crisis is the fact that the crisis is constructed and operates as a controlling myth of American culture, and instead of developing programs to foster lifelong literacy, most public discussions of literacy focus on simple, binary definitions of literacy (literate/illiterate), teacher accountability, standardized testing, and mechanistic, skill and drill solutions which may produce better test results but do little to foster literacy practices. (2000)

Taylor rightly points out that one of the effects of mythologizing the literacy crisis is that it keeps the focus on institutional responses rather than on literacy practices. Literacy is not something that is achieved and then surpassed, either at the level of the individual or at the level of a society: it is a process, not a condition. Just as literate people must continue to learn to read and write throughout their lives—as new situations for reading and writing develop—so too must societies continue to engage and refine their foundational cultural reproductive processes that take form as new lifelong literacy programs. Literacy is not a static quality, but a set of competencies that must be practiced and expanded throughout an individual's life.

Highly related to the first proposition, the second assertion, that technology can solve the problems of illiteracy, also rests on a set of simple equivalences. The term "illiteracy" is defined as an absence of basic reading and writing skills, but more recently has been expanded to include a lack of computer skills and information skills. When addressing the lack of traditional typographic reading and writing skills, this proposition often mistakenly diagnoses the problem as a lack of access to technology. The teleology is evident: technology is cast as the solution for a problem caused by a lack of technological access. If it were the case that this proposition only focused on computer illiteracy, then the proposed technological solution might be warranted.[41] But the lack of basic reading and writing skills is already a consequence of a complex arrangement of factors, where it is often difficult to determine whether the lack of a particular set of skills is the cause or the effect of disempowering social and economic situations. Moreover, even in the case where the problem is defined as a lack of technological access, the programs that propose simple technological solutions often fail, not because access isn't important in some democratic sense, but because the solutions fail to take account of the many factors that set up (or discourage) the conditions of motivated technological use, and the development of literacy practices within a given technocultural context. By overly privileging the object, or the device-form of technology—the computer or network access, for example—the other elements that make a technology meaningful are either overlooked or discounted.

Consider the banner reports about the failed use of educational technologies in the K-12 classrooms throughout the United States. Despite the spending of billions of dollars on technology for U.S. schools, the promises that justified these expenditures have not materialized.[42] The reason cited most frequently is that these technologies were never properly integrated into the K-12 curricula such that the educational objectives of various courses of study could be supported by the introduction of computer technologies into the classroom. One crucial missing element of the "technology as solution" proposition was totally overlooked: that of the training and hiring of technologically literate teachers and support staff. Busy teachers were not given time or training in the use of the new technologies necessary to help them develop appropriate pedagogical techniques that would have allowed them to address their educational objectives. As many observers and critics have complained, the technology was often literally dumped into these classrooms as a magic bullet, to solve a problem that wasn't entirely technological in nature.[43] This approach often leads to the formation of objectives for literacy programs that are exclusively defined in terms of increasing technological access, which is considered some sort of panacea. In the worst cases, the real hope is that access to the technology will be the means to some measure of social rehabilitation: it will keep kids off the streets and out of gangs. The focus on access obscures two important considerations: that computer and digital technologies reconfigure what it means to be literate; and that literacy discussions often serve as alibis for the institutionalization of administrative and social control programs.

My interest in unpacking these propositions is not so much to map the fault lines of the interesting and complex set of debates surrounding the creation of objectives for new literacy programs, competing definitions of literacy, or the deployment of educational technologies; rather it is to further develop the insights required of a robust technological imagination.[44] To this end, I espouse an approach that refutes the opposition of technology and literacy, in favor of an understanding that builds on the notions that the concept of literacy always implies a technological dimension; that literacy itself must be considered a social technology with cultural and political implications; and that new technologies reconfigure what it means to be literate. For example, Myron Tuman (1992: 8) was one of the first to articulate that computers will reshape "not just how we read and write, and by extension, how we teach these skills but our very understanding of basic terms such as *reading, writing* and text." In the intervening years since Tuman's observation we have witnessed how discussions about technology and literacy have taken up more nuanced questions about changing forms of knowledge production, new epistemological subject positions, and transformed notions of textuality. The discussion has moved from a preoccupation with instrumental considerations having to do with computer literacy as a foundation for employability, for example, to more complex discussions about how digital technologies can address the cognitive implications of multimodal learning. These notions are crucial not only for developing pragmatically effective educational practices, but also for elaborating how technologies function culturally. Literacy is a socially shaped and historically specific technology of cultural fitness: this is what I mean when I use the phrase, "the technology of literacy." Literacy programs enact a process of social engineering, for which the inputs are a specific set of cultural values, objectives, and modes of expression, and the desired output is a certain kind of culturally and materially competent person.

The phrase "literacy of technology" implies something else. All discussions about literacy are also discussions about technology—as a set of material conditions, expressive tools, communication devices, and the processes of technocultural reproduction and transformation. Thus, to continue to talk about the relationship between literacy and technology as a relationship between two distinct terms would be off-target, just as I argued in the introduction that the discussion of technology as somehow separate from culture was an untenable philosophical proposition. In making this argument, I join other scholars in asserting that it is more useful to talk about the concept of technological literacy as a way to discuss the specific set of expressive competences that are both invoked and repro-duced in the use of new technologies.[45] Rather than promoting a specific definition of technological literacy, I offer instead an analysis of how new technologies participate in the invocation of present literacies, and the innovation of literacies for the future.[46] I do this because I'm interested in elaborating how the notion of technological literacy can inform the work of designers of new technologies, museum exhibits, and other forms of interactive experiences.

In order to understand the way in which technological literacy is both an enabling condition and an outcome of the development of innovative technologies, consider how the XFR exhibit drew on certain assumptions about the technological literacies already mastered by the museum-going public. Taken together, the interactives that comprised the XFR exhibit assumed that readers would be able to read text presented in English; that they would understand how to use a range of technological interfaces such as a touch-screen, a joy stick, push-buttons, a steering wheel and a velocity pedal; that they would understand highly conventionalized relations be-tween image and text; and that they would understand how to read the meaning of a technological form. These competencies were resources for the design of the XFR interactives that were deployed for the purposes of providing a meaningful, yet defamiliarized, reading experience.[47] This is one of the ways that technological development draws on prevailing cul-tural understandings in the service of producing innovation. The design of *The Reading Wall* certainly relied on the reader's familiarity with cinematic conventions of the animated image, concurrently evoking a poetics of reading. Although this poetics may have been evoked by the experience of reading the wall, it was not a poetics about the wall per se. It was a poetics about the nature of reading itself. Even though the pedagogical impact may have been lost on all but the most astute readers, this interactive communi-cated something about the technocultural process of meaning-making. In reinforcing a reader's literacy, it acknowledged the reader as a member of a particular social group: the textually literate. In this way, the readers' base-level textual literacies had already transformed them into competent mem-bers of a particular culture.

In interacting with the digital episodes, readers encountered a highly conventionalized aesthetics of information design that replicated elements of print-based information architecture, but reinvented them in a new technological form.[48] In interacting with the wall, readers were presented with a unique form of epigraphic writing that explored a new use for walls in digital culture. In framing its story as a technologically mediated conversation between the static printed background and a digitally animated foreground, this interactive also experimented with the creation of a new mode of historical presentation. This is an example of the doubled-nature of technology as simultaneously replicative and expressive; it is also an example of how the process of technological designing always involves the reproduction of technocultural understandings. I generalize from this example to assert that all interactions with new technologies both replicate previous understandings and express new possibilities. In the process, these interactions serve as the occasion for learning new competencies. This is how new technological literacies are shaped. In the process of designing new technologies, developers design novel occasions for the rehearsal and practice of technological competencies, while they also create the conditions for the acquisition of new technological literacies. There are two general implications that follow from this set of assertions: one focuses on the implications for designers and technology developers, while the other focuses on the technocultural work performed by exhibitions of innovation. Before moving on to a specific discussion of the process of exhibiting innovation, I need to tease out the significance of these assertions concerning the work of designers and technology developers.

One of the guiding themes of this book is a meditation on the role that technologists and designers play in the creation of a common culture. This chapter implicitly argues that designers should pay attention to the technological literacy of the intended users of the technology-under-development. How one does this—or the timing of such considerations—is not an issue of methodology or design protocol; rather it is an insight of the technological imagination, exercised in the process of technology development. To address this question consciously—of the technological literacy of the intended users—raises a set of related questions: how does one design for audiences (and their literacies) that don't yet exist? How does a designer design new technologies that require skills (literacies) that are not yet common? How do new technologies reconfigure the literacies that will be common in the future?

While it is the case that these are interesting theoretical questions, the answers are not to be found in theoretical formulations, but will be addressed by what gets designed. This is one of the reasons for the creation of this transmedia book: the print chapters provide descriptions of works that were designed to be experienced by readers in a particular setting. For example, the website section that offers opportunities to browse animations of the interactive wall books still only approximates the experience of reading the books on the physical walls. The dynamism of the information design and information architecture is demonstrated more clearly in the media-rich environment of the web than it is through textual descriptions. Even as I say that though, I must assert that the theoretical working-out of the implications of a consideration of technological literacy will only unfold in the practical engagement of designers, technologies, users, and specific social contexts.

I argue that it is part of the ethical responsibility of technology and new media designers to engage these questions about technological literacies. Such questions serve as a reminder that all new technologies, and new media experiences, do significant work, both in reinforcing specific technological literacies and in refashioning the technological literacies of the future. Given that technological literacies are the material practices whereby people participate in creating their connection to a broader culture, these are life-making and life-enabling skills. As such they are not to be taken lightly, or dismissed as an epiphenomenon of technological design, but must be understood as central to the way in which culture is expressed, reproduced, and transformed.

Public Interactives and Learning in/the Future

The legacy of the early cabinets of curiosity not only include contemporary science and technology centers, as well as temporary spaces such as those created for spectacular World Expos, Olympic Festivals, and national expositions, as well as more permanent places such as regional cultural centers and special topic museums. All these institutional forms, for however long they last, are increasingly engaged in presenting exhibitions that feature emerging technologies and cutting-edge science, both as the topics for exhibits and as the technological form of presentation.[49] Just as innovation has become an important topic for these cultural institutions, so too have innovative technologies become an important design resource.[50]

As I described earlier, we can discern a couple of key historical shifts in the pedagogical mission of the science and technology museum, from an initial focus on the enculturation of the non-elites (the broad cultural purpose of early museums according to Bennett) to an emphasis on the disciplining of the *civic identities* of the masses within emerging nation-states (MacDonald). More recently we can see the development of a new pedagogical approach that understands that the display of innovative science and technology can be deployed as a resource in informal educational efforts to support the development of creativity and creative-problem solving skills for individual museum visitors.

This approach resonates with a broader technocultural preoccupation concerning DIY (do-it-yourself) practices. The launch of magazines such as *Make* and *Ready Made*, the appearance of DIY fabrication shops, the rise in the number of design and construction television programs, the development of personal manufacturing on-line services, and the wide availability of desktop design and fabrication applications announce the growing influence of an emerging technocultural formation focused on the creative capacity of the individual to make the world manifest in material form. This contextualizes the growing interest, on the part of science and technology centers, in exhibiting innovation, and in fact reinforces it. Exhibitions that feature innovative new technologies offer the stage for making explicit the connections between the creative practices of everyday life and the creative practices of the production of scientific knowledge and new technologies. In this way, exhibit visitors are symbolically called to participate, as amateurs or professionals, in the practice of knowledge creation and technology development.

I employ the phrase "public interactives" to identify the broad category of exhibits that use innovative interactive technologies for communication with a range of public audiences. Public interactives include specific instances of public art that go by the name of "urban screens" (McQuire, Martin, and Niederer, 2009). This new media form includes public installations of large screens in civic spaces as well as screens embedded in architectural facades. Public interactives also refer to information kiosks, public computer terminals, and augmented reality experiences. Many of these examples incorporate the use of touch screen, swipe cards, and RFID tags to engage users in digitally mediated interactions in public spaces. In the context of museums and other cultural institutions, public interactives refer to those exhibits that incorporate new technologies such as podcasting, text-messaging, and social networking applications. These interactives are explicitly designed to facilitate the development of new knowledge by connecting people in different ways to the mission of the museum. They are also used to connect people to one another as members of the public of the museum: these technologies infrastructure the creation of the museum's publics. My interest in public interactives as a new genre of infrastructure for the creation of publics is directed toward understanding the role that these interactives will play as sites for the active reproduction of technocultural understandings, mythologies, values, and the circulation of new knowledges. They are part of apparatuses for the production of technological literacies of the future. As ensembles of places, objects, subjects, beliefs, and experiences, these intereactives are critically important cultural technologies in their own right, in that they create contexts for the development of understandings about the meaning of emerging technologies and the role of technology in an imagined future. In addition to providing entertainment value and novelty in museums and other cultural places, these interactives are poised to become the infrastructure of the creation of what will come to be known as "public culture" in the future.

four

Designing Learning

The University as a Site of Technocultural Innovation

 Shift work is a fact of life in a 24/7 age. Unlike shifts that start and end with the punch clock, working the paradigm shift is one long now. The Singularity—a science fictional concept that describes the time when the acceleration of technological and social change exceeds our human ability to keep pace with the changes—is already upon us.[1] Twitter is our killer app. The aphorism, the only constant is change, is now our meditation mantra.

Unlike the great paradigm shifts of the past whose epicenter was the scientific academy, much of the current shift work is going on elsewhere than in our formal educational institutions: in corporations such as Google and Apple that have introduced new technology platforms; at ventures such as Linden Labs that launched the virtual environment called Second Life; and in small scrappy applications such as Club Penguin—a massively multiplayer online role-playing games (mmorpg) for children (now owned by Disney). Most of this work involves the use of digital networks and new media technologies. All of it addresses new modes of knowledge construction and emerging forms of cultural reproduction. Given the distributed nature of this shift work, and the rapid adoption of digital media, the challenge for those of us engaged in the profession of education, not yet willing to abdicate our responsibilities as cultural stewards, is how to coordinate these efforts such that the paradigm-shifting efforts contribute to significant and beneficial social changes.

The broader paradigm shift has been characterized in different ways. Educational theorists describe it as a transition from a paradigm of "teaching" to one of "learning" (Barr and Tagg, 1995: 12). Scholars and historians who work with digital archives speak of a shift from a paradigm of scarcity to a paradigm of abundance.[2] Media theorist Henry Jenkins expands on both of these notions to suggest that the paradigm shift we are in the midst of now has inaugurated a new cultural logic, based on a reconfigured relationship between people and media: no longer simply spectators of media productions, we have become media creators ourselves.[3] As he elaborates:

> Convergence does not occur through media appliances, however sophisticated they may become. Convergence occurs within the brains of individual consumers and through their social interactions with others. Each of us constructs our own personal mythology from bits and fragments of information extracted from the media flow and transformed into resources through which we make sense of our everyday lives. Because there is more information on any given topic than anyone can store in their head, there is added incentive for us to talk among ourselves about the media we consume . . . consumption has become a collective process . . . none of us can know everything; each of us knows something; and we can put the pieces together if we pool our resources and combine our skills. (2006a: 3–4)

This shift in our relationship to media—from passive spectators to active participants—involves the process of productive consumption. Just as we harvest bits and fragments of information from various media flows, so too are we called to actively contribute to the information streams we fish in. This is one of the connotations of the use of the term "prosumer" as the name for a person who is as much a producer as consumer of media experiences.[4] For Jenkins, this paradigm shift is marked by a transition from individualized media consumption to the formation of "consumption communities" that enable new forms of participation and collaboration

(80). Convergence for Jenkins lays the groundwork for the creation of a culture of participation.[5] He goes on to suggest that one of the key consequences of this paradigm shift is the rise of a collective intelligence that derives from collective practices of information exchange and meaning-making. The hallmark of this paradigm shift is its foundational assumption that intelligence is a distributed multimodal ability, developed, practiced, and expressed through the use of technologically mediated informational and social networks.

The specter of a superlative collective intelligence fires the imagination of science fiction writers as well as post-humanists, who take the notion of The Singularity seriously. The Singularity is a moment of significant discontinuity with what has come before; it is brought about by the acceleration of technological progress, as defined by increases in artificial intelligence and the speed of computer networks. In many science fiction tales, The Singularity results in the birth of a superhuman AI species that transcends and, in some cases, annihilates the remnants of humanity. In the darkest post-humanist scenarios, human beings are at least an endangered species, if not outright extinct. In the milder post-singularity story worlds, humans mutate and accommodate themselves to a lower berth on the intelligence chain-of-being; life after The Singularity, in this version of the post-paradigm-shift future, represents the next stage of human evolution in which we are no longer agents of our own destinies.[6]

For mathematician and science fiction author Vernor Vinge (1993), *The Singularity* manifests as superhuman intelligence.[7] Vinge believes that although such a development is inevitable, its disposition is not. He takes issue with the post-humanists who celebrate the decorporealization of the human being and the victory of mind over matter. As a self-professed "technological optimist," he asserts that human beings are still the initiators who have the "freedom to establish initial conditions, [and] make things happen in ways that are less inimical than others." He proposes that we focus attention on an alternative paradigm of superhuman intelligence he calls "Intelligence Amplification" (IA). This approach differs from artificial intelligence (AI) programs in that it concentrates more stridently on the creation of more robust human-computer interfaces.[8] The nuanced difference between the two approaches (AI versus IA) according to Vinge is that the IA approach keeps the human being positioned as an empowered agent within the unfolding technological project rather than (as he claims for AI) at the periphery as an entity to be modeled (human intelligence) and, as the stories would have it, eventually discarded.

While the apocalyptic rhetoric of the science fictional accounts has certainly fomented lively debates about the nature of the relationship between human beings and the technologies we spawn, my interest here is not to wade through these debates again, but to focus attention on a near-term set of issues that arise on this side of our ascension (or collapse) into The Singularity.[9] Like Jenkins and Vinge, I believe that this paradigm shift proffers important opportunities to positively shape the conditions of human life in the future. In this chapter, I am specifically interested in the implications of this paradigm shift for the cultural reproductive work of the university. I argue that if it is to remain an important site for the creation of knowledge in a networked digital age, the university must not only produce the rhetoric of innovation; it must also support the development of new pedagogical practices and the integration of new structures of learning.[10]

In Thomas Kuhn's (1970) famous account, paradigms take hold in the academy, where they are gradually institutionalized through the production of new experiments, theories, articles, books, methods, and educational programs.[11] When Kuhn was writing, the academy was at the center of a constellation of institutions and practices that served as the context for the production of scientific knowledge. While Kuhn's account included reference to the role of affiliated organizations—such as professional associations, government bodies, and publishing institutions—the academy was taken-for-granted as the center for the production of knowledge. Indeed, while this may have been true for the great paradigm shifts of the past century (and certainly of the scientific paradigm shifts that Kuhn focused on), this is NOT so true of the current shift. What we now realize is that the academy is but one site among many where significant learning and knowledge production happens. This is one of the first lessons of the current paradigm shift.

The practices that define this current paradigm shift focus on new forms of knowledge production, dissemination, and learning: few if any are based on the traditional practices of formal educational institutions. This has two general implications. The first is that to understand the paradigm shift—characterized by a transition from teaching to learning, or by Jenkins's logic of convergence—we need to take seriously the learning practices that are going on in places other than in the academy. If it is true, as I asserted earlier, that the hallmark of this paradigm shift is its assumption that intelligence is developed, practiced, and expressed through the use of digital informational and social networks, then we need to examine how learning happens when people engage in these networks. The second implication, and for my purposes the most relevant, is that we need to then think about how these practices might be incorporated into the university such that it can contribute to important cultural transformations. The changes necessary for the new paradigm to take root within the academy will involve more than the introduction of new textbooks or new technologies into traditional educational settings. Fundamentally, we need to stop thinking about new digital technologies as the channels through which education is delivered, and instead explore the ways in which these technologies are implicated in the reconfiguration of knowledge production across domains of human culture. The aim then is to take these insights as the basis for rethinking structures and pedagogies within formal educational institutions.

The sections of this chapter unfold parallel discussions. The first section of the chapter considers the identity of those who are poised to participate in these new learning efforts, the students and teachers, to examine how their sensibilities and dispositions are already in flux as a consequence of paradigm shifts already in motion. The backdrop for these discussions concerns the education of the technological imagination—the broad and consistent topic of this book. In a second section I present a model of technocultural innovation that is abstracted from work going on in the emerging field of the digital humanities. These efforts include the development of new educational programs, transformative (technology-based) research, pedagogical experimentation, and new modes of outreach and dissemination. In particular, I focus attention on the logic and ethics of interdisciplinarity, especially on the role that humanists can and should play in the process of technological innovation. Finally, I consider the horizon of our current shift work, which I take to be the horizon of The Singularity itself: the creation of a Global Culture of Learning. This science-fictional construct comes not from writers of science fiction, but from some of our most eminent scientists and global thinkers. It emerges from discussions about the development of the Open Educational Resource Movement. As the title suggests, the key notion is the creation of a distributed network of learning resources. In this vision, the university is but one site of learning among many that offer designed experiences for the purposes of knowledge construction. This doesn't suggest the end of institutions of learning, but their proliferation. I speculate on the characteristics of new spaces that should be developed as part of global distributed networks of learning that could work in conjunction with universities to serve as places where learners, across generations, can commingle. The learning that occurs in these places involves the body, in the process of making things, as well as in the cross-generational and physical making of community.

My broad objective in this chapter is to sample the expanse of the paradigm shift work already underway that is part of the emergence of the digital humanities. Of course, the reexamination of the role of the university in a digital age involves a wider set of issues than the ones I focus on here. For example, I do not explicitly discuss related issues, such as the waning cultural authority of the professoriate, the notion of education versus credentialing, or the organization of formal education within a specific national context. Instead, I examine a range of practices that are already going on at the edges of the academy that implicitly embrace the mission of cultivating the technological imagination among its students and teachers. I assert that if the university as a whole were to properly accommodate these edge practices—to allow them to transform the core of the institution—the university would make a significant contribution to the process of cultural transformation at the heart of the current paradigm shift. From the development of new identities and dispositions, to the transformation of the way we think about technology, to the labor required for specific projects of institutional reformation, the range of shift work we need to engage in and support is magnificently and dauntingly far-reaching. This is a worthy ambition for the exercise of the technological imagination in a digital age.

Learning in a Digital Age:
New Contexts + New Habits = New Subjectivities

The young people who are now showing up in American university classrooms have been labeled as ranking members of the born-digital generation. This moniker is used by researchers John Palfrey and Urs Gasser (2008: 4) to characterize the cohort of young people who were born after

1987. The use of "born-digital" was influenced by the phrase "digital natives and digital immigrants," developed by Marc Prensky—which in turn had been influenced by one of Douglas Rushkoff's phrases—that extended the metaphor of geographic immigration to the consideration of those who were born into a digital landscape.[12] Even though the degree of access to network information flows available in their school classrooms or their homes differs according to family economic position and geographic location, born-digital students are members of the first generation to grow up in a world that included portable computers (laptops, 1985), network communication applications (AOL, 1989), and creative graphics applications (Photoshop, 1990). By the time they reached school age, say between 1993 and 1997, the web (WWW, 1991; Mosaic, 1993) was already being touted as an educational resource. Given this contour of the technocultural scene of their birth, it is reasonable to assert that their beliefs and assumptions about the way learning occurs would have been significantly shaped by their early encounters with pervasive digital worlds and network technologies, and the ubiquity of creative and responsive environments.[13]

Yet, as David Buckingham rightly points out, it is important to be aware of the significant differences within the group who comprise the so-called born-digital generational cohort.[14] Teasing out these differences is a complex process. For example, students of certain social classes may not have had access to computers in the home, but could have encountered computers in schools. We need more research to identify how the different scenes of access affect learning attitudes and practices. Moreover, access—in homes or in classrooms—does not always translate into use and mastery. Research suggests that girls and boys growing up with similar access to computers show different levels of interest in computing, gaming, and other technology-based practices.[15] The members of this cohort who have not had direct access to computers and networks still have been targets for advertisements and media messages that reference digital technologies. We might ask how has the ubiquity of computers and digital technologies, as phantasms of post-capitalist consumer culture, influenced their basic understandings about the power of technology—and their imaginations about what is possible in the future. Even though they may not have born-digital technology skills, youth in this generational cohort will have been cajoled to adopt born-digital attitudes. As members of this generational cohort move around their technocultural landscapes, regardless of whether or not they have access to new technologies or any experience using creative digital tools, their imaginations have been subtly structured and shaped differently. The question that has preoccupied a number of scholars recently concerns the nature of this difference.

Those who have studied youth who use different kinds of digital technologies, note several significant shifts in the texture of their daily lives. These shifts concern practices of moving among networks, of creating a sense of self, and of engaging in new forms of sociality, each of which has been identified as a defining characteristic of the born-digital generation. For example, when youth learn to use new instant messaging programs, text messaging, and on-line chat spaces, they are learning not only new communication applications but also how to navigate new spaces of social life. In the process, they learn new cultural rituals of self-fashioning. As they engage in repeated experimentation with these technologies, born-digital youth create elements of the self through text, avatars, and on-line representations. The "self" is literally distributed throughout various digital networks: in the form of online accounts in different social spaces (*MySpace*, *FaceBook*, and *LookBook*, for example), through photographs and videos stored and shared through different sites (*Flickr* and *YouTube*), through game play and virtual world participation (*World of WarCraft* and *Second Life*), and through creative portals (*Scratch*, *Garry's Mod*, and *Outer Post*). Extrapolating from the observation of their online practices, we theorize that for these network denizens identity is best understood as a fluid construct that emerges through the performance and staging of multiple personae. They are the quintessential decentered postmodern subjects, with identities marked by differing intensity flows and shifting affinities. While it has been more than a decade since researchers first took up the question of "life on the screen," and the implications for the creation of identity, what we've come to appreciate is how the acquisition of new habits, practices, and notions effects the formation of subjectivity and the creation of new subject positions (Turkle, 1997: 15).[16] It is these new subject positions that must be considered in the reconfiguration of formal learning environments.

For example, many members of the born-digital generation understand themselves as just-in-time learners, confident that when they need to know something they'll know where to find it. These young people understand how to mine their networks, both digital and social, for their information needs. Many of them treat their affiliation networks as informal Delphi groups.[17] The statistical phenomenon of Delphi groups demonstrates that even when a factual piece of information is not known to each person the aggregate mapping of responses from group members tends to cluster around the correct answer. For these youth, the process of thinking now routinely—and in some cases, exclusively—relies on social network navigation. Just as the creation of a self emerges through the navigation of different information flows, so too does the creation of knowledge. As they navigate intersecting digital networks, they are exposed to different knowledge communities: those of peers, popular pundits, parents, media shills, informal teachers, and formal educators.

I am not alone in being curious about learning habits members of the born-digital generation develop through their travels through intersecting digital networks. In an effort to shift my own thinking about the identity of the members of this generation, who are or soon will be students in my university classes, I have started to think of them as "Original Synners."[18] In tagging them with this identity (borrowed from science fiction author Pat Cadigan), I see them as fluid subjects-in-formation, who create knowledge through their travels within different media flows. While some of them have well-developed media prosumption habits, and are already competent at creative synthesis practices such as remixing and modding, this isn't true across the board. In fact, what remains striking to me about this generational cohort is that even in 2010, there are many who show no interest in making their own media beyond customizing application dashboards. For all their experiences in traversing multiple media flows, many of the born-digital cohort seem content to consume what others produce, or simply rearrange options that others have already vetted. When I use "Original Synners" to characterize my students, it helps me remember that one of the key learning objectives for my pedagogy is to coach them in the process of becoming "original synthesizers" of information that is produced within different media flows.

"Synners" also connotes another important element of the born-digital generational identity: a basic sensibility of transgressiveness emerges from the repeated experience of fluid boundaries. Their successful navigation of media flows and distributed learning and social environments requires the fluid mutation of interests, identities, and affiliations. While this may vex those born before the ubiquity of digital networks, this mutability is exactly what we need them to foster, because it is the foundation for a lifetime of learning and success in a rapidly changing knowledge-based world. Mutable subjects are the only ones who will thrive during The Singularity. The challenge for them, and for those of us involved in the design of learning practices for the future, is how to support and channel this mutability in creative and productive ways.[19] Our pedagogical protocols must acknowledge and embrace the essential mutability of the subjects of digital technologies. On this point, it is useful to return to the work of John Dewey (or Paolo Friere and Lev Vygotsky, for that matter) for inspiration in helping us revitalize our thinking about education in a digital age that is grounded in an appreciation of the subjective experiences of Original Synners.[20] Dewey ([1938] 1998: 25) was adamant that a robust educational theory had to be grounded in a notion of experience, yet he was also careful to clarify that "while all genuine education comes about through experience," it does not follow that "all experiences are genuinely or equally educative." The project for educators, he argued, is to explicate the relationship between experience and learning.

Here we might turn to those scholars who examine the experiences of young people who participate in specific online communities. Consider the work of Douglas Thomas and John Seely Brown, who analyze the emerging epistemological sensibilities of young people who live, learn, and play among different kinds of digital and embodied networks. Thomas and Brown (2008) identify these emerging sensibilities as a disposition: "Dispositions are not consciously chosen and enacted (any more than a glass chooses to break when dropped on a hard surface). Dispositions are triggered because they are deeply embodied states of comprehension that we act upon at a tacit level. Dispositions are the means by which we make sense of our experiences, a 'grasping of disjointed parts into a comprehensive whole.'" In particular, Thomas and Brown (2007: 149) examine the implications of shifting and mutable subjectivities of those who participate in massively multiple online games (MMOGS). These games often involve the navigation among complex layers of game information; visually represented as "dashboards" or information overlays, these game spaces involve players in the navigation among multiple contexts of meaning. Thomas and Brown note that experienced participants develop heightened abilities to navigate the multiple epistemological contexts invoked by these games; in the process particular dispositions are triggered. Borrowing the notion of "conceptual blending" from Mark Turner (1998: 11), Thomas and Brown describe the epistemological experience that unfolds for a player in a MMOG wherein the imagination is engaged in the creation of a complex sense of reality, simultaneously physical and virtual, real and imagined, social and private, digital and corporeal. In reflecting on the specific epistemological quality of conceptual blending, Thomas and Brown (2007) argue, "whether it be in worldwide multiplayer games like *World of Warcraft* or new online tools such as *Wikipedia* or *Facebook*, the similarity among all of these spaces is the ability of people to create, shape and produce knowledge on a constant basis." While this notion of conceptual blending is only one of the dispositions created through the experience of online game playing, it is one that is particularly well attuned to the cognitive demands of a rapidly changing world. Bringing this insight to bear on the experiences of Original Synners, we might say that when they participate in online network cultures, especially those that involve complex virtual environments such as online games, they are not merely synthesizing information from disparate sources, but creating entirely new experiences of knowing and being.

Original Synners not only navigate intersecting media flows, they also navigate among learning spaces. For many young people, learning no longer happens within a specific physical location—the formal school classroom or the after-school program.[21] While this may have always been true to some extent, learning places now include domestic environments, various school locations, as well as recreational facilities, religious centers, and cultural institutions (to name a few). Through the use of digital media, homes and schools provide digital access points to websites created by cultural institutions and entertainment companies that sponsor on-line learning activities. Since the advent of the World Wide Web, the physical place of school has given way to a proliferation of online educational places that represent entirely new spaces for learning.

French sociologist Michel de Certeau (1984: 117) makes a poetic distinction between "space" and "place" when he writes: "a space is a practiced place." A place has stable boundaries and a fixed location; a space is created in time through actions and practices. In this sense, school is a place; and learning is a spatial practice. This insight is not merely theoretical. It captures something important about the nature of learning in a digital age. Through the use of the Internet, educational places are now part of broadly distributed digital learning spaces. When learning design researcher Katie Salen provocatively asks "Where is school for the born-digital generation?" she invites us to shift our thinking about education from a focus on the physical place of school, to a consideration of the nature of learning spaces that emerge from the digital connections among physical places, virtual environments, and mobile practices of access and interaction.[22] In posing this question, she draws our attention to the fact that young people move among and through many learning sites as part of their daily routines. As they physically travel from home to school, then on to after-school programs, they may have also virtually traveled through a dozen other learning sites, such as online virtual environments (such as *Whyville*), social networking sites (*MySpace*), and cultural portals (*Youth2Youth* at the Whitney Museum of American Art in New York City). For all their differences in actual access to technology and tools, the spaces of learning have multiplied for this generational cohort and the movement among them has become seamless, a matter of clicks rather than the transport of bodies by school buses.

Figure 25 illustrates a model of the space of learning for the born-digital generation as a networked distributed learning environment.[23] The diagram represents this space as a network created through the connections among different nodes (home, recreation, school, after-school, museums, and libraries) that are distributed geographically as well as temporally. Temporal distribution means that although they are always part of the network by virtue of their web availability, the nodes are accessed and experienced by learners at different times as part of their travels through the mesh of digital sites. This environment actually comprises several diverse elements: 1) physical places; 2) virtual places; 3) designed learning activities; 4) opportunities for social interactions; 5) information resources; and 6) access entry points. This is an example of a technocultural assemblage—as I described in the introduction—that is constituted through activities, institutional practices, physical structures, and virtual spaces of possibility.

A networked distributed learning environment differs from "distributed learning" in at least two ways. The notion of distributed learning often implies a one-way discussion where the intent is to disseminate learning materials (a lecture, a structured set of activities) from a central place (the educational institution) to individuals who are distributed geographically

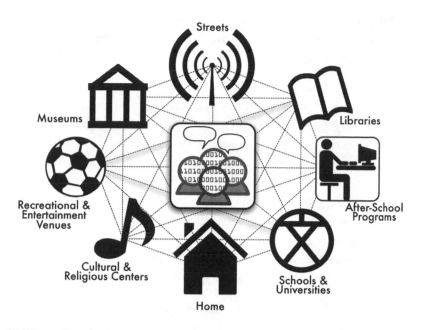

Streets

Museums

Libraries

Recreational &
Entertainment
Venues

After-School
Programs

Cultural &
Religious Centers

Schools &
Universities

Home

25. Where Is School for the Born Digital Generation? (Illustration by Anne Balsamo)

at a distance from the center. Moreover, discussions about distributed learning typically focus on the nature of learning experiences that take place through different channels of communication, such as through embodied face-to-face meetings, television, video, or the web. The notion of a networked distributed learning environment, on the other hand, implies a two-way model of conversation that can involve one-on-one dialogue as well as many-to-many interactions. Based on this model of the structure of learning activities, we would focus not so much on the efficacy of different channels of communication but rather on the affordances for learning that are provided by different nodes within the learning network.

This was the focus of a research effort I coordinated in 2008 that investigated the use of digital media in libraries and museums, to address the question of how these institutions are changing to take advantages of the learning opportunities provided by these new technologies.[24] We know that these cultural institutions have important educational objectives. At the broadest level, what we learned during our year-long investigation is that these institutions are keenly interested in the use of digital media to augment two important aspects of their missions: to develop new activities for informal education; and to broaden participation in digital culture. For example, in her study of the use of digital media in museums, communication researcher Susana Bautista notes that

> technology today allows museums to explore their goals of "education, study and enjoyment" in previously unimaginable ways, reaching out to a much larger and wider community than their physical museums could ever support. . . . Many museums are now using tools that more deeply engage audiences with the thousands of images they are posting online from their collections. Once audiences have created their own collections, they can share them with friends (often sent as postcards), "publish" them online for the public to view, comment on and rate, learn more detailed information about them, tag them as a collective activity, and in general, make these images personally relevant to their individual interests and proclivities. (Bautista, 2009)

The use of social networking applications by museums creates communities of interest that are anchored in some way by the museum's collections or holdings. These communities in effect extend the educational reach of the museum because they enable people to learn not only from museum staff but also from one another. This is an example of a specific affordance of learning enabled by the use of digital media within the context of a particular cultural institution (the collection-based museum) as a node within a distributed learning environment.

In my role as a teacher within a formal university setting, I am particularly interested in the learning affordances provided by this institutional form. The university might be usefully characterized as a learning ecology that supports the activities of certain types of participants (identified as faculty, students, support staff), whose work is shaped by specific structures, conventions, and rituals of knowledge production. This ecology spawns various communities of interest. As students, Original Synners encounter knowledge structures such as disciplines, curricula, critical frameworks, and methodologies. Disciplinarity is an institutionalized practice of knowledge reproduction and verification. As they are educated within the context of a discipline, students gain proficiency in using disciplinary discourse. Taken in its broadest sense, becoming proficient in a discipline means learning specialized terminology, methods of analysis and critique, as well as expressive practices of description, argumentation, and poetics. Students learn to speak the discipline. Moreover, they are guided—by virtue of structures such as general education requirements and minor programs—to engage in conversations with those from other disciplines who do not use the same language, or hold the same cultural values or intellectual commitments as they do. The objective of these structures is to encourage them to become deeply multilingual, not only in the use of a disciplinary discourse, but also in their understanding of different disciplinary logics and global contexts. For example, students need to be taught how to imagine different contexts, other than the one within which they are currently immersed, for the purposes of evaluating and making sense of truth claims. And because they are already global citizens by virtue of their consumption habits and residence in particular national contexts, students need to understand how the global flows of information and capital affect people in other geographic and cultural contexts. One of the learning affordances provided by the university is the demonstration of how knowledge is produced in dialogues among disciplines and in creative collaboration with experts and peers who come from distinct disciplinary backgrounds.

Providing the foundation for the development of skills of creative and critical synthesis is one of the most important learning affordances offered by the university to those whose learning emerges through their travels across media flows, among distributed learning sites, and in dialogue with contradictory sources of disciplinary authority. In this sense, the ability to read a variety of information sources critically, and integrate this information, is not an outmoded text-based literacy.[25] As members of the born-digital generation, they acquire a taken-for-granted epistemological framework: data equals information equals knowledge. The role of the university is to refine this epistemological formulation. Data mining does not necessarily yield valid information, and information requires a context in order for it to count as knowledge. The ability to apprehend contexts, to recognize patterns, and to reflect on the constitution of meaning is the foundation for the production of incisive critiques of information flows. From these critiques emerge a set of questions about what is not yet known and what is yet to be done. Theirs is a daunting learning agenda: they must acquire an appreciation for the depths of disciplinary knowledge, but not get mired in the merely academic, so that they can forge connections across disciplinary contexts, in the service of creating new understandings and formulating new questions to guide their lifelong learning pursuits.

Following this, I argue for the importance of another disposition that I identify as "the technological imagination," that I believe needs to be more fully cultivated in Original Synners. As I elaborated in the introduction, this imagination involves the development of a cognitive capacity to think with complexity about the nature of technology and the process of technocultural innovation. In the next section I offer a model of the university as a site for technocultural innovation that is based on examples of paradigm-shifting work coming out of the digital humanities that contributes to the cultivation of the technological imagination.

Technocultural Innovation of the Digital Humanities

As I asserted earlier, the academy is but one node in a distributed learning network, a specialized node that represents a concentration of resources in the form of creative and critical intellectuals, physical structures, and broader institutional affiliations. It provides an important infrastructure for knowledge production in a digital age. Infrastructure includes not only the technological and material substrate, such as brick and mortar buildings, digital network connectivity, and computing resources, but also immaterial forms: universities both inherit and reproduce standards and conventions of knowledge production; they structure and codify conventions of practice—of education, teaching, research, and administration; they are embedded within other networks, such as the ones formed by government mandated schooling and professional credentialing. The university is itself a cultural technology; as such, it is a privileged site of technocultural innovation.

The diagram in figure 26 represents the key stages of what might be best described as an academic circuit of technocultural production based on the work going on in the digital humanities.[26] These stages name the elements of a cycle through which new technologies, new literacies, and new knowledges, are produced. This model blends insights that come from different discursive registers: university strategic plans; the process of technology innovation; philosophies of literacy; and the design of educational curricula.

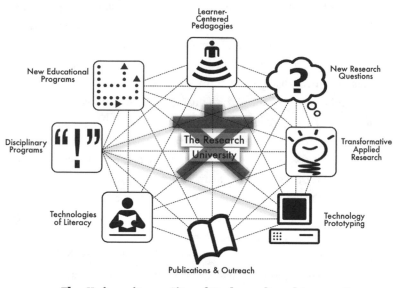

Learner-
Centered
Pedagogies

New Research
Questions

New Educational
Programs

Disciplinary
Programs

The Research
University

Transformative
Applied
Research

Technologies
of Literacy

Technology
Prototyping

Publications & Outreach

The University as Site of Technocultural Innovation

26. The University as a Site of Technocultural Innovation. (Illustration by Anne Balsamo)

This model rests on an understanding of the doubled efficacy of formal educational programs, both to disseminate disciplinary knowledge (traditional literacies and established knowledge bases), and to evoke the creation of new knowledges and new literacies. One domain focuses on the creation of new programs that provide opportunities for students and faculty to learn how to use technologies, tools, and applications for the production of multimodal forms of expression. Another domain of work in the digital humanities focuses on the development of new research questions based on the development of new technology prototypes.

Disciplinary Programs: These are an important part of the infrastructure of the contemporary university that organize knowledge,
reproduce prevailing cultural understandings, and demonstrate
methods of analysis, evidence creation, reasoning, and question formation. They are important for the creation of foundational structures of knowledge creation.

New Educational Programs: These grow out of the development of new
questions that cannot be addressed within the context of a previous

disciplinary program of study. These are essentially new pathways for the creation of new knowledge and new research questions.

New Research Questions: The formation of interesting research questions is a process of exercising the technological imagination in conversation with disciplinary traditions and the conditions of possibility enabled through the use of new technologies.

Transformative Applied Research: Applied research is a term used to describe research that has a pragmatic or social agenda. This type of research is always transformative because it explicitly seeks to intervene and reorder current cultural arrangements.

Technology Prototyping: The creation of experimental technologies, prototypes of devices, applications, systems, or hybrid assemblages is a stage within the process of innovation.

Publications and Outreach: The protocols of technology and knowledge transfer from the university into other networks are undergoing transformation through the use of digital media, the development of new genres of digital scholarship, as well as the creation of new partnerships between the university and other constituents.

Technologies of Literacies: There is a category of technology development that focuses on the development of new meaning-making applications, tools, and devices. Because they focus on new forms of meaning-making and new protocols for the circulation of meaning, these technologies are implicated in the development of new literacies.

The guiding set of ideals for this model is an approach to learning that is identified as "learner-centered." This approach emphasizes the development of pedagogical practices that engage students as active learners. As educators, we have the responsibility of designing learning environments and institutional practices that foster the acquisition of dispositions students will need for a lifetime of network navigation and mutable self-fashioning. I argue that in order to fulfill this responsibility, we must become the change we advocate by making a commitment to becoming lifelong learners ourselves. Just as the notion of Original Synners helps to shift our ideas about the identities and dispositions of students, so too should the notion of teachers as lifelong learners inspire a reconsideration of the effort required of teachers to develop new dispositions and knowledge-making practices, such that they remain effective teachers for Original Synners.[27] The language of learner-centered pedagogy recasts both students and teachers as collaborative participants in learning activities. To be responsible collaborators, faculty members, instructors, and teachers must develop their skills in the use of new digital applications and tools. Drawing on observations of the learning experiences of Original Synners, we can identify three characteristics required for the creation of new educational programs, pedagogies, and institutional structures:

> *Media-rich*: Incorporating the use of multiple modalities of expression, including textual, visual, audio, dynamic, interactive, and simulated
> *Hybrid*: Combining networked and physical spaces that blur the lines between academic and everyday social, creative, and expressive practices; crossing traditional generational and cultural boundaries
> *Open*: extensible, participatory, non-proprietary, collaborative, distributed, many-to-many, multi-institutional, global

To illustrate the broader model presented in figure 26, I discuss several digital humanities projects at the edges of one formal educational institution in the United States: the University of Southern California.[28] These projects share a set of cultural values and philosophical commitments that take seriously both the dispositions of Original Synners and the educational needs of lifelong learners. Even as I offer these examples of edge projects, I do not promote them as a set of best practices of digital learning: the innovations described here are context specific and continually in a stage of reinvention. This is as it should be, for in a digital age, it is unimaginable to think that any single set of best practices will address the varied learning needs of youth situated in different geographic, national, and institutional contexts. Nonetheless, these examples describe experiments in the development of new programs and pedagogies that are inspired by changing practices of networked communication and digital knowledge making.

New Programs: Multimedia Across the Curriculum

As I argued in chapter 3, literacy is a community-based metric. This suggests that the way in which new literacy programs take shape will be influenced by specific institutional contexts. For example, the Institute for

Multimedia Literacy (IML) at the University of Southern California has, for more than a decade, served as a test bed for the development of new curricula and new pedagogies involving the production of multimedia literacy education activities and projects.[29] Because it is housed within the context of the USC School of Cinematic Arts, IML's approach to multimedia literacy draws deeply on cinematic approaches to the creation of dynamic modes of expression, as well as on the design of interactive media, ranging from games to immersive and mobile experience design. IML undergraduate programs are built on the assertion that in order to be fully literate in today's world, students should be able to read and write using the languages of multimedia as readily as they read and write using text.[30] The learning objectives that guide IML courses engage multiple intelligences: the social, cultural, and emotional—as well as the cognitive and the technical—in the service of exploring new modes of digital authoring.[31] The goal of the IML programs and research is to explore the full range of expressive potentials offered by moving images, sound, and interactive media, with a continuing emphasis on the integration of text as part of the expressive palette of multimedia.

Participants in IML programs learn to write multimedia by first learning to read it critically. Students develop proficiency with the modes of formal analysis required for the critical evaluation of a wide range of multimedia artifacts, including images, video, sound design, information visualization, typography, interface design, and interactivity. In addition, students become familiar with the major theoretical frameworks guiding the development of contemporary multimedia applications and interactive experiences. IML instructors introduce students to a broad range of multimedia genres—such as argumentative, documentary, essayistic, experiential, game-based, narrative, and archival forms—by performing expert critical readings of these media-rich cultural works. The performance of expert readings of media rich documents is a critically important pedagogical technique because it is by watching these performances that students learn how to read new forms of expression and how the conventions of these forms cohere as new multimedia genres.

Based on these demonstrations and performances, students are taught to evaluate the rhetorical strengths and weaknesses of different genres for serving different communicative objectives. As students become critical readers of multimedia, they also learn to produce it in a scholarly way.

Students gain experience in both individual and collaborative forms of multimedia authorship. In IML classes, students learn to choose appropriate media platforms for their projects, including video and audio productions, interactive DVDs, websites, games, exhibitions, and installations. One of the key concerns of multimedia pedagogy is ensuring that students avoid the uncritical adoption of commercial or entertainment media conventions. In their own projects, students are required to justify their authoring and design decisions to demonstrate that their use of media and techniques are appropriate to their overall communicative goals. Thus, students learn not only how media-rich documents and modes of expression are constructed, they learn how to create them using a range of media design tools (cameras, sound devices, animation programs, game engines, storyboarding, and presentation applications). This wide range of authoring modes necessitates a highly skilled and diverse support structure, which includes teaching assistants, technical support staff, and student mentors, in addition to full-time faculty.[32]

Rather than positioning multimedia literacy or scholarly multimedia as an emerging field, the IML developed strategies to integrate multimedia literacy efforts within existing disciplines and academic practices. IML classes are taught within disciplines as diverse as history, philosophy, religious studies, geography, linguistics, and anthropology, as well as more traditionally visually oriented fields such as cinema, communications, visual arts, and art history. The methods used by IML instructors, which draw from the fields of cinema studies and communication, are readily adaptable to fields within the humanities and social sciences, many of which are in the process of adapting to accommodate audio / visual expression, as well as different forms of electronic publication and technologically enhanced teaching. Multimedia, in these contexts, functions to catalyze and promote innovations in research and pedagogy already emerging organically within various fields; IML programs are explicitly designed to be transformative of the educational experience of students across the university. The design of these programs incorporated important insights from writing across the curriculum programs, for example in the use of pedagogies that promoted peer-to-peer learning.

In addition to the development of undergraduate educational programs, the IML also developed events that focused on the education of a new generation of graduate-student teaching assistants and faculty in strategies that enhance traditional academic practices through the use of media-rich modes of expression. In-service seminars and workshops on "Transforming Teaching Using Multimedia" were specifically designed to address these other important groups of learners whose educational needs are often overlooked by the university.[33] This effort supported the integration of multimedia literacy across the disciplines because it served as a bridge to integrate faculty members' and graduate students' teaching interests with their research interests. As they learned new literacy skills, faculty and graduate students were encouraged to rethink their scholarly publication and authoring practices using the affordances of new media to not only become multimedia literate, but also to explore how the use of digital media might enable the creation of new scholarly insights and the development of new genres of scholarship.

New Pedagogical Experiments: Back-channeling in the Classroom

For Original Synners the process of knowledge creation happens across diverse settings, in formal institutions as well as through informal social and technological practices. The multiplication of learning spaces is enabled in part by increased access to high-speed data networks, but perhaps more important is the increasing familiarity and ubiquity of collaborative online activities. Just as Thomas and Brown turned their attention to a consideration of the dispositions created in the course of online game playing, other researchers are investigating those particular experiences developed during game playing that may have a bearing on learning in complex media environments.[34] An analysis of the game playing experience of young people suggests that in addition to providing dynamic visual, auditory, and sometimes bodily stimulation, interactions within game worlds also offer opportunities for players to express emotions, engage in structured goal setting, and gain a sense of accomplishment and social belonging. Higher-order competencies include learning the ability to strategize, respond tactically, problem solve, interpret, use hints and aides, and abstract general principles from specific situations. Moreover, for youth of school age, the bounded nature of a game world holds their attention in a way that traditional classroom activities often do not. Many games require participants to move between multiple planes of reality: the world of the game, the strategy, the goal, the other players, and the real world. Gamers learn by cycling through information spaces: they learn to iteratively scan multiple spaces and to adjust their activities in line with new information. In this way, games teach and condition a disposition of partial attending. In the process, the performance and temporality of attending is transformed. This type of attending is not easily accommodated by traditional classroom practices. This suggests that although there is great interest among educators across the spectrum in the development of educational games, also now referred to as "serious" or "learning" games, the deployment of games as an educational activity is going to require a broader refashioning of the expectations for students' classroom behavior.

The pedagogical task here is to design classroom activities that take advantage of those new habits and modes of attending that are learned through the use of new digital media. Indeed, Linda Stone (2006), former Vice President of Microsoft's Virtual Worlds research group, argues that the new disposition of attending common among gamers—a disposition she refers to as "continuous partial attention"—can be an extremely powerful mode of engagement.[35] The notion of "continuous partial attending" has stimulated experiments with the opening up of classroom space to multiple information flows. For example, some of the classes offered by the Interactive Media Division (IMD) at the University Southern California use multiple wall-sized screens as windows onto different kinds of media flows.[36] Some screens might display web pages; other screens present a text messaging back-channel space; other screens display prepared image and slide sets. Rather than wrestling with students to command their attention to a single-channel of communication (the "sage on the stage" classroom model), by incorporating publically viewable multiple screens for the display of different kinds of visual material, the pedagogical structure of the classroom seeks to enjoin the experience of continuous partial attending. A typical IMD class session involves an instructor (or discussion leader) who displays a set of digital slides or bookmarked urls on several screens, a "Google jockey" who commandeers another set of screens for the purposes of annotating and questioning the classroom conversation by surfing through websites and online resources, and an IM backchannel (displayed on another set of screens). The use of multiple screens enables multiple conversations to happen simultaneously. The viewable backchannel subtly changes the rituals of classroom communication (Hall and Fisher, 2006). In a similar way, the display of web searches, through the use of Google or other search engines, is a pedagogical technique that embraces the web as an important media flow that has value to add to classroom-based learning experiences.[37]

The physical architecture of the IMD classroom embraces the hybrid nature of digital learning activities. The physical classroom space includes fourteen screens, creating a panoramic room environment in which any one of the screens—or all of them—can be accessed by a cluster of personal computers, commercial-grade DVD players, or individual laptops (see figure 27). The room accommodates up to 30 participants—students, faculty, outside speakers—who sit either at a large conference table or at individual workstations arrayed around the perimeter of the room. Some set of screens is visible from every seat in the room. The creation of this classroom, referred to as a "digital atelier," was the result of the applied research projects, of several IMD faculty, on the development of environmental and immersive panoramic displays. Special software enables the panoramic display of an image across all fourteen screens. Thus, the screens can be used as individual displays for images or digital content, or as tiled parts of a single panoramic image.[38] In this way, the research interests of IMD faculty resulted in the development of innovative technologies that in turn serve as the platform for pedagogical experiments, not only in the use of new modes of digital display, but also, and more importantly, in the integration of diverse digital media flows into the classroom.

As Stone (2006) points out, when individuals participate in multiple information streams, they learn to reinvent themselves as nodes within networks who are capable of contributing to information flows as well as receiving them. Through interactions in a backchannel, an individual's agency in the classroom expands in interesting ways. Simultaneously interpellated as listener, audience member, and peer, the student oscillates between technologically mediated subject positions. None of these positions is purer than the other: by oscillating among these subject positions, the opportunity for the creation of new insights emerges as different sets of cognitive skills (such as those skills associated with listening and entering text), are simultaneously activated and rapidly expressed in a temporal oscillation of attending (between listening and texting). As a wild departure from the staging of communication in a traditional classroom, the early IMD backchannel experiments suggest that the multiplication of information flows can productively stimulate meaningful interactions among

27. The Zemeckis Media Lab in the Interactive Media Division at the University of Southern California in 2008. (Photo by Vince Diamante)

students-as-peers in a classroom space. This classroom ecology of multiple media flows explores the epistemological experience of conceptual blending. All participants—students, presenters, teachers, and visitors—have to find ways to meaningfully engage the multiple levels of reality and mediated information that unfold during a classroom session. Indeed, some participants find the back-channeling practice extremely distracting, and when the conversation on the backchannel devolves into sniping, in-jokes and tangents, it's difficult to understand what whole can be usefully created from the disjointed flows and conversation streams.

Howard Rheingold has argued that although they are extremely promising, the existing cultural vernaculars that emerge in peer-to-peer social networking practices (such as IMing) are not always applicable to academic contexts. To use these tools effectively, teachers must not only understand the technological potential, but also the kinds of structures needed to focus the energies these tools unleash. In particular, teachers need to introduce into these open classroom spaces critical methods of reflection and assessment that consider the nature of interactions unfolding across multiple reality planes. In this version of the open classroom, the role of the educator is rather like a maestro, whose artistry is to orchestrate the creation of a meaningful experience. This experiment demonstrates a fundamental rethinking of the classroom, not as a bounded physical space within a fixed institutional geography, but as a mixed-reality learning ecology that is malleable, plastic, and able to open onto a variety of digital media flows.[39]

On the Nature of Transformative Research

One of the outcomes produced by new educational programs and pedagogical experiments in the use of new technologies is the creation of new research questions. The digital humanities has been one of the domains within the university that has embraced the imperative to develop research questions that address social issues.[40] This approach is sometimes referred to as applied research, but it should also be understood as *transformative* because the research is designed to explore new possibilities and new social arrangements.[41] The outcomes of transformative research are diverse, taking shape through the formation of public policies, social services, cultural narratives, as well as new technological applications and devices.

One of the major impacts of transformative research in the digital humanities is a reconfigured understanding of the nature and structure of multidisciplinary collaboration in the university. Considered together, these projects argue that transformative research requires multidisciplinary collaboration that is radical in scope. All too often projects that claim to be "interdisciplinary" have actually only engaged a narrow range of disciplines: computer scientists in collaboration with engineers in robotics programs; business professors and engineers in innovation studies; medical researchers and social work practitioners. Recall when C. P. Snow (1963) first described the gulf between the sciences and the humanities as a "two culture" problem. He implored educators to find ways to bridge the divide. He took pains not to blame one side or the other for their failure to communicate, because he believed that neither "the scientists" nor the "literary intellectuals" had an adequate framework for addressing significant world problems. Although there have been noteworthy attempts to bridge this divide, in the fifty years since the publication of Snow's manifesto, the perception prevails that the "literary intellectuals"—who we would now more commonly refer to as humanists—have little of value to say about significant world problems. As techno-humanists Cathy Davidson and David Goldberg (2004) point out, those who call for interdisciplinary collaboration focused on global social problems frequently disregard the necessary participation of humanists in these discussions.[42] Because contemporary social problems are often defined from the beginning as requiring technological solutions, the failure to include humanists in these calls for interdisciplinarity betrays an all-too-common belief that the humanities have nothing useful to contribute to projects requiring technology development.

Two decades ago, it was social scientists (mainly sociologists and anthropologists) who confronted a similar disregard when they asserted the importance of studying human factors in the development of new information systems and networks. Over time, frequent border crossings bridged the gap, as social scientists collaborated with computer scientists, especially in the area of artificial intelligence, to investigate the social impacts of computing.[43] Based on the work of social scientists such as Lucy Suchman, Susan Leigh Starr, Les Gasser, and early work in STS, there is wider appreciation for the social dimensions of technology development and deployment. This approach defines innovations as socio-technical achievements.[44]

While there is still much to be done on this front, the range of participants engaging in technological border crossing work has expanded to include humanists and technologists who agree that understanding the cultural aspects of technology design, use, deployment, implementation, maintenance, and disposal is absolutely fundamental to the process of forming appropriate and adequate technological solutions to complex social problems.[45] As Davidson and Goldberg (2006) elaborate, "the humanities engage three broad sets of questions: those of meaning, value and significance. *Meaning* concerns interpretation of data, evidence, and texts. *Value* ranges over the entire field of cultural, aesthetic, social, and scientific investments. *Significance*, implicating both the former two, raises questions of representation, in the sense of accounting for (explanation) and of capturing, in the sense both of offering a faithful rendition (description) and of making broad claims (generalization)." As such, they need to be taken into consideration both during the diagnosis of social problems, and in the design of innovative technological solutions.

The contribution of the humanities to the process of technological innovation not only involves a set of methods for the interpretation of meaning—such as the method of hermeneutic reverse engineering I described in the introduction—but also establishes frameworks for understanding the value and significance of technology-based social and cultural practices.[46] These practices are the means by which social and cultural life is reproduced: communication, ritual, language, symbolic production, and tool-use. The increasing complexity of contemporary social and global problems requires the application of multiple frameworks of analysis: these problems clearly demand multidisciplinary approaches, and some require the development of new technologies. We also know that technology alone will not solve these problems, however. The development of technologies that are from the beginning informed by social, cultural, policy, and environmental analyses can form the basis of more nuanced and complex technological solutions. The kind of technological solutions that result from multidisciplinary research are not going to be (solely) complex technologies, but complex *hybrids* of technological objects, services, and applications, along with social and cultural implementation plans.

This implied horizon of contemporary cultural and humanistic studies of technology is the creation of multidisciplinary frameworks within which to create more nuanced and complex technological interventions.[47] Fundamentally, this work maintains a commitment to the deep analysis of the ideological effects of cultural arrangements. This involves more than simply analyzing the cultural values manifest in technology: it investigates the way in which technologies are implicated in maintaining a dominant social order, perpetuating conditions of oppression, and reconfiguring the conditions of human existence. The best of this work also seeks ways to intervene in the technological reproduction of structures and relations of power, transforming technology to be more democratic and empowering. Although this work draws deeply on a full range of cultural criticism, it recognizes that the process of doing things differently with technology must engage theory as well as practice.[48]

In an effort to move beyond the familiar rehearsal of Snow's two-cultures analysis—for the purposes of elaborating the kind of structures and protocols that would facilitate truly transformative research—consider the following discussion of the role of different disciplinary specialists, in collaborations that have as their aim the creation of technocultural innovation. Regardless of whether the research focuses on social problems or the identification of creative possibilities, transformative research that involves technological innovation must engage participants whose interests span the disciplinary spectrum: humanities; social and cognitive sciences; arts; engineering; and sciences. Each of these disciplines brings something important to the research effort.

Special role of humanists: Contribute expertise in the assessment and critique of the ethical, social, and practical affordances of new technologies; provide expertise on the process of meaning-making, which is central to the development of successful new technologies; provide appropriate historical contextualization.

Special role of artists: Contribute expertise in the performance, expression, and demonstration of technological insights; provide skills in different modes of engagement: the tactile; the visual; the kinesthetic; and the aural.

Special role of social scientists: Contribute expertise in the assessment of social impacts and in the analysis of institutional, policy, and global effects of the development and deployment of new technologies; provide methods for analyzing social uses.

Special role of engineers and computer scientists: Contribute expertise in the innovation of new devices and applications; provide analytical skills in the assessment of problem formation and solution design; demonstrate methods of design, creation, and prototyping; recommend specific tools, processes, and materials.

Special role of physical scientists: Contribute expertise in the development of new theoretical possibilities; provide methodologies for assessing and evaluating implementation efforts and for formulating possible (theoretical) outcomes; develop experiments with new materials; contribute understanding about environmental impacts.

One of the difficulties in fomenting truly interdisciplinary technological research is that the logic of institutionalization actually works against multidisciplinary collaboration. (Here I use the term "multidisciplinary" to name the constitution of collaborative research teams; the term "interdisciplinary" names the kind of research produced by multidisciplinary teams.) Consider the definition of "institution" formulated by political scientist Robert Keohane (1989: 3): a "persistent and connected set of rules (formal and informal) that, along with norms and beliefs, prescribe behavioral roles, constrain activity, and shape expectations." When participants come from different disciplines, cultural contexts, and geographical locations, it is difficult to create shared rules, norms, and beliefs. This is especially the case when the project is to establish a creative, peer-based, and novel environment for technocultural innovation and the production of new knowledge. Scholars trained in different disciplines have diverse rule-sets. Academic disciplines provide the cultural contexts that instill professional norms and beliefs about the practice of scholarship, research methodologies, and paradigm conditions. When people come from different disciplines and domains, even when they share a common language, it is not surprising that their underlying beliefs and norms differ greatly.

A successful project of transformative research involves creating the conditions whereby participants explicitly understand and commit to the goal of creating shared rules, beliefs, and norms. This process must not evacuate the most valuable part of having multiple disciplines represented. People with distinct perspectives must be free to contribute insights that come from their individual experiences. For this reason, the project of building new institutional structures that support multidisciplinary collaborative teams must explicitly include attention to how the teams are going to develop shared understandings, which need to be based on a deep respect and valuation of disciplinary or cultural differences.[49] The social coordination required to create these teams—and to support their collaborative work—is a crucial element in producing successful research outcomes. Not only must each participant embrace collaborative work, but they must also actively work against the facile division of labor that would have the humanists doing the critique, the technologists the building, and the artists the art direction. While there is a special role to be played by each participant, they must all be willing and eager to learn new skills, analytical frameworks, methods, and practices.[50] A personal commitment to lifelong learning is the foundation for these collaborations. Moreover, each participant must be willing to uphold the ethical foundation of multidisciplinary work. When people with different disciplinary or even interdisciplinary backgrounds come together, it is important they acknowledge that everyone has something to contribute to the collaborative effort, and that there is something important for each to learn from the other. The following describe the foundational ethical principles of multidisciplinary collaboration:

Intellectual generosity: The sincere acknowledgment of the work of others. This acknowledgment must be explicitly expressed to collaborators as well as through thorough citation practices. Showing appreciation for other people's ideas in face-to-face dialogue and throughout the process of collaboration sows the seeds for intellectual risk-taking and courageous acts of creativity.

Intellectual confidence: The understanding that one has something important to contribute to the collaborative enterprise. This is the commitment that makes one accountable for the quality of an individual's contribution to the collaboration. Everyone's contribution to the collaboration must be reliable. It must be thorough and full of integrity; it must refuse short cuts and guard against intellectual laziness.

Intellectual humility: The understanding that one's knowledge is always partial and incomplete and can always be extended and revised by insights from other collaborators. This is the quality that allows people to admit that they don't know something without suffering a loss of confidence or a blow to their self-esteem.

Intellectual flexibility: The ability to change one's perspective based on new insights that come from other people. This is the capacity both for play and re-imagining the rules of reality: to suspend judgment and to imagine other ways of being in the world, and other worlds to be within.

Intellectual integrity: The habit of responsible participation that serves as a basis for the development of trust among collaborators. This is a quality that compels colleagues to bring their best work and contribute their best thinking to collaborative efforts.

The output of transformative research that involves multidisciplinary teams may take several forms: as innovative technological devices, applications, research monographs, presentations, demonstrations, performances, or installations. It will also yield insights into the nature of multidisciplinary collaboration. The guiding strategy for this research is that it must take culture seriously, both as the context for the formulation of the research question and as the domain within which significant technological developments will unfold.

The phrase "technologies of imagination" has been used by prominent sociologist of science Bruno Latour (2007) to refer to the digital environments within which we leave traces of our imaginations through our habits of interactivity: for example, in the games we play and through the avatars we deploy in virtual worlds. I employ the phrase to describe the genre of technologies that serve as the scaffolding and platforms for the education and exercise of the technological imagination. As I use the phrase, technologies of imagination enable the exercise of creative thinking, across disciplinary domains and sites of expressive practices, through the design of new technocultural learning networks that take place in mixed-reality learning spaces. The aim of developing technologies of imagination is to encourage the physical and embodied exploration of new technocultural possibilities.

Let me parse this set of assertions. In the first sense, technologies of imagination are a genre of technology that enables creative thinking. Following this, the genre includes virtual worlds such as *Second Life, Whyville,* and *World of Warcraft,* simulation play environments such as *The Sims* and *Spore,* as well as tools and applications such as APIs (Application Programming Interfaces) that enable people to create novel technological experiences through the expressive forms of mashups, remixes, and mods. These technologies of imagination enable users to reassemble existing technocultural artifacts, creating something new, thus serving as a stage for the exercise of the technological imagination.

In the second sense, the genre of technologies of imagination also includes the social and pedagogical practices that shape patterns of participation in digital networks. As participants engage in repeated activities of network use, they develop new cognitive capacities. When teachers and informal learning designers develop activities that involve the use of online materials and social networking applications, they are also creating technologies of imagination. Pedagogical protocols for the use of online networks are technologies of imagination, in that they structure the activities through which students participate in new technocultural learning networks.

In the third sense, technologies of imagination include the creation of mixed-reality learning spaces such as the virtual spaces that enable peer-to-peer connections. It is clear that these spaces are important places of learning. Even as these virtual spaces multiply, and time spent inside them increases, learners still thrive and enjoy the social experiences that take place in embodied spaces. In fact, researchers who study the development of gamers' expertise note the importance of shared common physical space.[51] Unsurprisingly, people enjoy playing online games in the physical presence of other gamers. The coming together in a shared embodied space for the purposes of sharing technological experiences remains a vital component of game playing. In a similar way, participation in small groups that share a physical space is a powerful element in digital learning experiences; the physical space is understood as a mixed-reality learning space that allows for the conceptual blending of the physical and virtual.

The design of mixed-reality learning spaces also involves the creation of other kinds of technologies of imagination, such as mixed-reality learning devices (blending the physical and the virtual), digitally augmented physical environments (involving the use of sensors and responsive architecture), and digital learning objects, each of which provides different modes of network connectivity and social participation: some to local social networks; some to distributed networks comprising other learning participants; and some to networks of resources and materials. Considered together, technologies of imagination serve as platforms for the exercise of the technological imagination. In short, the reason to create technologies of imagination is to enable the technological imagination to unfold and take flight, to enable people to learn how to use technologies, how to think creatively and with complexity about the development of new technologies, and how to imagine new horizons for technocultural practices. Technologies of imagination should draw people into participation within different overlapping networks of social communities and digital materials, for the purposes of expanding our collective sense of the horizon of technocultural possibilities.

New Forms of Scholarship and Outreach

Another key contribution of the transformative research coming out of the digital humanities is the development of new forms of publication, dissemination, and outreach. Research in the digital humanities has not only produced new theories, technologies, and educational materials, but has also served as the occasion for developing new ways of communicating the meaningfulness of the research to broader audiences, using fresh expressive modalities. Along with the prototyping of new technologies comes the experimentation with new genres of (digital) scholarship.[52]

One such experiment is the journal *Vectors*, edited by Tara McPherson and Steve Anderson. *Vectors* provides a persistent online space for the experimentation with new genres of multimodal scholarship.[53] Subtitled "A Journal of Culture and Technology in a Dynamic Vernacular," *Vectors* publishes scholarly projects that explore the visual, affective, and sensory aspects of research that uses the expressive languages of multimedia. Drawing on the lessons learned from other digital publication efforts, such as the refereed online journal, *Kairos*, which explores the intersections of rhetoric, technology, and pedagogy, articles appearing in *Vectors* are peer-reviewed and fully interactive.[54] One of the unique aspects of *Vectors* is the way its development process engages the work of authors, designers, and technologists, all of whom collaborate on the creation of individual articles.[55] For these multidisciplinary creative teams, the authoring and designing processes have fully merged. Although there is often a lead scholar who guides and produces the article, the authoring/designing effort is deeply collaborate.[56] As Tara McPherson (2010: 210), the *Vectors* editor, explains, the "creation of spaces for innovative digital scholarship allows for a shift in focus from the end product to the process of scholarly thinking." This shift leads to a focus on the creative acts of making knowledge using the affordances of digital tools. "Hands-on engagement with digital tools," she argues, "reorients the scholarly imagination, because scholars come to realize that they understand their arguments and objects of study differently when they approach them through multiple modalities" (211). By bringing new forms of literacy into their practices of scholarly production (of communication, publishing, and argumentation), they come to think differently about the topic of investigation.

In producing articles for *Vectors*, authors develop new literacies acquired through the process of collaborative design thinking. The circulation of these works of scholarship also require new literacies on the part of readers, reviewers, and critics who have to relearn how to read these new expressive forms. Through the development of new reading, writing, and designing skills, new literacies are codified; these literacies eventually provoke the redesign of educational programs. These programs and projects, in turn, draw on existing technological literacies, while they also necessarily shape the literacies of the future. It is through the reformulation of literacies that the digital humanities participate in significant techno-cultural innovation.

New Literacies

In different ways, these digital humanities projects contribute to a multi-faceted effort to cultivate a robust imagination through the development of new educational programs, the innovation of new technologies, and experiments with new pedagogical techniques. Each involves the creative and thoughtful use of new tools, new communication technologies, and design methods. The model of creativity that supports the praxis of innovation in the digital humanities is built on the following principles:

- Creativity is at base a social activity (Csikszentmihalyi, 1996).
- People can learn to be creative by modeling practices, habits, and attitudes of creative thinking-in-action (Sennett, 2008: 9).
- The genesis of a "creative act is the escape from one range of assumptions to another" (Mitchell, 2003: 31).
- Technologies are an expressive medium: people think through and with tools, and the tools enable new insights and cognitive connections. In this way technologies collaborate in the creative process (Papert, 1980; Coyne, 1995: 304).

As I noted in the introduction, design researchers who investigate the sources of influences on creativity argue that sharing a cultural context with one's collaborators is an important aspect of the expression of novel ideas (Eckert and Stacey, 2000: 531). In fact, Mihaly Csikszentmihalyi (1996), in his social model of the creative process, argues that culture, as a widely shared symbolic system, is the generator of creativity. He asserts that designers mediate between culture and society (the social context of the design situation) to manifest creativity.

Disciplines also influence what counts as creativity. Included as part of a discipline's culture are practices of thinking and making that manifest creativity. Moreover, what signifies an idea as novel and creative differs across domains. For example, in the arts, creativity manifests in a novel form of aesthetic expression; in business, it is realized through entrepreneurial activities; in the sciences, it is demonstrated through well-formulated hypotheses and elegant proofs. Creativity is a cultural construct; the signs of creativity, innovation, and novelty are expressions of domain-specific cultural sensibilities. Learning to be creative is in part a process of learning what the meaning of creativity is for a specific domain. The notion of transdomain creativity promotes the understanding that creative thinking is central to the development of new ideas in every discipline and domain of human activity, although the practices that yield new and novel ideas within a given discipline or domain may differ.

I argue that transdomain creativity is important for the cultivation of the technological imagination because it provides a framework for the development of new practices that lead to new literacies. Designing thinking is one of the names given to the collection of practices that enable the production of new (creative) insights about the nature of technology. Richard Buchanan (1992: 5), one of the founding figures in the field of Design Studies, asserts that design is a "new liberal art of technological culture." In making this assertion, Buchanan returns to the work of John Dewey to remind us that Dewey promoted an understanding of technology as "an art of experimental thinking" (8). This leads Buchanan to profess that design thinking is of utmost value in complex technological culture. In essence, he reframes Dewey's assertion to suggest that design is the term for the activities whereby technologies are used as experimental thinking materials. Technologies are understood as an expressive medium. This assertion lays the groundwork for thinking about design as an important body of knowledge that should be incorporated into basic educational programs, as a "new liberal art" for the twenty-first century (5).

Incorporating design activities and thinking into the discussion about twenty-first century skills is not only a strategy for fostering creativity in different disciplinary contexts. It is also a way to train the technological imagination of those who are active within participatory cultures. With this in mind, let me turn to the list of twenty-first century literacies Henry Jenkins (2006b: 4) has identified as the most important set of skills required for robust participation in contemporary culture. While the term "design" isn't explicitly referred to in his list, it is reasonable to suggest the notion of design—as the name given to a particular set of skills such as information gathering, creative thinking, improvisation, and tinkering— is absolutely fundamental to the broader cultural shift Jenkins is concerned to elaborate. It is important to note that these new skills do not compete with traditional print-based literacies, but rather build on and complement them.

Jenkins (2006b: 4) itemizes the key literacies of the twenty-first century in the following terms: play, performance, simulation, appropriation, multitasking, distributed cognition, collective intelligence, judgment, transmedia navigation, networking, and negotiation. Following each of Jenkins's descriptions (in italics), I offer a brief elaboration about how that skill manifests in the process of designing:

Play—the capacity to experiment with one's surroundings as a form of problem-solving

> While problem solving is not the only motivation for engaging in designing activities, the identification of a problem and of the constraints that define a problem space are important aspects of design thinking.

Performance—the ability to adopt alternative identities for the purpose of improvisation and discovery

> Designing involves improvisation with materials and stories. Sometimes this activity is referred to as "tinkering." Designing incorporates non-purposive engagement with potential materials.

Simulation—the ability to interpret and construct dynamic models of real-world processes

> Designing involves the creation of prototypes of new ideas, technologies, applications, and experiences. Sometimes these prototypes take the form of digital simulations, other times these prototypes are worked out in material form. A wide range of tools, including new varieties of digital design applications (Rhino, Maya, Processing) and new visual and multimodal authoring programs (Sophie, Scratch) expand the form factor of prototypes that offer models of real-world processes and objects.

Appropriation—the ability to meaningfully sample and remix media content

> Design practices enact the logic of technocultural reproduction, as previous materials (media content, built forms, functional systems) are borrowed and replicated as elements of a new design. In the process of appropriating previous materials, the meaning of the new design is reworked as a consequence of situating the materials within a new expressive context.

Multitasking—the ability to scan one's environment and shift focus as needed to salient details

The meanings that designers create are mediated through the production of objects that can be material as well as digital, representational as well as gestural, and theoretical as well as physical. In this sense, objects also participate in the designing process by evoking knowledge, stimulating discussion and the production of discursive understandings, and by manifesting the matter of the world. This requires that the designer have the capability of rapid attention shifting, from the world of objects to that of abstractions, from the social world of meaning creation to the various channels through which media flow.

Distributed Cognition—the ability to interact meaningfully with tools that expand mental capacities

Designing involves the realization of knowledge claims through the use of a range of prototyping tools and through the creation of different kinds of evocative knowledge objects (EKOS). In engaging with objects, human participants create provisional understandings that are conveyed in story form to one another. Objects must be continually reproduced as meaningful entities and participants throughout the designing process. Through the co-creation of objects, narratives, identities, and dispositions, a set of shared social understandings emerges about the designing process itself.

Collective Intelligence—the ability to pool knowledge and compare notes with others toward a common goal

Designing is inherently multidisciplinary. It requires the construction of creative and productive relationships among humanists, artists, engineers, and technologists—each of whom has something necessary to contribute to, and to *learn from*, the experience of collaborative multidisciplinary design and technology development.

Judgment—the ability to evaluate the reliability and credibility of different information sources

As part of the designing activity, designers seek to identify the multiple contexts within which technologies take shape and have effects. This involves a consideration of how all participants in a proposed design—designers, users, and generations yet to be born—are implicated in the materialization and dematerialization of the technology-under-development. The range of expertise required for the assessment of a design includes not only deep understanding of technical principles and protocols, but also incisive knowledge about the psychological, social, political, and institutional contexts that make the innovation meaningful, relevant, and effective.

Transmedia Navigation—the ability to follow the flow of stories and information across multiple modalities

Designing involves the production of socio-technical-cultural assemblages. The elements of the assemblage are reworked in the process of designing. Using reverse engineering methods, designers employ a set of techniques for analyzing an existing technology to determine its constitutive parts and pieces and the interdependencies among functional components. By working backwards from the construction of a functioning technology, a designer gains useful information for the creation of a novel technological instance. In thinking about the notion of transmedia navigation, the designer might apply a set of techniques that I call *hermeneutic reverse engineering*. Here what is "reverse engineered" are the elements that contribute to the meaning of a given problem space or technology-under-development. These techniques focus on uncovering the layers of sedimented meaning as well as the meanings that circulate through different media channels.

Networking—the ability to search for, synthesize, and disseminate information

Designing involves practices of cultural analysis for the purposes of explicating the cultural matrix within which something makes sense. The process of cultural analysis uses basic techniques of description, analysis, and elucidation. To *describe* something adequately requires the use of specialized vocabulary and knowledge of diverse cultural vernaculars. The step of *analysis* can involve formal methods of linguistic and grammatical parsing, or the decoding of visual symbols or representations. The step of *elucidation*—of interpretation—involves the creation of an account of the way in which meaning coheres through the association among various signifying elements. Just as the practices of reverse engineering focus on identifying constitutive components of a functioning technology or system, these steps identify the main elements of signification that invest a particular design with meaning.

Negotiation—the ability to travel across diverse communities, discerning and respecting multiple perspectives, and grasping and following alternative norms

To understand technology fundamentally, one needs to apprehend it from multiple perspectives: the historical; social; and cultural; as well as the technical; instrumental; and material. This breeds a more nuanced understanding of the topic at hand. Design thinking is augmented with training in the history of technology, the development and use of critical frameworks for assessing technologies in their various forms, and disciplinary approaches that provide skills for the detailed assessment of global technocultural contexts, such as international studies, policy studies, and anthropology.

By engaging in practices of design thinking, participants in learning activities are encouraged to develop a robust imagination about what could and should be done differently with technologies that already exist. In this sense, the traditional role of critical thinking is expanded. No longer an end in itself, criticism of what has already been done is a step in the process of determining what needs to be done differently in the future.[57]

The Horizon of Singularity: A Global Culture of Learning

In the early 2000s, when many universities were focusing on branding and tightening control over classroom activities, faculty and administrators at MIT took an unconventional approach to rethinking the role of the university classroom in a networked age. Instead of chasing tuition revenue streams that might come from distance education, the university created an innovative model of learning that took advantage of the information flows provided by digital networks. MIT's OpenCourseWare (OCW) project, initially supported in the early 1990s by the Hewlett Foundation, took seriously the institution's mandate to develop a model to "advance knowledge and educate students in science, technology and other areas of scholarship that will best serve the nation and the world in the twenty-first century."[58] In doing so, MIT abandoned the one-to-many distance education model in favor of an approach that seriously and creatively addressed its cultural mission as a leading technocultural educational institution. What began as a large-scale web-based electronic publishing initiative quickly transformed into a new model of education that took advantage of the many-to-many communicative logic of the World Wide Web.[59]

By the early part of 2005, the OCW project had grown into a worldwide movement. As a consequence, the OpenCourseWare Consortium was established to provide resources and expertise on how to make course materials available, how to promote the development of open source tools and software to support these efforts, and how to find ways to sustain Open-CourseWare projects over time. The OCW Consortium seeks to create a vast archive of freely accessible course content, including syllabi and a portfolio of readings, with supplemental materials from a wide range of educational institutions. What is remarkable about this movement is the speed with which it coalesced and took hold across a broad spectrum of university contexts. Its reach is worldwide, with exceptionally active participation by institutions in France, Japan, and China. The many-to-many aspect of this rapidly expanding global network is of particular importance here. Rather than simply exporting cultural capital from American universities to the rest of the world, this movement encourages multi-directional exchange and cross pollination of ideas, resources, and pedagogies.[60]

A comprehensive review of the new Open Education Resource (OER) movement, written by international technocultural experts Dan E. Atkins, John Seely Brown, and Allen L. Hammond for the Hewlett Foundation, assessed the efforts and impact of the early efforts of various OER projects. In their review, the authors point out that the next stage of development of this movement will focus on community building, so that the "movement will create incentives for a diverse set of institutional stakeholders to enlarge and sustain this new culture of contribution (2007: 3)."[61] From the consideration of the cost of the initial production of OpenCourseWare materials (approximately $25,000 per course based on the MIT model), to a discussion of issues of digital preservation and archiving, the OER movement raises several issues that are at the heart of the current paradigm shift: how to sustain the momentum of early projects; how to expand the efforts to important global areas such as Africa and South America; and how to create a community of users, both within and outside formal educational institutions, for the purposes of truly revolutionizing the educational landscape.[62] The report ends with an itemized list of the issues that still need to be addressed, in order to realize the profound possibilities the OER movement has inaugurated. Among the most inspiring claim is the authors' call for the development of a truly global "culture of learning" that can prepare people to "thrive in a rapidly evolving, knowledge-based world . . . This world demands creativity, innovation, and entrepreneurialism from all of us . . . The OER initiative has been a vehicle for building a culture of sharing. We now propose that OER be leveraged within a broader initiative—an international Open Participatory Learning Infrastructure (OPLI) initiative for building a culture of learning" (35).

The Open Participatory Learning Infrastructure (OPLI) is an ambitious global initiative designed to address the dramatic increase in the need for educational programs over the next decade. To describe the scale of the educational project we will collectively face in the upcoming years, the authors point out that, in 2007, there were more than thirty million people qualified to enter a university for whom there are no places available; by 2017, that number will grow to more than one hundred million (33). As they surmise, in order to meet the higher education demands of this growing population of potential students, "a major university needs to be created every week" between now and then (33).[63] Given that we don't have enough brick and mortar buildings to school the qualified population at this point in time, it is obvious that the shortage of formal institutional education programs will become more pronounced. The OPLI builds on key elements of the paradigm shift already underway, such as the promotion of open code and content, as well as the development of media-rich learning environments, but it pushes things further by calling for the creation of an infrastructure to support the evolution of global educational opportunities.[64] The broad aim of OPLI is the development of a decentralized learning environment that permits participatory learning, provides incentives for participation at all levels, and encourages multidisciplinary and cross-cultural learning. In short, the authors call for the creation of a new socio-technical-cultural formation that involves the design of cooperative and complementary organizational practices, investment in technical infrastructure, and the formation and codification of new social norms of participation and learning.

Firmly grounded in a paradigm of abundance, the hope for the development of the OPLI is that it will spawn the creation of a network ecology that encourages participatory learning. To do so necessitates the development of new digital learning objects, as well as protocols for their continual revision, and access to special collections of instruments, archives, and cultural expertise. These are the key elements of the infrastructure that will have to be designed to mediate between "open-source content" and the knowledge-making activities of network participants. The importance of this infrastructure cannot be underestimated. The dream for this infrastructure is that it will be self-renewing in that every use of a particular learning object provides feedback about the effectiveness of the learning experience. Participants would thus be involved not only in their own learning, but in helping the OPLI learn as well by refining learning objects, modding them, and annotating contexts of use. While the shift work to enable the development of the OPLI is already underway, there is much more to be done, both inside and outside the academy. Rather than promote the development of a new centralized global educational system, the OPLI seeks a different horizon: the creation of learning alternatives that take place on the edges of formal educational systems. As the authors rightly point out, these edge shifts will eventually propagate, changing the core system of what counts as education and, more importantly, what counts as learning in a rapidly changing knowledge environment.

It is clear that as the reach of the OER movement expands, new technologies need to be developed that will enable participants to make sense of the abundance of knowledge available through the OPLI. These technologies include the development of expert pathways, robust indexing capacities, and detailed users' guides. The granularity of the resources available through open education repositories is an issue that needs further investigation. As the authors of the Hewlet OER assessment report claim: "How would we handle a 'success disaster' in which, for example, a teacher now has access to 100 elementary calculus courses? We need incentives and mechanisms to promote creation and access to fewer instances of the same course, but with more support material, more commentary, more examples" (Atkins, Brown, and Hammond, 2007: 22). While the logic of the network suggests that its value is enhanced by every instance of new content, it is easy to see how the simple collection of 100 instances of a learning object is not going to ensure a valuable learning experience for all participants at all levels. The signal-to-noise ratio is simply too high. The process of evaluating the quality of 100 individual digital learning objects swamps the learning effort from the outset. What is needed is the development of middleware learning protocols that can provide an assessment of the quality of different kinds of digital learning objects, guiding users to the ones most appropriate for their particular learning objectives.

The creation of effective digital learning objects must become a focus of design-research projects. In this sense, the aims of the OPLI will be helped by the emergence of learning designers, who may or may not be formally trained as teachers, but who can create pathways and digital learning materials that include both reliable content and suggestions for use in different contexts by different kinds of learners. To live up to the most ambitious goals of the OPLI, which holds forth the ideal of a self-modifying system, where learning materials are transformed based on feedback about effectiveness and applicability, these learning objects will include talk-back functions that can capture and interpret the traces of use left behind by users. The OPLI requires the development of a range of new technologies of imagination that focus on content (digital learning objects), context (pedagogical techniques, learning objectives), and system-based modification protocols designed to recursively amend the materials, such that they too learn through use. I describe one effort to create such a learning object in the conclusion, using it as the occasion to reflect on the affordances of the print book in comparison to those of the digital object.

The effectiveness of the OPLI will also require the development of local networks of people who share a set of physical resources, such as tools, instrumented spaces, and creative materials. These local learning networks need not be attached to formal educational organizations; in fact, one of the rich opportunities to explore is how informal learning institutions, such as museums and libraries, might serve the mixed-reality physical space needs of these local learning networks. The notion of mixed-reality refers to two aspects of learning within informal learning spaces: the nature of learning objects made available within these places; and the nature of the physical learning spaces. We need to develop new spaces of making that will allow people to create things together. To connect to broader distributed learning networks these spaces will also need to include a range of digital technologies, such as computer workstations and video and audio recording equipment. While it is likely that many of the participants in these spaces will be equipped with mobile devices, to serve the broadest range of people the space must be fully networked as well. Outfitted with these objects, tools, and network capabilities, the spaces provide the context for important embodied social experiences, such as the peer modeling of digital learning practices and the performative presentation of digital productions for embodied audiences.

Tinkering with the Future: Making Spaces to Make the Future

As I briefly discussed in chapter 3, the notion of "tinkering" is at the heart of several emerging cultural movements, such as the Maker's Movement, DIY Culture, and the resurgence of interest in handicrafts. In early 2008, an article in the *New York Times* described the Bay Area Maker's Faire as a gathering of "folks from all walks of life who blend science, technology, craft and art to make things both goofy and grand."[65] Later that year, the *Los Angeles Times* published a piece about the rise of "craft-making" among young artisans, noting that the burgeoning growth of "craft websites have fostered a global network based on cooperation rather than competition."[66] Even as these seemingly old-fashioned practices gather steam, taking form as new cultural movements, they also point out an important under-theorized consideration in discussions about the relationship between digital media and learning: the role of the body in the process of learning and making culture. As the set of practices at the center of these cultural movements, tinkering is a mode of knowledge production that involves the hand, the use of tools, and mentoring relationships among people in close physical proximity. Tinkering in the twenty-first century also involves the use of digital networks, tools, and materials. For this reason, I argue that tinkering should be a topic of discussion in any conversation about the development of twenty-first-century literacies. Tinkering names an important set of practices for developing the technological imagination.

Promoting tinkering as a mode of twenty-first-century knowledge making involves the creation of new mixed-reality spaces and informal learning protocols that support the development of communities of interest that may also coalesce as communities of practice. This project entails the development of specific elements:

- A creative, communally accessible physical space that provides the tools necessary for common tinkering practices.
- A creative, communally accessible physical space that provides ac-

cess to creative digital technologies (graphics production, video-making, etc.).

- A community-based physical space that supports the development of learning relationships between members of different generations (youth and adults).
- A network of institutional professionals (librarians, museum docents, for example) who can mediate between learners, mentors, physical spaces, tools, and technologies to foster communities of (tinkering) practice.

Fundamentally, these spaces would provide access to commonly used tools (hammers, saws, and wrenches, for example) and simple machines (sewing machines, sanders, and lathes). Beyond these simple tools, these spaces would also make available a range of evocative knowledge objects, such as commercially available interactive toys, robot-assembly kits, microprocessor design kits, and simple fabrication systems.[67]

There are already several examples of spaces that provide these kinds of tools and technologies within local communities. For example, the open-access public workshop called the TechShop in Menlo Park, California, provides core tools, as well as advanced machines, to members who pay a monthly subscription service to use the tools and facilities.[68] Founded in 2006 with the mission to support the fabrication needs of innovators and tinkerers, the TechShop provides a range of tools, machines, and equipment so that members can build, fix, or create any kind of project. Housed in a fifteen thousand square foot light-industrial space, the Menlo Park TechShop provides every manner of basic hand and power tool, as well as equipment for fabrication, machining, electronics, sewing, wood working, welding, and finishing. Special tools for automotive work, plastics molding, and rapid prototyping are also available. The TechShop staff provides basic and advanced instruction on the use of all equipment, as well as a range of services in 3-D printing, project and prototyping consultation.

While the current model of the TechShop is as a commercial enterprise, a non-profit version called hackerspaces has developed in different locations across the globe. A hackerspace is a physical location where people gather to collaborate on computer-based projects to make electronic art, digital devices, and computer applications. There are several hackerspaces across the world that go by different names, for example: Noisebridge in

San Francisco; Pumping Station One in Chicago; Metalab in Vienna; Cyberpipe in Ljubljana. Unlike the TechShop's focus on the physical fabrication of things, hackerspaces primarily function as spaces that support those who want to make digital applications and small electronic projects by providing access to computer systems, game consoles, and video- and audio-making equipment.

In addition to the physical spaces, we need to develop communities of interest that connect learners with mentors, for the purpose of sharing knowledge about the use of tools and tinkering techniques. Social networking applications are key to this effort. For example, *The Public School* is an inventive program offered by TELIC Arts Exchange in Los Angeles. It functions as a social networking backend, connecting those who want to learn with those who have something to teach. *The Public School* has no fixed curriculum. It works on a simple model: a class is proposed by someone who has either a desire to learn or something to teach. These "school topics" are listed on a website. Other members of the public can indicate interest in a particular class topic. When a critical mass of people expresses interest in a class, *The Public School* representative engages a teacher and finds a place for the class to meet (see figure 28). As the website claims: "*The Public School* is not accredited, it does not give out degrees, and it has no affiliation with the pubic school system. It is a framework that supports autodidactic activities, operating under the assumption that everything is in everything."[69] *The Public School* provides a mechanism to connect learners and teachers; when enough of these connections are made, its facilitators work on finding a physical location for embodied meetings. This is easiest when the topics only require face-to-face communication, but when the topic involves instruction in the use of physical tools and materials, obviously a different kind of space is required that is stocked with the necessary equipment.

When I imagine combining the affordances of physical make-spaces with the use of a social networking application such as *The Public School*, I see the creation of the type of community make-spaces that could serve as the mixed-reality infrastructure of the OPLI. In this vision, the mission is to enable residents to gain skills and experience in exploring new technological possibilities where community members can congregate one-on-one or in small learning groups. This level of community-based open access to a physical workshop is necessary to enable people to gather in the presence

THE PUBLIC SCHOOL process

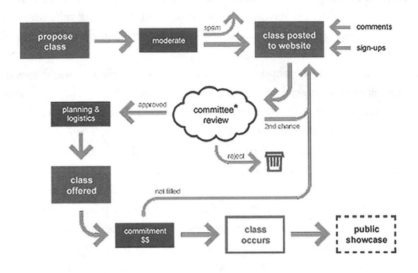

28. Diagram of *The Public School* process at TELIC Arts Exchange in Los Angeles. (www.telic.info)

of tools and materials. An important aspect of the gathering is the social experience of conversation and camaraderie. These social experiences provide the backdrop for peer-to-peer learning and teaching. While watching other people work with materials and tools, new makers are subtly encouraged to start experimenting as well. This provides the stage for the possibility of being captivated by an idea and a possibility. The use of digital networking tools gathers people as participants in a community of interest; the physical space enables this community to also become a community of practice. This is the infrastructure for the exercise of the technological imagination. These spaces enable participants to gain skills and experience in hacking the present in the service of creating new futures.

The establishment of community-based make-spaces equipped with a range of tools and fabrication machines, that rely on social networking applications to provide the infrastructure for community building, would result in a new institution form—call it the community garage or the tinkering shop—that extends the cultural work of the community library in important ways. As a partner to the library, these community centers become places for the making of technologies, the making of relationships, and the making of physical communities. One of the missing ingredients in this vision—and there are others—is a process for connecting learners with the people who can help nurture the technological imagination to think differently about our technocultural futures. While the foregoing discussion of tinkering was developed in terms of the relationship between tool use and the exercise of the technological imagination, for the purpose of creating new visions of the future, it skirted an important aspect of the embodied experience of collaborative making—the opportunity to engage in cross-generational discussions about the connection of the future, the present, and the past. As I elaborated earlier in this chapter, one of the important aspects of the technological imagination is its appreciation of the pasts of technology development. In light of that assertion, let me end this chapter with a brief polemic: it is time for us to confront the implications of the intense presentism of digital learning experiences. As members of the born digital generation navigate different media flows, they are immersed in the sense of the now and the next. Their media landscapes treat the past and history as no more than cultural memes at best, or as decorative materials at worse. As was true in the analysis of postmodern logics of pastiche, history is often treated as a mere repository of images, slogans, and remixable clips (Jameson, 1991: 17). Issues of historical context, the specificity of media, and the development trajectory of technological possibilities are difficult to convey in the wash of images that is the vernacular of remix culture. While we might be right to be wary of the ideological work performed through the dutiful rehearsal of grand narratives of history—of empire or of progress, for example—there remains a challenge of how to engender the development of a historical imagination for those whose learning happens through surfing media flows. Our pasts, "the past," are important elements of cultural reproduction. Dewey's ([1938] 1998: 23) question should haunt us: "How shall the young become acquainted with the past in such a way that the acquaintance is a potent agent in appreciation of the living present?" We need to invent ways to enable Original Synners to gain an appreciation for the pasts that are not about nostalgia, dutiful recitation of received wisdom, or the bland reproduction of old tropes.

This is where the particular contexts—and learning affordances—offered by the community library serve increasingly important roles in the digital future.[70] These cultural institutions perform important archival service in maintaining the official histories of, among other things, technologies, innovation, creativity, and idea formation. Libraries, like universities, are specialized nodes within distributed learning networks. These institutions are ideally situated to contribute to the development of the technological imagination through the support of tinkering practices and the creation of mixed-reality make-spaces. Community-based libraries can initiate and support the formation of social relationships between mentors and learners. By doing such, these cultural institutions offer intriguing learning affordances that can foster corporeal skills of tinkering, and the creative prototyping of visions of the technocultural futures. When tinkering make-spaces are located in proximity to these institutional contexts, there are exciting possibilities for connecting the making of the future, through tinkering, with the histories of making of the past, in the form of informal as well as official narratives of cultural memory. These pasts may take the form of tinkering techniques that are passed along from a mentor to a learner, but they also may take the form of embodied histories of technology-learning that open onto understandings about the historical contours of technology development.

I began this chapter by posing the question of what is changing in our current paradigm shift. Noting the accelerating rate of change, converging on a singularity no longer seems like a far-fetched science fictional scenario. As many have astutely observed, participating in convergence culture develops new dispositions, which inevitably serve as the cognitive and epistemological framework of learning in the digital present. I invoke the tag Original Synners to identify those individuals who have developed these new dispositions through their experience participating in digital networks. This general background served to set the stage for a discussion about the role of the university as a specialized node within distributed learning networks, which can inspire and develop the technological imaginations of Original Synners. While the trajectory of this chapter ranged over a wide territory, from a discussion of new subjects of the technological imagination, to a call for the design of new technologies of imagination, most of the projects I considered in detail were those that are going on at the edges of formal institutions. Our shift work is a remix project in its own right, where we strategically select and combine elements from a range of theoretically grounded innovations, for the purposes of developing new literacies, peda-gogies, and programs. The efforts I discussed in this chapter creatively engage the dispositions of those who learn and work in digital networks. In different ways they manifest the labor involved in paradigm shift-ing. Whether it's a shift from a culture of consumption to a culture of participation—as Jenkins argues—a shift from a culture of teaching to a culture of learning, or a shift from the University 1.0 to version 2.0, this labor requires significant personal stamina and creativity to find resources, sym-pathetic colleagues, and (sometimes) institutional work-arounds. Make no mistake, working on the edges is often lonely business. The core of the University 1.0 has not yet embraced these edge-projects. But I believe that in order to be responsive to changing knowledge environments, and to the needs of those who will soon be enrolling in its programs, the university will need to transform in significant ways. From a reconsideration of its mission and its interest in technological innovation, to its sense of its constituents (Original Synners and Lifelong Learners), and its role as one site within a distributed global learning network, the university, as an ideal type of learning institution, needs an operational, technical, and epistemological upgrade and reboot. With these projects, the building of the University 2.0 has begun.

The Work of a Book in a Digital Age

 Why write a book in an era obsessed with net worked digital communication? There are personal, professional, and cultural reasons. I'll leave the personal reasons for last. For humanists, the book remains the privileged signifier of academic credibility. Curiously, the value of the book as a testimony to scholarly trustworthiness is not due to the size of the audience it reaches immediately, which is likely to be smaller than the other forms of technological media, such as the museum exhibits and websites that I have discussed in this project. Rather, its value is tied to its particular affordances that allow for the expression of complex explanations of abstract ideas and of critical analyses of particular texts, applications, and situations. I am interested in how the book functions in relation to new modes of dynamic knowledge production, and to new forms of cultural experience that are occasioned by the use of digital networks. While I understand how I might communicate the insights that emerge from a critical analysis of an interactive application, it is less clear how I might convey, in print, the way in which these insights might be used to redesign an application differently. As one last example of hermeneutic reverse engineering, let me describe the process to design a digital learning object using semantic mapping applications.

Semantic mapping tools are knowledge-making devices that offer a set of interactive possibilities—for lexical data representation, linking, expansion, and compression—that can be used to elaborate relationships among key terms and concepts. All semantic mapping applications are built on a deep structure that establishes relationships among elements—terms, definitions, and connotations. As with the case of dictionaries and encyclopedias, the cultural work of these lexical artifacts is profound, yet elusive (Kramarae and Treichler, 1985: 3). Their taken-for-granted stature as denotative works masks the way in which cultural assumptions are in fact reproduced as semantic truth.

Consider, for example, the popular semantic mapping application called the Visual Thesaurus™ created by the company ThinkMap (originally called Plumb Design, Inc.). This application graphically represents the meaning of a term as a cluster of words linked by graphic lines connecting definitional nodes (see figure 29). In the following figure, the term "technology" is mapped as a set of connections between the words "engineering science," "applied science," and "engineering" (see figure 30).

A close reading of its definitional nodes reveals interesting assumptions about the relationship between technology and culture. For example, when a user continues to unfold the map of the meaning of the term "technology," new phrases are revealed, such as "aeronautical engineering," "automotive engineering," "computer technology," and so forth. Exploring this set of connections linked to the term "technology" illustrates a tight semantic coupling between it—as a broad category—and the professional domains of engineering; in this way, the visualization application promotes an instrumental and highly truncated annotation for the term.

The first reference to a term that explicitly invokes the domain of culture doesn't occur anywhere within the immediate collection of nodes connected to the term "technology." The user has to follow the path of connections that leads from the term technology to the term "profession," to find the nodes for "literature," "architecture," "journalism," and "politics." The term "technology" moves to the periphery and remains linked only to the nodes of "engineering" and "engineering science."

Tracking the use of gendered pronouns in various sections of the Visual Thesaurus™ reveals a subtle distinction in the assignment of value to

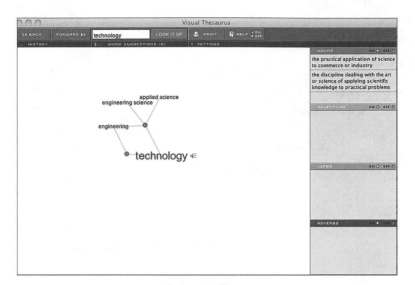

29. Screen shot of the Visual Thesaurus™ semantic map of the term "technology."
(www.visualthesarus.com)

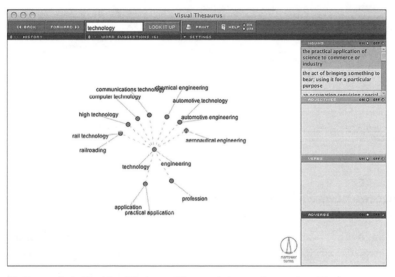

30. Screen shot of the Visual Thesaurus™ expanded semantic mapping of the term
"technology." (www.visualthesarus.com)

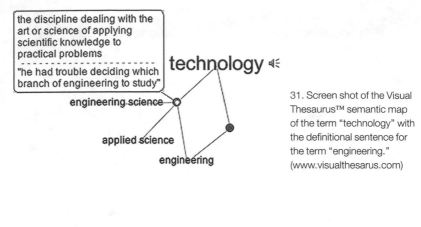

the discipline dealing with the art or science of applying scientific knowledge to practical problems
- - - - - - - - - - - - - - - - - - -
"he had trouble deciding which branch of engineering to study"

technology

engineering science

applied science

engineering

31. Screen shot of the Visual Thesaurus™ semantic map of the term "technology" with the definitional sentence for the term "engineering." (www.visualthesarus.com)

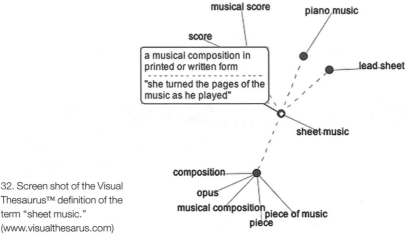

musical score   piano music

score

a musical composition in printed or written form
- - - - - - - - - - - - - - - - - -
"she turned the pages of the music as he played"

lead sheet

sheet music

composition

opus

musical composition

piece of music

piece

32. Screen shot of the Visual Thesaurus™ definition of the term "sheet music." (www.visualthesarus.com)

different genders. For example, the definitional sentence that illustrates the meaning of "engineering" invokes the masculine pronoun: "he had trouble deciding which branch of engineering to study" (see figure 31). When the term "major" is selected—the following definition/illustration couplet is revealed: "the principal field of study of a student at a university"; "her major is linguistics." Further exploration reveals that female pronouns are used in references to linguistics, literature, and the bar exam, but the masculine is invoked in the engineering sciences, doctoral programs, frontier brain science, and geology. One of the more perplexing gendered references is the definitional sentence for "sheet music" (see figure 32).

Amusing as these examples are, it is precisely these unsurprising and taken-for-granted assignments of gender identity, embedded within a visual lexicon, that reveal a particular cultural bias to this technological application. Technology is defined as distinct from the disciplines and practices of culture, and this visual map rehearses a familiar gendered distinction between technology and culture more broadly. Just as we learned to appreciate the deeply cultural, and often ideological, work of dictionary making, in critically examining new meaning-mapping applications we see the re-inscription and reification of a set of cultural understandings about gender and technology (Kramarae and Treichler, 1985: 8). So even as it visually maps technology and culture as separated by several degrees of linkage, the application cannot help but demonstrate the inseparableness of these concepts.

Imagine a different network of linked terms, one that is explicitly designed to illustrate the relationship between technology and culture. In this version of a semantic map, the term technology is visualized as a network of linked and related elements and manifests a definition of technology as a structured cultural arrangement. The design of the application called *Learning to Love the Questions* (LLQ) draws on multiple theories of the relationship between technology and culture in creating a graphic web of significance that includes terms, definitions, and key questions about the cultural implications of specific technologies (see figure 33). Its purpose is to help users think with more complexity about the cultural aspects of technology. In designing the first version of the LLQ, I explored the possibilities of interactive semantic mapping applications for the representation of theoretical understandings; in the process, the understandings were reworked in dialogue with the expressive capabilities offered by the tool.[1]

The *Learning to Love the Questions* application makes use of the representational affordances of semantic mapping applications for the purposes of new knowledge creation. The labor involved in creating this application included learning how to read a new lexical form—the interactive semantic map—modifying interpretive techniques appropriate for this form, developing a language to describe the meaning that is created and expressed through the new form, and becoming proficient in several authoring applications.

This application visualizes the definition of technology as an articulated cultural formation. The formation comprises different elements that connect to others in multiple ways; each element contributes to the overall meaning of the term "technology." The elements of a technological

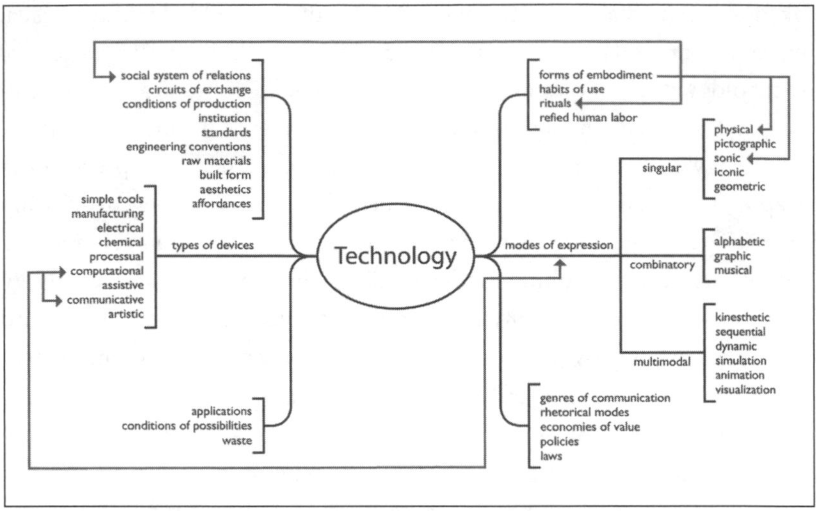
social system of relations
circuits of exchange
conditions of production
institution
standards
engineering conventions
raw materials
built form
aesthetics
affordances
simple tools
manufacturing
electrical
chemical
processual
computational
assistive
communicative
artistic
types of devices
Technology
applications
conditions of possibilities
waste
forms of embodiment
habits of use
rituals
refied human labor
physical
pictographic
sonic
iconic
geometric
singular
modes of expression
combinatory
alphabetic
graphic
musical
kinesthetic
sequential
dynamic
simulation
animation
visualization
multimodal
genres of communication
rhetorical modes
economies of value
policies
laws

33. An early prototype of the interactive application called *Learning to Love the Questions* created in Freemind.

formation include taken-for-granted aspects of technology, such as a built-form, a set of functionalities, applications, and intended uses, as well as those technical elements that may become sedimented within a particular technology: standards; codes; conventions; conditions of production; and raw materials. Technological formations also include a range of elements that might be typically considered as cultural and social in nature: forms of embodiment, habits of use, rituals, reified human labor, aesthetics, economies of value, and circuits of exchange. In its first iteration, LLQ was a simple graphic elaboration of a set of related terms. A second iteration organized the key elements according to models of the circuit of culture (Johnson, 1986: 47; DuGay et al., 1997: 3). The final iteration expresses the semantic relationship among elements in the application as a series of questions (see figure 34). The learning objective that inspired the design of the interactive experience (of engaging in questions instead of definitional terms) was to stimulate the technological imagination to think with more complexity about technology. The aim was to design an interactive: a "reverse oracle" that, when queried, provides questions instead of answers. This application is an example of a digital learning object that enables users to record their experiences in using the application. Sections next to the semantic web graphic allow users to leave traces of their path through the

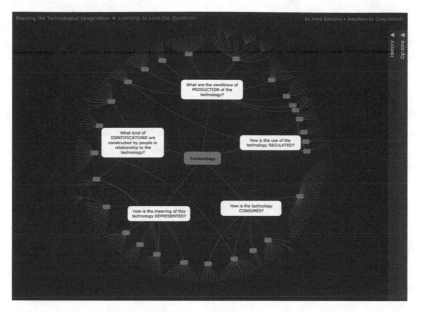

34. Screen shot of the interactive application called *Learning to Love the Questions*.

web of questions, make notes in response to particular questions, and add new questions to the underlying database. Over time, as users leave their notes and responses to various questions that are posed in terms of a particular technology, other users who are interested in the same technology will be able to access the question paths and the notes left by earlier seekers. In this way, the digital learning object will learn from the people who use it. This modest effort to design an innovative technocultural object—a learning object that learns through use by learners—is another small example of the technological imagination at work.

The LLQ is a manifestation of cultural theory and a new mode of digital scholarship: the creation of interactive semantic maps.[2] The skills required to understand semantic maps—learning how to read them, modifying interpretive techniques, developing a new language to describe their hermeneutic work, and becoming proficient in new interfaces—are also the base set of literacies required of anyone who wants to participate in the intellectual communities that are central to digital culture. The time investment to gain these skills is significant. As I argued in chapter 4, it is important for scholars and teachers to keep current with the expressive modalities of digital culture. This involves learning not simply how to read new modes, but also how to author them as well. There is a payoff for the individual, in terms of increased digital capabilities and skills, but the more important outcome is achieved in contributing to the design of cultures in the future. The same technologies that provoke the development of new educational programs and pedagogical techniques also serve as platforms for new ways of knowing, and for new practices of knowledge construction. Just as students are developing new literacies through the use of new tools for the creation, representation, and dissemination of knowledge, so too are researchers using these tools for the circulation of ideas and the development of new forms of scholarly participation. Many researchers are experimenting with multimodal forms of expression, made possible by digital technologies, to create new modes of scholarship. These, in turn, require the development of new forms of publication and dissemination. It is also the driving motivation for the creation of this transmedia book project.

The Work of This Book

This print book is a boundary-object: it was never one thing.[3] From the beginning, I imagined it as a multimodal information system that both follows and revises the genre conventions of the academic monograph. It adheres to the genre conventions of a scholarly project in that it elaborates the cultural and theoretical significance of a set of specific technological artifacts, professional design-research practices, and institutional formations. It is a project that is designed to enact its own theoretical assertions about the importance of taking culture seriously in the creation of new technologies. The limits of the print book form were tested in the process of developing analyses of the technologies discussed in each chapter. Deciding what would be textually represented and what would be better expressed in a digital mode was part of the iterative design of the entire project. The result was the creation of a transmedia book that includes material distributed on diverse kinds of media, including DVD, video, and the web. One could say that the print book serves as an avatar for the digital materials that are also part of the project known as *Designing Culture*. It is a pointer to other media and other modes of knowledge dissemination.

In some cases the digital materials were explicitly discussed in these print chapters. In chapter 1, I described the design of the interactive multimedia documentary *Women of the World Talk Back*, which was initially created in 1995 for presentation at the NGO Forum held in China, as part of the Fourth United Nations World Conference on Women. Cast as a project of feminist media activism, the design of this project explicitly drew insight from feminist cultural theory. I used this example to elaborate the process of rearticulation: where the aim of the designing practice was to remix the significant elements of a given technological formation in such a way as to change their meaning and cultural valence. One of the particular innovations included in that project was the development of short video pieces called *Video Dialogues*, which used the conventions of public service announcements—sound bite statements, illustrative b-roll, and multiple talking-head shots—to communicate the key themes of the UN conference. These pieces were designed as primers (a pedagogical genre) on important feminist topics of global interest. The meaning of these primers has changed in the ensuing years since the UN conference. When first created they served as briefing statements about the key UN conference topics; now they are digital memory traces of an event far removed from the pages of contemporary newspapers and personal experience. Originally the project explored the design of a ritual of interactive communication, yet now it signifies a specific moment of creation that was thoroughly influenced by specific historical forces and opportunities. Interacting with it now, viewers may get a sense of what the designers had hoped to accomplish, but can never fully apprehend what the pieces meant at the time. The work of the print chapter is to elucidate the context of the creation of this multimedia application, and to reflect on its theoretical and cultural implications as an example of a design approach I call hermeneutic reverse engineering. By including it with this book project, viewers can investigate the way in which the project's theoretical aims were aesthetically and figuratively expressed.

The relationship of the print book to the website is both more intimate and less material. The book and website serve as portals to one another. In chapter 2, the discussion of the institutional context of the creation of the XFR exhibit is followed by an analysis of the design of individual interactives. While each of the XFR interactives can be isolated as a singular element of the overall exhibit, with a proper name and a list of technological components, it is more accurate to describe each interactive as a plurality of affordances, signifying elements, and evocative effects.[4] This kind of description is not easily accommodated by the conventions of a print book. The website, on the other hand, serves as a useful platform for the presentation of dynamic archival material. The *Designing Culture* website includes video clips of the each of the interactives in use, which allows readers to see the way in which the interactives engaged museum visitors through eye, hand, and body. While the print chapter included a brief textual and image-based description of the evolution of RED: *The Reading Eye Dog*, for example, it couldn't show the object-in-action, which was another aspect of its meaning and significance.

In addition to serving as the repository for archival material about an exhibit that lasted only three years, the website also allows for the detailed annotation of each interactive in terms of its technical specifications, a description of its content, and a reflection on its broader cultural implications. On this last point, the website includes an analysis of each interactive, addressing the four questions of McLuhan's tetradic framework of analysis, which probe the poetics and implications of a particular medium: 1) What does it enhance or amplify? 2) What does it erode or obsolesce? 3) What does it retrieve that was previously obsolesced? 4) What does it reverse into when pushed to the limits of its logic? McLuhan's mode of exegesis is poetic and interpretive. He formulated his "four laws of media" in the form of questions in order to provoke insights about the diverse and contradictory effects of media. His four questions allow for the creation of understandings about how media and technologies more broadly are both/and.[5] On the website, the use of a blog interface allows for the multiplication of interpretations, where the ones I formulate can be augmented, contested, contradicted, or refined by other readers. This interactive application enables the collaborative analysis of the plurality of meanings evoked by each XFR interactive.

At the center of chapter 3 is a discussion of the information design and cultural implications of one particular XFR exhibit: *The Reading Wall* and the "History of Reading" episodes I authored/designed for it. The design of this speculative reading device was influenced by the traditional notion of walls as monuments that record and preserve the history of a culture. This interactive bore the responsibility of conveying the histories of reading and writing for the entire XFR exhibit; it manifested this responsibility in its built form, its digital content, and its mode of interactivity. While the print chapter fills in the historical and institutional contexts that influenced the design of the digital application, missing is a specific description of the poetics of interactivity that augment the symbolic meaning of the reading experience. The digital episodes were created as multimodal accounts of historical narratives that were animated by the movement of the display along the wall. When the reader moved the display from one episode to the next, visual elements appeared, lingered, and eventually disappeared. The actual reading of historical material—comprising text, words, images, captions, titles, and dates—takes place in one temporal space, the present time of the reader. As the time of the reader's present gives way to the next moment, and the next episode is assembled, the past—in the form of the episode just read—dissipates: it has no presence any longer on the digital display. These dynamic animations are reproduced on the website in a section devoted to *Interactive Digital Wall* books. The three-part application on the "History of Reading" built for the xfr exhibit was the first of several interactive pieces created for this new reading technology. Although they are reformatted for viewing on a standard computer screen, the web applications allow a viewer to see the way that the screen space was populated with text and image, and how these elements become animate through the reader's interaction. Two additional interactive wall books are included as well: a fourteen-episode application called "Science for All Ages," which addresses the history of science, and an application called "Deslízate en el Tiempo," a Spanish-language history of the development of communication technologies. While the mode of interactivity is different on the computer screen than it was when using an actual *Interactive Digital Wall*, these web simulations provide the viewer with an approximate experience of reading the wall, enabling the assessment of the poetics of animated text and images that both reproduce and extend notions of page-based literacy.

Chapter 4 reflects on the paradigm shift work that focuses on rethinking the nature of learning in a digital age. I begin with a discussion of some of the signal characteristics of the dispositions of young people who have grown up with ubiquitous access to digital networks, and then elaborate how the technological imagination—as one of these important dispositions —might be cultivated by incorporating design thinking into learning activities. I review the changing context for learning in a digital age by describing a model of a distributed network of learning, and discuss the way the contemporary university contributes something important to this learning environment. The university is an important site for technocultural innovation, and I am especially interested in how the digital humanities contributes to this cultural work of the academy. To this end, I consider a model of how the research university's interest in technological innovation might be productively tied to an educational mission that focuses on the training of the technological imagination. We need the university to engage this mission: in so doing it will serve as a significant site of cultural transformation.

The university is one site within a distributed learning network, offering a concentration of resources in the form of creative and critical intellectuals, who can contribute important work as expert learning designers. I discuss a genre of technology called "technologies of imagination," which can serve as platforms for the exercise of the imagination. I am particularly interested in how these technologies—what Atkins, Brown, and Hammond (2007) refer to as "digital learning objects"—can be used to augment learning in different sites. The *Designing Culture* website offers a collection of digital learning objects that include information about how they might be used in different learning contexts. The section of Video Primers includes a selection of short video "postcards from the edge" that address different topics relating to culture and technology. These short video pieces employ the editing conventions of dynamic film trailers to convey key lessons about digital culture.

The work of this book, then, is to focus on the work of the digital age as materialized in the practices of designers, innovators, prosumers, educators, and other shift workers. My preoccupation with the labor involved in designing culture is probably a manifestation of my working class sensibility. I remain continually impressed by the sheer volume of creative energy, mental engagement, and physical effort that is involved in the production of digital culture. Designing is a social practice of meaning-making, whereby the relations among elements that constitute a technology are replicated, transformed, codified, and disseminated. Designing not only shows the influence of culture—in terms of language use and symbolic resources—but also functions as one of the central activities whereby culture is given material form. For this reason, everyone who is engaged in practices of technological innovation is also implicated in the process of designing the cultures of the present and of the future. In the end this book project argues that we need new ways of thinking about technology, culture, education, and the multidisciplinary practices of cultural reproduction that take form as media rich documentaries, public interactives, creative pedagogies, digital scholarship, and new technologies of imagination.

In closing, I return to the question, Why write a book in an age of digital abundance? The print-based book is a layered set of conversations that manifest as rhetorical strategies, citation conventions, and poetic expression, straightforwardly following a conventionalized textual architecture. Students, peers, and supervisors are literate in the ways of the printed book: they know how to decipher the knowledge production and representational strategies deployed there; therefore, they know how to read the object for signs of intelligence (or wrong-headedness), scholarly credibility (or blindspots), and creative thinking. I respect the sensibilities of this audience and understand how their sense of the meaning of *this* book is shaped by institutional considerations, as well as by the pleasure of owning and collecting objects. Authoring this book was a part of my professional practice. It sets up the conditions of possibility for the creation of social relationships mediated through this object; it serves as an interface among different groups of people who apprehend it as readers, users, reviewers, collectors, and designers. I am a humanist by training and a technologist by vocation. My identity is coproduced through the oscillations of these professional experiences and practices. As an expression of this doubled identity, I offer this book as an evocative knowledge object (EKO)—an object to think with—that combines the material and the digital, the abstract and the representational. The knowledge it evokes is not contained in the book, the author, *or* the reader, but is manifested through the physical interaction and engagement with objects that take different forms: materially; digitally; visually; and textually. Compared to other EKOs, the print book has a low signal to noise ratio: it is well suited to the work of exegesis and elaboration.[6] It is not easily deployed for the purposes of presenting dynamic motion and processual poetics. While this print book circulates as one element among many, including a range of digital materials, I know that its meaning now will differ from its future meaning, when those digital elements have disappeared.

I have a recurring dream in which I'm lecturing in a cavernous room about some theoretical point. People hover nearby: sometimes they come close to listen. I sense interest in them; their bodies move with energy. I get more animated, but the volume of the space swallows my voice, so I start talking louder. Eventually I'm screaming theory. Recently I've been screaming about design to unknown computer scientists. Last year I was screaming about technology to female students. Eventually I wake up with a metaphoric sore throat, exhausted but weirdly invigorated. I wrote this book to lower the sonic volume of my dreaming life. I think of it as a calling card on a noisy planet, a time machine, a space ship, and a bearer of tradition. It is a way for me to be present in some version of the future. As a cultural artifact, it will outlive me. This is my personal hope for the future of the book in a digital age.

notes

introduction: **Taking Culture Seriously**

1 The Organization of Economic Co-operation and Development
(OECD)—a consortium of ministries from 30 countries—develops "rules of the game" for the creation of a global economy that
focuses on the creation of policies that support technological innovation. See OECD (2004). There are several recent books that
examine the relationship between national policies and innovation productivity: see especially Clark and Tracey (2004); Hagel
and Brown (2005); Tavares and Teixeira (2006); and Schmoch,
Rammer, Legler (2006).
2 The World Economic Forum publishes an annual report on global
competitiveness that ranks countries according to the "Networked
Readiness Index," which measures the degree to which countries
make use of their information-computer technologies (ICT) resources. The metric evaluates a country's capacity to develop
policies and an interrelated system of education, research and
development, and technological diffusion. To the extent that the
elements of the system (number of graduates in science and technology educational programs, national infrastructure and pen-
etration of use of ICT's, as well as investment in research and
development) work in concert, the greater the level of global competitiveness is. In 2005–2006, the United States ranked number
one. In 2006–2007, its ranking dropped to seven. The top three
countries in 2007 included: Denmark, Sweden, and Singapore.
These figures come from *The Global Competitiveness Report 2006–
2007* (Lopez-Claros, Porter, Schwab, Sala-i-Martin, 2006).

3 Since the early 1990s, Singapore has been working on a billion-dollar investment strategy to create the conditions for the development of a cradle to grave "Innovation Lifestyle" that will enable the country to become a "science-oriented nation with a knowledge-based economy." The small city-state is poised to spend more than $15 billion (U.S.) to stimulate innovation in biosciences, and approximately $330 million on innovations in Interactive Digital Media. The strategy relies on investing in global brands to seed new industries and technology-transfer enterprises: Microsoft, SAP, Electronic Arts, Lucas Films, as well as MIT, Johns Hopkins, NYU, Carnegie Mellon, and USC, among others. The per capita figure was calculated based on a 2005 population figure of 4,425,720. During 2006–2007, I was involved in several discussions with Singaporean colleagues about the government's strategy to invest in interactive digital media. For an official overview of the country's investment in biomedical innovation, see Brantley (2001). The early reports on the level of investment in interactive digital media have disappeared from the web since 2007. As of 2010 there are no official statements available about the amount of funding to be devoted to innovation in digital media.

4 The per capita figure was calculated based on a total amount of $5.9 billion dollars, divided by the 2007 population figure of 303,266,913. See "State of the Union" (2006).

5 The map of India included in the Windows 95 OS displayed a small territory in a different shade of green from the rest of the country. The territory is, in fact, strongly disputed between the Kashmiri people and the Indian government, but Microsoft designers inadvertently settled the dispute in favor of one side. Assigning the territory—roughly eight pixels in size on the digital map—a different shade of green signified that the territory was not part of India. See Best (2004).

6 After India banned Windows 95 OS, Microsoft had no choice but to recall two hundred thousand copies. The cost of this blunder was measured in dollars and good will. See Best (2004).

7 As of 2006. See Arrington (2006).

8 *Kairos* publishes "webtexts" that can include video or hypermedia: http://kairos .technorhetoric.net/. *Vectors: A Journal of Culture and technology in a Dynamic Vernacular* publishes interactive, multimodal works of scholarship http://www .vectorsjournal.org/. *Postmodern Culture* accepts submissions with full-motion video and animations: http://muse.jhu.edu/journals/postmodern_culture/. *Digital Humanities Quarterly* will accept "experiments in interactive media": http://digitalhumanities.org/dhq/. *Internet Archaeology* will accept video as well as databases: http://intarch.ac.uk/.

9 Probably the best known and longest running program, the McLuhan Program in Technology and Culture at the University of Toronto, was established in 1963. Since 1996, Georgetown University has offered a Masters of Arts program in Communication, Culture and Technology. Washington State University has a major in Digital Technology and Culture. Georgia Institute of Technology has an

undergraduate major in Science, Technology, and Culture. University of California at San Diego offers an undergraduate core sequence in Culture, Art, and Technology. King's College at the University of London offers a Masters program in Digital Culture and Technology. At Brunel University of West London, the Centre for Research into Innovation, Culture, and Technology (CRICT) has been at the forefront of educational programs for more than a decade. In 2010, MIT announced a new program in "Art, Culture and Technology."

10 The Korea Advanced Institute of Science and Technology (KAIST) launched the Graduate School of Culture and Technology in 2005 to train students to "actively practice culture technology and explore the emerging convergence between the arts, humanities, and technology." It currently offers M.S. and Ph.D. degree programs.

11 One of the key questions in these debates focuses on the nature of creative labor—its benefits and costs for the workers who populate this new class—and the methods adopted by governments and corporations to both incubate and profit from this labor. Richard Florida (2002: 16) first introduced the concept of the "no-collar worker." Around the same time, Andrew Ross (2003) conducted an ethnographic investigation of the culture and work practices of collarless creatives. John Hartley's (2005) edited volume on the "creative industries" collected essays by an impressive range of cultural theorists and critics to digest the implications of this new class formation. Other central participants in these discussions include Geert Lovink and Ned Rossiter. See Rossiter (2006) and Lovink and Rossiter (2007).

12 Sometimes, as in the case of the Microsoft product referred to in the index statement, the cultural implications of a technological innovation escape notice until too late—the offending product entailed a costly recall. The map of India blunder was not the company's only cultural stumble. Through another release of its famous operating system, Microsoft again learned the cost of cultural ignorance. A Spanish-language version of Windows XP OS, marketed for Latin American consumers, presented users with three options to identify gender: "non-specified"; "male"; or "bitch." In a different part of the world, with yet a different product, Microsoft again was forced to recall several thousand units. In this case the recall became necessary when the Saudi Arabian government took offence at the use of a Koran chant as a soundtrack element in a violent video game. The reported estimate of lost revenue from these indiscretions was in the millions of dollars. See Best (2004).

13 The work to cite here is voluminous. For those who are unfamiliar with this field, an introduction to its early formation can be found in Williams (1981), Hall (1996), and Grossberg, Nelson and Treichler (1991). Earlier in my career, I wrote several articles that discussed the specific encounters between a particular tradition of cultural studies (the one associated with the Birmingham, U.K. Centre for Contemporary Cultural Studies—CCCS) and various U.S. academic institutional programs (Balsamo, 1991, 2000b; Balsamo and Greer, 1993, 1994).

14 Sterling is careful to situate the contemporary formation within a historical frame of reference where he delineates the distinctions among a technoculture of artifacts, machines (which emerges roughly in the 1500s), products (post–First World War), gizmos (1989), and spimes (in 2004). "Spimes" is his term for manufactured objects that are material manifestations of extensive informational (immaterial) fields.

15 In making this claim, I am informed by both Steven Johnson's (2002) work on emergence, and John Thackara's (2005) consideration of the social purposes of designing.

16 The resonance with C. W. Mills's notion of the "sociological imagination" is intentional here. He defined it as a quality of mind that

> enables its possessor to understand the larger historical scene in terms of its meaning for the inner life and external career of a variety of individuals. It enables him to take into account how individuals in the welter of their daily experience, often become falsely conscious of their social positions . . . For that imagination is the capacity to shift from one perspective to another—from the political to the psychological; the examination of a single family to comparative assessment of the national budgets of the world; from the theological school to the military establishment; from considerations of an oil industry to students of contemporary poetry. (1959: 5–7)

Teresa De Lauretis, Andreas Huyssen, and Kathleen Woodward edited an important volume titled *The Technological Imagination: Theories and Fictions* (1980) that explicitly explored the notion of the technological imagination in the history of art and literature. See also Benamou (1980) and Woodward (1980). In one of the earliest discussions of the cultural formation of digital humanism, Arthur Kroker (2001: 114) reviewed Marshall McLuhan's contribution to the study of technology, claiming that "McLuhan's mind was a magisterial account of the technological imagination itself." David Kratzer (1997) uses the term to argue for the continued importance of practical skill building in architectural education. Agnes Heller (2005) invokes it as one of the two main characterizations of the imagination within modernity; the other being the "historical imagination." See also Honey et al. (1991). Don Ihde (2008) discusses the fallacy of referring to the designer's intention as the source of a design's plan. He speaks specifically of the mediation of "technological imagination," what he defines as a historically constituted mode of fantasy (56). I think we are in agreement on these points. As I've argued, the rationality of a design approach is a post-hoc fabrication that might refer to intentions, but cannot be reduced to them. The technological imagination is a creative resource that is evoked in the designing process; it is culturally and historically shaped, and imperfect as a source of prediction.

17 Cultural theorists refer to this as a "conjunctural analysis," where the objective in creating an analysis is to assess the meaning of a technology at a particular historical moment (at a particular conjuncture of time). For examples of this

approach, see the work of theorists such as Jennifer Slack (1989), Greg Wise (1997), Kim Sawchuk (1999), Martin Allor (2000), and Charles Acland (2007).

18 The term "cultural reproduction" was used by Pierre Bourdieu (1984) to describe the way in which cultural values are replicated from one generation to another, usually through educational systems, which function (according to Bourdieu) to reproduce the values of a ruling class, thereby ensuring the continuation of relations of oppression and domination. For a discussion of the way in which Bourdieu's thinking inspires other insights about the positive aspects of cultural reproduction, see Jenks (1993). As Michele Barrett (1988: 21) reminds us, there are at least three "analytically distinct referents of the concept [of reproduction] —social reproduction, reproduction of the labor force, or biological reproduction." Barrett's attention to the different logics of reproduction was in fact the basis of her feminist critique of classic Marxist theory: she argued that with its focus on modes of production and the world of public wage labor this theory betrayed a masculinist bias. By reminding her Marxist colleagues of the important notion of social reproduction, qua Althusser, and by extension the role of biological reproduction in the maintenance of relations of power, she argued that the social spaces of capitalism were gendered spaces of determination and possibility.

19 Susan Leigh Star and Geoffrey Bowker (2002) describe the importance of understanding the social and theoretical role of infrastructure in analyzing new media formations. Star, in particular, is a leading theorist of infrastructure as an emerging area of research within STS and new media studies. See also Star and Ruhleder (1996).

20 Leah Lievrouw and Sonia Livingstone (2002) succinctly describe a framework for understanding new media technologies (ICTs) that acknowledges the rich interweaving of media technology, human action, and social structure. Their elaboration complements the one I offer in this chapter:

> By new media we mean information and communication technologies and their associated social contexts, incorporating:
> — The artifacts or devices that enable and extend our ability to communicate
> — The communication activities or practices we engage in to develop and use these devices
> — The social arrangements or organizations that form around the devices and practices (2002: 7)

21 In the introduction to their edited collection, Wiebe Bijker and John Law (1992: 3) state unequivocally that: "all technologies mirror our societies. They reproduce and embody the complex interplay of professional, technical, economic, and political factors." Indeed, the work collected by Bijker and Law, by noted sociologists, historians, and philosophers of technology such as Bruno Latour, Michel Callon, Trevor Pinch, and Thomas Misa, offers varied, but remarkably consistent accounts of socio-technical production of technology. As Bijker and Law elaborate, even though their authors come from different disciplinary traditions, they

share a set of central assumptions about the study of technology. Let me para-
phrase their list of these shared assumptions:

— That technological change is contingent and messily so in that there is no
"grand plan" or invisible hand ultimately guiding the technology-under-
development

— That technologies emerge from complex social situations that are often
marked by controversy and competing social interests and investments

— That the technology that emerges often embodies a strategy for the negotiation of these differences and conflicts

— That the network of forces of determination must too be managed strategically so that the particular technological arrangement is stabilized

— And finally, that the technological is an emergent phenomenon. What
results—the technology—is not reducible to individual acts or strategies,
but is an effect of the entire ensemble of actions, forces, and negotiations.

For a discussion of tensions between the social shaping of technology perspective
(represented by Bijker and Law) and the diffusion of innovation model, see
Lievrouw (2002). See also Winograd (1986), and Winograd and Flores (1986).

22 Gilles Deleuze and Felix Guattari offer a complex theory of assemblages in their
book, *A Thousand Plateaus* (1987). Manual daLanda (2006) takes on the task of
elucidating how the notion of "assemblage" allows for new insights into the
complexity of social arrangements. In contemporary cultural studies, the term
"assemblages" is used in nuanced distinction from the term "formation." Early in
the development of cultural studies, Raymond Williams (1961) introduced the
term "formation" to describe the complex organization of a historically contingent cultural arrangement. This notion was further elaborated as an outcome
of "articulations." Stuart Hall (1996) uses the term "articulation" as the name for a
structured totality that is neither inevitable nor unending. According to Hall's
account, the unity of a structured totality (its sensibleness, meaning, and manifestation) is a construction, constituted by connections among different elements that make up a formation. Drawing on earlier work by Hall, Jennifer Slack
(1989: 331) develops the notion of technology as articulation, stating that technology should be studied "as a non-necessary connection of different elements that,
when connected in a particular way, form a specific unity." Jennifer Slack and
Greg Wise elaborate the relationship between articulation and assemblages in
their book, *Culture and Technology: A Primer* (2002).

23 Although Lucy Suchman (1996, 2002) does not use the term "articulation," the
analyses developed in both her first and second books (1987, 2007)—based on
her empirical anthropological investigation of service agents, users, and managers
in relation to photocopier machines—remain for me the richest accounts of the
dynamic complexity of articulatory practices in (situated) action. See also Strauss
(1985) and Bannon and Schmidt (1989).

24 For example, design philosopher Richard Coyne (1995: 307) identifies the use of
metaphor in designing practices as a technique that "sets up a distance that is also

a space for imaginative thought." In this case the creative deployment of an expressive form—the metaphor—enables an important epistemological move within the designing process. The metaphor creates an epistemological space for creating new possibilities.

25 Although the focus of Krippendorf's (1995) discussion is to elaborate the notion of product semantics as a structure for understanding how technologies and artifacts communicate symbolic meanings, his broader point is important for my argument here: that design is the process of meaning-making. He discusses the underlying principles of design appropriate for the information age in his book, *The Semantic Turn* (2005).

26 The work of articulation—the process through which meaning is constructed by the forging of associations and of semiotic codings—expresses a nuanced similarity to the process of second-order signification discussed by Roland Barthes (1970), where the meaning of any one sign within a system of signs is in part constructed through the association with other signs, both through associations of identity (equivalence) and difference (dissimilarity).

27 Strathern (1992) is careful to situate this "reproductive model" in a particular Euro-American view of procreation. Nonetheless, she notes that it offers an interesting approach to think about such issues as continuity, change, potentiality, and the future, both as these apply to the intellectual work of anthropology as a discipline, and as they identify the key processes of cultural reproduction. To be certain, the nature of these processes is difficult to define precisely because they refer to differences that are manifested over time and understood relationally, either as a relation between two states—the meaning of continuity, for example implies an equivalence between two states or moments—or, as in the case of the concept of potentiality, as a relation between what is possible and what is manifested.

28 In fact, it is more frequently the case that technological formations are constantly in the process of breaking down and unraveling. In his book, *Normal Accidents: Living with High-risk Technologies* (1984), Charles Perrow refers to these breakdowns as "normal accidents." The question for him is not why do things break down, but rather, how is it that they don't break down more often given the tenuous coherence of the formation. The work of cultural institutions—educational organizations, advertising, marketing—is often involved in the business of maintaining the arrangements of a dominant technological order. This is, to some theorists, the real work of ideology: to keep the meanings in place that prop up a dominant ruling structure.

29 As the philosopher of technology Carl Mitcham (1994: 110) explains, the formulation of the nature of technology in this way is at root a metaphysical debate: "At some level of abstraction technology does appear to be one and autonomous; all technology is technology with a broad historical trajectory that appears to transcend particular times and places. At another level the diversity of technologies belies any strong unity; unity appears no more than nominal. The root issue, a

metaphysical one, concerns the different realities present in the different levels of analysis." See also Mitcham and Mackey (1972).

30 Although it is not referred to as a "hermeneutic circle," the schematic offered by Per Galle (1999) of the "generic artifact production process" incorporates many of the elements of a hermeneutic understanding of design as the process of meaning-making. He adds an important emphasis on the mediating role of design representations, such as the sketch and the design brief. These symbolic representations play an important role in bringing the artifact into material existence by mediating among "artifact-ideas" and artifact production. Winograd and Flores (1986) turn to hermeneutical theory for philosophical insights into the process of creating artificial intelligence systems, supporting the assertion that design is a meaning-making activity. For a critique of Winograd and Flores, see Suchman (1994).

31 Design researchers assert the importance of a shared cultural context for the expression of novel ideas. Culture, in this sense, provides the broad framework of "meaningfulness" and "novelty" (Eckert and Stacey, 2000).

32 For a discussion of the cultural significance of designing, see Julier (2000), Margolin and Buchanan (1998), and Margolin (2002).

33 Scott Minneman, a former research scientist at Xerox PARC, investigated the moment-to-moment communication among designers to examine the way in which technical reality is socially constructed through the mediation of representational objects (among other things). In contrast to the traditional understanding of design as a series of logical steps that yield rational solutions, Minneman (1991) offers a more complex account of the social process of design where designers negotiate alternative realities, construct plausible—but always provisional —accounts of the design task, and subtly confront the limit-conditions of the material world as well as the contingent nature of technical specifications. Minneman makes explicit reference to the way these social practices both perpetuate and alter the culture and values of a particular social setting.

34 Feenberg (1995: 4) elaborates the role that social negotiation plays in the designing process; as he points out, "technological rationality doesn't spring fully formed from the mind of the technologist nor from the results of an experimental manipulation of materials." He notes that, "the design process is the place where the various social actors interested in a developing technology first gain a hearing ... Technologies, like other rational institutions, are social expressions of these actors."

35 Whereas the instrumental significance of design is well documented in the histories of the development of technologies of mass production, until relatively recently there was less discussion about the cultural significance of design. This has changed within the past twenty years, during which several notable conferences and anthologies have been devoted to the question of the relationship between design and culture. See, for example, Sparke (1992).

36 While the consideration of the cultural role and responsibilities of designers is a

frequent topic among design theorists who study graphic and digital design, it is less widely discussed within engineering-based design programs—which is probably a remnant of the institutionalization of the "two culture" divide that C. P. Snow lamented more than 50 years ago. While there is a growing body of work in engineering-design research that now explicitly considers cultural questions in the elaboration of theories and philosophy of design, this research has not yet widely influenced the development of curricula in engineering or interactivity design. Sometimes the reference to culture is implicit, as when design researchers discuss designers' use of metaphor and symbols. In other work the notion of culture is quite prominent, although there are subtle differences in how the term is invoked. In ethnographic studies of designing practice, for example, the notion of culture is used in two ways: 1) as the term for the organizational context for the proposed design, as in design for products that have to fit the "culture of BMW" or the "culture of IBM"; or 2) as the context of the working environment of the design group themselves, as in the "culture of IDEO" or the "culture of PARC." This usage of the term draws on an anthropological notion of culture as the set of practices and sensibilities of a bounded social collectivity. A volume of the journal *Design Studies*, devoted to the topic of ethnographic design research, included several insightful articles: Lloyd (2000); Baird, Moore, and Jagodzinski (2000); and Burton (2000). For philosophers of design, such as Terrence Love (2000), the term *culture* has been invoked to describe designers' milieu. In other work, culture is described as having an influence on the internal processes of designers, and is manifested in the form of shared sources of inspiration or shared cultural references (Eckert and Stacey, 2000: 531). Another way that the term culture is used is as a property of a national (or geo-political) identity and context. Although less frequent, these discussions focus on the increasingly important, yet stubbornly elusive process of designing across cultures where, for example, a U.S.-based design team is designing products or services for clients and consumers in another country (Ellsworth, Magleby, and Todd, 2002).

37 Bucciarelli (1994: 159) describes design as involving "the process of achieving consensus among participants with different 'interests' in the design . . . those different interests are not reconcilable in object-world terms." Consensus is accomplished, according to Bucciarelli, through the use of a particular rhetoric of the object that renders the object meaningful in deterministic terms. Certain materials or components are said to favor certain conditions: for example, "this circuit board will be happiest in a ventilated environment." As Bucciarelli notes, an important part of the designing process is to communicate these understandings of the object-world to others. This rhetorical turn produces closure for the negotiation process: "we know this to be true therefore there is no more need for discussion." Contradictions are settled by the rhetorical strategies of design participants. Bucciarelli suggests that a better way of describing the communicative act of designing is to use the term "story making."

Story making is a better metaphor—story making about voltages and currents, tank dimensions and air pressure . . . This story making is constrained by these mundane concepts and features in that they must behave deterministically in accordance with an accepted set of principles and rules, and there is general consensus not only on what they are (voltage, stress, pressure) but also on how to measure their character in hard, quantitative terms. Nevertheless, there remains much to be constructed of their relationships and interactions in particular circumstances within object-worlds. The elements are there, but their synthesis requires rhetorical skill and creative effort (1994: 88).

For a similar analysis of the role of story telling in designing practice, see Deuten and Rip (2000).

38 I am aware that to invoke the term "hermeneutics" in this formulation—to name a set of research and design protocols—is to open the door to a set of debates and philosophical discussions about the ontological nature of human experience, the role of language (and sociality) in the process of human becoming, and even the possibility of a science of interpretation (among other issues). Variously defined as the science of "textual interpretation," or more broadly as a system of inter-pretation, I use it to claim a role for humanistic participation in the process of technological innovation. For as Cathy Davidson and David Goldberg (2004: B7) assert, humanists possess a diverse set of skills useful for the creation of new technologies: "historical knowledge, linguistic mastery, geographical precision, aesthetic production . . . as well as models of interpretation, comparison, and critique."

39 In proposing this approach, I draw inspiration from several key theorists of design who advocate the use of methods of cultural analysis for the purposes of creating a more nuanced understanding of the cultural work of designing. Winograd and Flores (1986) were among the first to discuss the relationship between hermeneu-tics and socio-technical design of complex systems. Richard Coyne (1995) eluci-dates a new philosophical framework for designing by drawing insights from Hans-Georg Gadamer, Martin Heidegger, and Jacques Derrida to provide a foun-dation for thinking about the role of language in the designing process. Terence Love (2002) identifies hermeneutics as one of the research paradigms that can contribute to the creation of a philosophy of design.

40 Hermeneutics is the study of the process and methods of interpretation of texts. The text, however it is constituted, is considered the platform and the medium for the creation and exchange of meaning among people, understood either as indi-vidual subjects or as collective subjects. Meaning is created in the interaction between subjects and texts; this process is often described as circular, where subjects bring previous understandings to the text—including presuppositions, understandings of the genre or category of the text, and other forms of tacit knowledge—and use these understandings in the process of creating a meaning for a new text. Although there are many strands of hermeneutics, the one that I draw from is a version known as critical hermeneutics, which takes as its founda-

tion the collective subject, whose interpretive acts are always influenced by the social collectivity and a particular history. While it is not the place here to rehearse the many interesting insights and debates within the field of hermeneutics, one of the key claims made by a specifically critical (as opposed to phenomenological) hermeneutics is that meaning is produced through social interaction, and is the consequence of social consensus. For a fuller elaboration of this perspective see Habermas (1979, 1981).

41 Although Geertz (1973) borrowed the phrase "thick description" from the philosopher Gilbert Ryle, it came to identify Geertz's signature approach to the practice of ethnography. See also Geertz (1999).

42 This resonates with Edward Tufte's (2006: 9) invocation of the practice of "intense seeing" which he defines as "the wide-eyed observing that generates empirical information." His book explores "how seeing turns into showing." This practice, common to both art and science, is the first stage of the production of knowledge.

43 Although it is tempting to deploy the term "deconstruction" as the name for a set of interpretive techniques for elucidating the meaning of a text or discourse, I want to avoid getting mired in debates about whether deconstruction is a method or an epistemology. Nonetheless it is an important set of discussions that bear on the fuller elaboration of the methodology of reverse hermeneutic engineering. For a particularly useful overview of the logic of deconstruction, see Belsey (1980). I also draw on Barthes (1970) and Abrams (1971). Although it's a bit dated, when explaining this methodological framework to engineering colleagues, I found it useful to refer them to Hawkes (1977).

44 In fact, "design for culture" is the mission directive for Onomy Labs, the start-up company that I co-founded in 2002 with former colleagues from Xerox PARC, Mark Chow, Dale MacDonald, and Scott Minneman. I would also use this term to describe the cross-cultural collaborative project called "design for wellbeing" that involves several universities and industry groups in the U.S., Sweden, and Japan. The project grew out of collaborations among design researchers at the Stanford University Center for Design Research (CDR) in the U.S. (under the direction of Professor Larry Leifer) and at the Polhem Laboratory at Luleå University of Technology in Sweden (directed by Professor Lennart Karlsson).

45 John Seely Brown has developed this notion of the radical potential of edge-projects in several talks and co-authored publications. As a point of reference for these ideas see Hagel and Brown (2005; 2008).

46 This assertion echoes an observation made by Teresa de Lauretis (1980) three decades ago, that technology has become "our context"—regardless of how one defines the identity of "our" in that statement.

47 Henry Jenkins (2006a) develops the notion of transmedia in relationship to the popular cultural phenomenon of telling stories across multiple media platforms: television, the web, graphic novels, mobile media, film, and toys.

48 Katherine Hayles (2002: 23) analyzes the development of specific interactives

that were part of the XFR exhibit to illustrate her notion of a "material metaphor." She specifically examines RED : *Reading Eye Dog* to consider how its material form reconfigured the "metaphoric structuring for the relation of word to world." Andrew Ross (2003) reports on his visit to PARC during the time when RED was involved in designing the XFR exhibit. He was interested in tracking the business value of having artists involved in technology development.

49 This move recalls Peter Lunenfeld's (2002: xv) notion of the "digital dialectic," the term he uses to name an analytical practice that grounds the "insights of theory in the constraints of production."

one: Gendering the Technological Imagination

Sections of this chapter first appeared in an article co-authored with Mary Hocks: "Women Making Multimedia: A blueprint for Feminism Action" in Beth Kolko (2003). I am grateful to Mary Hocks, Beth Kolko, and Columbia University Press for permission to include this material in this chapter.

1 See Summers (2005a). The editorial response was immediate: see, for example, Bombardieri (2005). Although the discussions have largely vanished, the blogosphere response was especially lively. The National Organization for Women circulated a call for a broader commitment to equality for women in science and technology: see Nelson (2005). On January 19, 2005, Summers issued a letter where he admitted that he was "wrong to have spoken in a way that has resulted in an unintended signal of discouragement to talented girls and women" (Summers 2005b). The Anita Borg Institute for Women and Technology staff created a web document called "Chronicle of a Controversy" that contains a transcript of Summers's original remarks and links to the text of his apology and to the news coverage of the controversy (ABI Staff, 2005).

2 The question of sex differences among males and females belongs to a different category of question that implies different research paradigms and protocols. While there is a significant body of feminist work on these questions, this research was not cited by Summers. See WISELI (2005).

3 Even the most cursory of investigation into the business scene in the U.S. in the late 1990s suggests that there were many women pursuing demanding, risky, and potentially highly rewarding business ventures (Office of Advocacy, U.S. Small Business Administration, 2003).

4 As summarized in the NSF report (2002) between 1991 and 2001, the government agency has spent more than $84 million in awards for projects that are part of its Program for Gender Equity. And yet, in the year 2000 the gender composition of the labor force in science and engineering indicated that the unemployment rates of women were higher than men in all STEM occupations and age groups.

5 An article in *Business Week* (Gogoi, 2005) described several efforts by technology retailers to attract a larger share of female consumers. The article quotes Jonas Tanenbaum, senior marketing manager of flat-panel displays for Samsung Elec-

tronics America, as saying: "We now recognize that the female consumer is influencing, if not controlling, 50 percent of all consumer-electronic purchasing today." The article also describes how the "Jill Initiative" at Best Buy is designed to transform the trend-savvy working suburban mom with a fair amount of disposable income, who's likely to shop at Target as opposed to Wal-Mart, into a big-time electronics buyer. With women in mind, Dell has increased the number of accessories available for sale on its site. "We started offering stylish jackets in different colors for the Pocket DJ at the direct request of our women customers," says Gretchen Miller, a director of product marketing for the Austin Texas PC maker.

6   The story about Purple Moon's acquisition by Mattel Inc. is recounted in Laurel (2001).

7   Autumn Stanley (1995) investigates and, sometimes for the first time, uncovers women's contribution to the development of five areas of technology: agriculture, computers, machines, medicine, and reproduction. The bibliography alone is an incredible and invaluable contribution to the history of technology.

8   For example, see Irigaray (1985), on the labor of becoming woman.

9   In addition to Autumn Stanley's work (see n. 7 above), Marvin (1988) also documents the systematic erasure of women from official histories of early communication technologies such as the telephone.

10 Donna Haraway's manifesto, first published in 1985, catalyzed an entire generation of feminist thinkers, encouraging them not only to critically engage the dominant technologies of the late twentieth century—communication and cybernetics—but also to carefully attend to the emergence of new technologies (Haraway, 1985). Spurred on in part by Haraway, as well as by a maturing sensibility about the importance of seizing "the master's tools," feminist critics across the globe have turned their attention to a range of techno-scientific disciplines; as a consequence we now have a significant body of trenchant criticism to draw upon in our encounters with a range of new techno-scientific phenomena.

Several feminist projects demonstrate the enactment of a gendered technological imagination. The following are a mere sampling of projects: In the U.S., there is the Paula Treichler's (1999) work on HIV / AIDS and medical discourse; Lisa Cartwright's (1995) analysis of the role of the cinematic gaze in the constitution of medical diagnostics; Katherine Hayles's (1999) analysis of our posthuman condition; and Alison Adam's (1998) description of how gender is inscribed in AI programs and systems. In Europe, feminist scholars have turned their attention to key issues, such as the gendered division of labor in a global information society (Mitter and Efendioglu, 1997), and the "gender mainstreaming" strategy promoted by the European Union (Behning and Pascual, 2001). Other noteworthy work by feminist scholars of technology include Nina Wakefield's (2008) ethnographic research on blogging, and Randi Markussen's (1996) work on feminism and Scandinavian design. In Canada, see Kim Sawchuk's (1999) work on embodiment and new media technologies; the study of digital cities by Barbara Crow et al.; and Janine Marchessault's (2007) research on art, digital media, and globalization. In Australia, see Elspeth Probyn's (2005) analysis of the cultural work of shame and media technologies, and Meaghan Morris's (2005) article on "humanities for taxpayers."

11 What is particularly useful for the discussion here is Barad's account of the nature of apparatuses: "Apparatuses are not inscription devices, scientific instruments set in place before the action happens, or machines that mediate the dialectic of resistance and accommodation. They are neither neutral probes of the natural world nor structures that deterministically impose some particular outcome." Barad elaborates Bohr on this point: "apparatuses are not mere static arrangements *in* the world, but rather *apparatuses are dynamic (re)configurations of the world, specific agential practices/intra-actions/performances through which specific exclusionary boundaries are enacted.* Apparatuses have no inherent 'outside' boundary. This indeterminacy of the 'outside' boundary represents the impossibility of closure—the ongoing intra-activity in the iterative reconfiguring of the apparatus of bodily production. Apparatuses are open-ended practices" (emphasis in the original, 2003: 816).

12 Several programs designed to foster collaboration among artists and technologists as peers also demonstrate these assumptions. See for example: Craig Harris's (1999) account of the artist-in-residence program at Xerox PARC; Michael Naimark's (2003) report for *Leonardo* journal on the opportunities and constraints of such collaborations; Michael Century's (2006) description of the studio lab concept. On the concept of artists as inventors see the edited volume by Dieter Daniels and Barbara Schmidt (2008) and Simon Penny (2008). On the topic of the management of art-technology research collaborations see Biswas (2008).

13 Panagiotis Louridas (1999: 523) makes a distinction between self-conscious and unselfconscious design, arguing that "unselfconscious design is design without designers. It is the prevalent form of design activity in primitive and traditional societies in which design professions do not exist." He reminds us of the anthropological term for this mode of unselfconscious design, *bricolage*, and wants to argue for the usefulness of the term as a way of describing the creative practices of the professional (self-conscious) designer. In this argument, the self-conscious designer replaces tradition (of the bricoleur) in designating the materials to design with, the problems to design for, and the solutions that will suffice. The consequence of the "designer as bricoleur" or the "design as bricolage" perspective asserts the importance of understanding the transformative power of the designer to change the world.

14 Mary Hocks worked at Spelman College, a historically black, women's institution, directing a technology-rich writing program. As Project Director of a Mellon Foundation grant, she wanted to design collaborative educational projects that integrated multimedia technology into the undergraduate curriculum; see Hocks and Bascelli (1998). I worked across town at the more traditional, engineering

focused, Georgia Institute of Technology, where I helped design a graduate curriculum in Information, Design, and Technology. I was especially interested in finding ways to combine feminist cultural theory with the development of new media as a way to inspire female students to get more involved in technology development (Balsamo, 2000a).

15 Occasioned by the receipt of an invitation to participate in the NGO (Non-Governmental Organization) Forum, a colleague from Georgia Tech's College of Engineering and I convinced the university to sponsor a delegation of students to attend the events in China. The members of the Georgia Tech delegation included: Anne Balsamo and Donna Llewellyn as faculty co-chairs; Kelly Johnson (graduate student in Information, Design, and Technology); Kristin Thorvig (undergraduate student in Science, Technology and Culture); Minh-An Arthur (undergraduate student in mechanical engineering); and Lisa Kravchuk (undergraduate student in electrical engineering). Mary Hocks and Phil Walker also traveled to China as part of the Georgia Tech delegation.

16 Although the 1995 UN Conference *Platform For Action* was not a binding document, governments were expected to commit resources for enacting the policies it outlined on the national level. The document was intended to serve as a guide for national legislation and to help shape international priorities in the future. The final *Platform for Action* was eventually published in print and on the Feminist Majority's website. By the year 2000, the document was no longer available anywhere on the web. Political follow-up work since the conference has continued through teleconferences, meetings, and additional conferences, both internationally, as well as nationally, in the form of published and online reports from the President's Interagency Council on Women (Institute for Global Communications).

17 At the time, Donna Shalala had just finished serving on President Clinton's cabinet as Secretary of Education. Elizabeth Colemen, the founder of the Maidenform Corporation, was still active in running her company. Veronica Biggins, an executive from NationsBank in Atlanta, was the chair of the U.S. delegation to the Fourth UN World Conference on Women.

18 Purple Moon developed such CD-ROM games as *Rockett's Tricky Decision* (1997), a "friendship adventure" aimed to encourage pre-teen girls to participate in a collaborative technological environment. Mattel acquired Purple Moon in 1999. Now the original Purple Moon website (http://www.purple-moon.com/) redirects to a site called: EverythingGirl.Com. For more information about the Purple Moon adventure, see Laurel (2001). Tamblyn's CD-ROM "She Loves It, She Loves it Not" is no longer widely available, although a copy of it is archived at the library at University of California, Davis. Information about Lynn Hershman's videodisk *Lorna* is available at her site, http://www.lynnhershman.com/.

19 For an engaging discussion of women's participation in the development of technologically based art practices and productions, see Malloy (2003).

20 Our first idea was to create an interactive presentation about the education of

women in science and technology, because this issue would be debated during the UN Conference. In the process of conducting background research on this topic, we learned about a videotape archive owned by Georgia Tech that included extensive interviews with international spokespeople and heads of state. Staff from the Georgia Tech communications office had conducted the interviews for the purposes of producing public service announcements (PSA's) about previous UN events, including the UN Conference on Environment and Development (or Earth Summit) in 1992, and the UN Conference on Population and Development in 1994. The archive consisted of 40 hour-long interviews with prominent international spokespeople, who, during the course of their interviews, often made strong statements concerning the global situation of women. In screening these interviews, we began to conceptualize the construction of a series of talking-head dialogues that would present one side of a conversation that offered an official view of the pressing issues facing women throughout the globe. Indeed, we isolated several dozen sound bite statements, which were eventually edited together to create four main video pieces featured in the *Women of the World Talk Back* project. To augment our found interview footage we conducted additional interviews with the 1995 UN Conference and NGO Forum organizers: Gertrude Mongela, the convener of the UN Conference, Irene Santiago, the convener of the NGO Forum, and UN representative Patsy Robertson.

21 Although Carey's broader point is to elaborate a specifically cultural theory of communication, in describing the notion of communication as ritual, he elaborates an alternative model of communication that resonates with feminist ideals. In Carey's words, communication as ritual is "the sacred ceremony that draws persons together in fellowship and commonality . . . and it focuses on the construction and maintenance of an ordered, meaningful cultural world" (1989: 18–19).

22 Although the project construction process was entirely collaborative, there was an undeniable institutionalized, hierarchical relationship among project team members. For example, both Mary and I served as Project Directors, while three Georgia Tech graduate students were employed as multimedia authors, graphic designers, and interactivity architects. As Project Directors, we provided the design, information structure, and content for the project, as well as some of the labor involved in video editing, graphic production, and interactivity authoring. Most of the multimedia authoring work was done by graduate students under our supervision; first in the graduate program at Georgia Tech, and then later at the University of Southern California. The original design team included three graduate students from Georgia Tech's program in Information Design and Technology: Kelly Johnson, a multimedia producer; Mary Anne Stevens, a graphic designer; and David Balcom, a multimedia author/designer. Soon after the project was launched, Phil Walker, a professional TV producer at Georgia Tech, became a significant collaborator, producing the interviews and the music soundtracks used in the project. With the help of a local musician, Bryan Arbuckle, Phil co-

wrote the music used in the project. In the second round of project production, IDT graduate student and multimedia director Sandra Beaudin and Professor Ellen Strain from Georgia Tech contributed additional graphic design and multimedia authoring. The most recent development on the project was conducted at the University of Southern California, under the production guidance of Veronica Paredes. The original project cost approximately $10,000, not including the many hours of labor donated by project team members at various times during its development. Given the typical costs of building multimedia projects, and the state of the technology at the time, this one was created very inexpensively. We kept costs down by using found video footage, free B-roll footage, and donating our own labor. Most of the budget went to provide stipends for student production work and to pay for the design of original musical and sound elements. Video editing expertise and the use of a professional editing suite were among the in-kind contributions provided by Georgia Tech.

23 The Video Dialogue, titled "Access to Education," featured sound bite statements from Jacqueline Pitanguy, Founder of CEPIA (Citizenship, Studies, Information and Action), a non-governmental organization based in Rio de Janeiro; Irene Santiago, Executive Director of the 1995 NGO Forum, New York; Patsy Robertson, Director of Information and Public Affairs for the Commonwealth Secretariat, London; Dr. Frederick T. Sai, President of International Planned Parenthood, Ghana; Halida Hanum Akhter, Director of the Institute of Research for Promotion of Essential and Reproductive Health and Technologies, Bangladesh; Father Juan Wicht, Jesuit Priest and Professor of Economics, University of the Pacific, Peru; and Gertrude Mongela, Secretary-General, UN Fourth World Conference on Women, New York.

24 For a fuller discussion of this analytical process, see Hocks (1999).

25 The Feminist Majority's website also provided general information about the conference and included publications such as *Putting Gender on the Agenda*, which summarized the purpose of the conference and the global networking opportunities that would be available during the 17 days of the NGO Forum. It was by reading daily updates on the Feminist Majority website that we learned that *all* lesbian-activist materials would be seized by Chinese customs agents.

26 Lucy Suchman (2005: 379) puts forth the notion of "objects-in-action" in which she focuses her critical attention on the "ways in which objects are not innocent, but fraught with significance for the relations that they materialize."

27 John Law (2002) assembles fractional accounts of a fractionated object, the military aircraft called the TSR2, offering a compelling demonstration of the beauty and power of theory to perform the world differently.

28 Pasty Roberston is currently an international media consultant and was the former Director of Information and Official Spokesperson for the Government of Jamaica. Excerpts from my interview with her are included in the Video Dialogues that are part of the *Women of the World Talk Back* documentary.

29 To my mind, the most thorough exploration of this question, and indeed of the

tension between theory and practice, is found in Paula Treichler's (1999: 2) work on AIDS, which is framed by the question, "what should be the role of theory in an epidemic?"

two: **The Performance of Innovation**

1 For a beautiful collection of the images of the future that now forms our archival memory of the projection of the future, see Canto and Faliu (1993).

2 Although literary critics disagree about the aesthetics of the term "scientfiction"—Samuel Delaney went so far as to call it "ugly"—they all acknowledge that Gernsback was singularly responsible for launching a new literary sub-genre (McCaffrey, 1990: 79).

3 The book series "Designing the Future," published by Creative Education, discusses the history and design of built space, including dedicated volumes on theaters, museums, skyscrapers, bridges, houses, and barns. The history of the future is documented in the buildings that we now inhabit, the monuments that we read, and the ruins that are consistently slipping away. See, for example, Koelsch (2001), and Halfmann (1999).

4 Technologies are always involved in creating "the future" before it is inhabited as "the present." Consider the coordination work involved in amassing the physical labor required to build cathedrals and monuments. This coordination work is a social technology that anticipates the future. So too is true of the use of CAD applications. The future, in the form of built space, is designed through the routine mediation of CAD-systems (Baker, 1993).

5 The management of innovation and organizational change is a topic of increasing interest in business schools across the U.S. The popular literature of business strategy books based on case studies of successful (and sometimes unsuccessful) organizations has grown exponentially since Peters and Waterman (1982) wrote their influencial book *In Search of Excellence*. In that book, the authors identify eight principles that they argued were key for successful business growth. What they didn't realize at the time was that the principles they identified were historically specific practices and not universal techniques that would sustain corporate growth for all time. Christensen (1997) contested most of the principles identified by Peters and Waterman in his own research and case studies of organizations that were poised to take advantage of new technological innovations, but that failed ultimately to do so.

6 For more information about the Institute for the Future, see http://www.iftf .org/.

7 Of course, well before then, Leland Stanford Jr. and his wife Jane had established their namesake university on 8000 acres of former agricultural and horse land. A fuller account of the mythologizing of the Santa Clara Valley would also look at the stories that circulate about Stanford's dream to build the Harvard of the West.

8 According to Pake's account, the original mission for PARC circulated among new

employees in xerographic form. The earliest document, dated April 21, 1970, was produced on a typewriter and outlined the "Role of Xerox Palo Alto Research Center." According to Pake, PARC would contribute the following: 1) Bring into Xerox and train top flight post-doctoral scientists, generating a pool of able people from which the rest of the corporation can select; 2) Set up a new center of science strength in the United States at a time when the nation is cutting back its science; and 3) Help save some of the brightest new Ph.D.s for future United States science by launching them on their careers in a first-rate science atmosphere. Pake's invocation of the nation, and its need for bright scientists, was not a widely popular theme at PARC, even as many of the researchers found support for their research from NSF and DARPA. Two other articles by Pake (1985; 1986) elaborated his vision for PARC and its historical accomplishments. The 1986 article outlines the crucial contributions PARC offered to Xerox, including the development of laser xerography (laser printing) and ETHERNET technology.

9　Two well-known accounts of the mythology of PARC both place the failure to capitalize on the invention of the Alto on the shoulders of corporate executives: see Smith and Alexander (1988), and Hiltzik (1999). Brown and Duguid (2000) also offer an encapsulated account of the ways in which Xerox "fumbled" in recognizing and valuing the knowledge that was produced at PARC in the early days of the development of the personal computer. The tone of these popular press books is in stark contrast to the set of "founding" documents written by PARC's first director, George E. Pake (see note 8 above). The invocation of the term "myth" to describe the identity narratives that were projected onto PARC and consciously performed by various people is not meant to connote untruthfulness or falsity: see Barthes (1970).

10　It is against this backdrop of an American Corporation's popular (public) history and the mythic legend of a particular place at the edge of the continental U.S. that my own biography and research profile takes an unexpected turn. In 1998, Rich Gold invited me to join the research staff at Xerox PARC to become part of a new group he had just formed at PARC called RED, which was getting ready to begin a large-scale group research project. On January 1, 1999, I moved to Silicon Valley, in part to see for myself what all the fuss was about.

11　This description of Suchman's project is taken from an unpublished research proposal that she generously shared with me for use in writing this chapter. The new project is called *Reproducing the Center: Performing Innovation at Xerox* PARC. Part of the project was published as Suchman (2005).

12　I frequently return to Carolyn Steedman (1987) as an example of how to write about the relationship between the biographical and the historical.

13　Long before he worked at PARC, Rich Gold had a vibrant art practice that included alternative identities. During the 1970s, his art practice included several avant-garde musical/art performances (he had academic degrees in electronic art and music) that explored and transgressed the boundaries between visual and sonic art forms. Early in his career he created a series of performances where he as an artist would *perform science,* using mathematical algorithms, for example, to generate permutations of graphic elements or physical assemblages. Although these works were enacted and performed in different settings, many of them became subjects of his publication/circulation project called the *Original Goldographs* (1975) (which were distributed via his website for many years, but are no longer available). Before he died, Gold finished a hybrid text-image project called *The Plentitude: A Power Point Book* (2007), which incorporated many of the insights disseminated in the *Original Goldographs.* His industry experience included a job as the head of the sound and music department of Sega USA's coin-op video game division, where he invented the award-winning "Little Computer People" for Activision, the first fully autonomous computerized-person application built for commercial consumption. Gold's "Little Computer People" were a born-digital species that preceded the commercial availability of Tamogochis or the Sims. Yet his contribution has fallen out of the historical accounts of the development of this area of digital media. Sadly, he remains largely unacknowledged as one of the key designers of innovative interactive devices. For example, before he joined PARC, Gold worked at Mattel where he directed the electronic and computer toy research group that created the Mattel PowerGlove. During his early years at PARC, he was the inventor or co-inventor on ten patents and the principle designer of the PARC Tab and the LiveBoard project. I hope that my brief overview of Rich Gold's work at Xerox PARC will encourage others to investigate the impact of his artistic practice and technological innovations.

14 An account of the plausibility of ubiquitous computing and of PARC's role in the development of this paradigm is offered in Buderi (2001). Brown's (2001) account of this paradigm was published as a (fictional) missive from the future—2020. The PARC tagline for ubiquitous computing as a new paradigm (attributed to Mark Weiser): "First there were computers, then they went away." For an account of the origins of ubiquitous computer at PARC see Weiser (1999).

15 In this role, Rich Gold was recognized as a kindred spirit to Gordon McKenzie, a long-time corporate provocateur who worked at Hallmark Greeting Card Company. His book was required reading for RED members (McKenzie, 1986). In it, McKenzie describes the need for large organizations to employ people who work against the grain of the organization, and who irritate or disrupt the standard operating procedures, such that creative "thinking outside of the box" remains a possibility. McKenzie and Gold were alike in their sensibility that it was possible and indeed necessary, within a corporate structure, to foster creativity through the employment and support of renegade thinkers and corporate iconoclasts.

16 Brown (1999: xi) described the PAIR program as an "experiment intended to keep PARC both a leader in innovation and relevant to the corporation."

17 During the first five years of the program the list of pairings included artists Jon Winet and Margaret Crane, who collaborated with researchers Scott Minneman and Dale MacDonald (later founding members of the RED group); documentary filmmakers John Muse and Jeanne Finely, who worked with noted organizational

anthropologists and PARC researchers Lucy Suchman, Jeanette Bloomberg, Susan Newman, and Randy Trigg; vocalist Pamela Z conversed with researchers David Levy and Michael Black on the topic of art and science; sound sculptor Paul De Marinis worked with the researchers in the ubiquitous computing group as well as with print scientists; installation artist and scholar Steve Wilson worked with researchers Jock Mackinlay and Polle Zellweger to explore the nature of online collaboration; interactive novelist Judy Malloy co-created a hyper-narrative with Cathy Marshall and installation artist Perry Hoberman. For a description of various PAIR projects see Harris (1999).

18 For a more critical assessment of such artist-in-residence programs, including PARC's PAIR program, see Schrage (2001).

19 Gold worked in this vein until he died suddenly in January 2003. He left a legacy of innovative art and technology projects that spanned four decades.

20 Gold's first attempt to create a new kind of interdisciplinary research collective was a short-lived group, formed in 1996, that went by the name CDI (Creative Documents Initiative), whose purpose was to investigate the nature of innovation. The people involved in CDI included researchers as well as creative production staff such as graphic designers, videographers, and photographers. One of the few, but most successful, CDI efforts was the PARC Identity Project. PARC's identity elements—logos, graphic monikers, names, and titles—had been created in an ad hoc fashion over many years and were (by the mid-1990s) hopelessly outdated. The CDI group took on this classic project of design work to create a new identity system for PARC, which included not only graphic elements, but also everything from phone scripts to signature files. In collaboration with Shelley Evanson, noted identity designer, CDI embarked on the adventure of orchestrating a community-created identity. The mixing of research and production was a logical move, given the emphasis of the group on creative documents, and not unlike the professional mixing that was the hallmark of the PAIR program. But the institutional strictures that defined the job characteristics of each type of employee proved to be an insurmountable obstacle. Production staff members were not artists-in-residence; they had to generate billable hours. Thus their participation in meetings (for example) became a costly endeavor: they had to charge some account for their presence at meetings. CDI (the group) couldn't afford the overhead. The financial and managerial challenges became a significant distraction. For the production staff, research was a low priority, for good reason; they were hired and rewarded for their production work. The research staff operated within an entirely different context; not only was there no expectation that their hours would be charged to a particular project or account, but they rarely kept track of the number of hours worked on any given project. As is true with many researchers, the length and contour of any single workday is determined by the nature of the research. Long hours and all-nighters were not atypical experiences for the research staff, as were half-day design meetings and weekend work sessions. In the end, CDI was disbanded largely because it proved impossible to

creatively redesign the institutional context that governed and rewarded different kinds of work practices. The members of CDI from 1996–1997 included Steve Walgren, Dan Murphy, Jennifer Ernst, Trey Galagher, Brian Tramontana, Mark Chow, Susie Mulhern, Amy Jacobson, Dale MacDonald, Steve Harrison, Maureen Stone, Beth Mynatt, Scott Minneman, Kim Edens, and for a short while, Maribeth Back.

21 As mentioned earlier, Rich Gold was a prolific writer. Among his many short thought-pieces was a statement called "How We Do Research at Xerox PARC." In it he identifies the seven stages of research: 1) The idea; 2) Reading; 3) Early prototyping; 4) Developing a thesis; 5) Conducting experiments; 6) Publishing and Patenting; and 7) Turn over (technology transfer out of research into development). Gold's (2000) history of PARC was published in *Dr. Dobb's Special Report* on the occasion of PARC's 30th anniversary. In this piece, he identifies the PARC researcher as the "PARC Sapien"—someone who has a strong sense of philosophy, "engages in a kind of visionary thinking and inventing for a world that doesn't yet exist but might come into being partly because of the inventions themselves," and who also "puts things into practice and builds real working models" (43).

22 Most of original RED members had participated in the CDI effort and had been— prior to CDI—research members in various PARC labs. Dale MacDonald had come from the Electronics and Imaging Lab (that eventually spun out to become DPix); Steve Harrison, Maureen Stone, and Scott Minneman had come from the Information Systems and Technology Lab; and Rich Gold and Beth Mynatt had come from the Computer Science Lab. One production staff member, Mark Chow, a videographer, had been a part of the CDI group, and was convinced to continue on as a member of RED. Eventually Beth Mynatt and Maureen Stone left RED and three new members were added: Maribeth Back, Matt Gorbet, and I.

23 The members of RED had expertise and experience from a range of disciplinary domains: Scott Minneman holds a Ph.D. in mechanical engineering; Steve Harrison was an architect by training and a design-engineering researcher; Dale McDonald was a chip designer, computer programmer, and a light artist; Maribeth Back was a sound designer; Mark Chow was a videographer; Gold was a toy designer and electronic musician; Matt Gorbet was an engineer from MIT's Media Lab; and I was a cultural theorist and humanist. By virtue of my interest in theory and methodologies of interpretation, I was considered a scientist within the context of RED and according to the organizational logic of PARC.

24 In this way RED differed from the other labs at PARC at the time that were strongly identified in terms associated with particular kinds of technologies or aspects of technological systems: the Computer Science Lab (CSL), the Information Sciences & Technology Lab (ISTL), Electronic Materials Lab (EML), Document Hardware Lab (DHL), and Systems and Practices Lab (SPL). As a research group, RED was not on the same level as a lab. Unlike other research groups, such

as Fluid Documents or Electronic Paper, the members of RED did not have appointments within any particular lab.

25 Rumor had it that Gold sealed the deal for the one million dollar project budget by convincing the marketing managers that the exhibit would be far less expensive than a Super Bowl commercial and would still reach the right kind of audience—technology fans in Silicon Valley.

26 Among the things we had to take into account in designing the exhibit were the editorial and exhibit guidelines produced by the Tech Museum that describe key elements of exhibits: 1) audience; 2) textual considerations, such as voice, language, vocabulary, label readability, the use of unbiased examples; 3) graphic conventions, including typefaces, font size, accessibility, information layout; and 4) exhibit "message" construction.

27 A representative sample of popular accounts of research going on at the time includes a report on PARC researchers Bernardo Huberman and Lada Adamic's research on website traffic in Markoff (1999) and an account of the work by Peter Pirolli and Stuart Card on their creation of foraging models of web surfing in Chalmers (2000). The range of material to be folded into an overarching narrative was not imposed on RED, although the process of selecting and recruiting research projects to be part of the RED project did uncover the different political investments on the part of PARC's central administration made in various research efforts. RED learned that some projects were off limits because of deadline pressures. This was most evident in the discussion with the researchers working on electronic paper. They were working under a brutal deadline to produce a workable prototype in time for the Xerox announcement of the formation of a manufacturing partnership with the 3M Corporation. The researchers were told in no uncertain terms not to waste one moment on the RED project. On the other hand, a group of researchers who collaborated with RED on the DataGlyph interactive was in danger of having their funding cut; working with RED helped keep the project alive a while longer.

28 The first exhibition installed in the Tech Museum's Center of the Edge Gallery was of art-technology pieces created at Interval Research Center. In fact, Interval artist/researcher Michael Naimark gave the address at the grand opening of the new Tech Museum on March 2, 1999. Another Interval researcher, Rachel Strickland, installed an interactive piece called "Portable Effects" where users could unload the stuff they carry with them, on their person, to see how much the baggage of everyday life actually weighs: see Strickland (n.d.; 2003). The second exhibit installed in the Center of the Edge Gallery was sponsored by AT&T and featured demonstrations of voice recognition technologies and applications. The installation was designed, developed, and installed by a professional exhibit fabrication firm, which created the exhibit as an example of experience marketing. In this installation, the emphasis was the new devices and applications that AT&T would soon make available to consumers. There was less emphasis on

the underlying research questions concerning voice recognition technologies, and more attention directed to the predictive availability of these devices in the near future.

29 In discussions with Michael Naimark, one of the featured Interval artist-researchers, I learned a bit about the difference between Interval and PARC as the organizational contexts for the creation of installations for the Tech Museum. Although there was really interesting art and technology work at Interval, which formed the basis for the Tech Museum installation, there was no pressure to use the Center for the Edge Gallery invitation as a stage for the performance of a story about the "innovative research" going on at Interval. Although the technological artwork was in fact a demonstration of innovation at Interval, this work was not always well received by upper management there. So although the Tech Museum tendered its first invitation to Interval, and trumpeted the technological art as evidence of creative innovation at the turn of the millennium, the reception of this work within Interval was not applauded as such. Michael Naimark, personal conversation, February 22, 2006.

30 Although I don't recall anyone explicitly describing RED's work in these terms at the time, it was clear that its aims at this point were consonant with the organizational processes involved in technology-transfer projects. Much later, when working under the auspices of Onomy Labs, we were actually hired by Sun Labs to employ the methods we had worked out in RED for the purposes of assisting a technology-transfer project at Sun. It was during this project that we learned how other industry professionals made sense of what RED was doing in creating the XFR exhibit at PARC.

31 I joined the group at the end of their yearlong study of the history of reading. Geoffrey Nunberg, who was also a member of the PARC research staff, had presented an overview of the field for RED. The bibliography that I inherited and added to included Altick (1983); Anderson (1983); Bolter (1991); Cavallo and Chartier (1999); Davidson (1986); Drucker (1995); Eisenstein (1980); Febvre and Martin (1984); Flynn and Schweickart (1986); D. Hall (1996); Johns (1998); Machor (1993); Manguel (1996); Martin (1988); McGann (1991); Nelson (1990); Nunberg (1996); Radway (1984); K. Smith (1995); and Williams (1961).

32 Robert Boyton (2000: 40), in *Time Digital*, announced the coming revolution, to be brought about by e-books, in its December 2000 issue. Wanting to have it both ways, the article simultaneously claims: "This is a transformative moment in print culture. Two revolutions are taking place—one for writers and the other for readers. The book is dead. Long live the book." One of the most concise accounts of the shiny future of e-books was offered by Steven Levy (2000: 96), who writes, "when Y3K pundits look back on our time, they'll remember it as the *Last Century of the Book* . . . As a common item of communication, artistic expression and celebrity anecdote, the physical object consisting of bound dead trees in shiny wrapper is headed for the antique heap. Its replacement will be a lightning-quick injection of digital bits into a handheld device with an ultra sharp dis-

play." Other accounts of the future role of e-books were careful to suggest that we shouldn't dismiss the printed word (just yet). This article also lists the (then) available handheld hardware for reading e-books: Gemstar's REB; Franklin eBookMan; Palm OS handhelds; Pocket PCs that use built-in Microsoft Reader and Peanut Reader (Harrison, 2001). In another article, journalist Henry Norr (2000) reports on the e-book publicity coming from the Seybold SF publishing trade show: "The show produced a flurry of e-book-related announcements, with Microsoft and Adobe cutting deals right and left to line up support for their rival formats. Meanwhile, scores of smaller players tiptoed warily across the stage, hoping to position themselves to share in the expected bonanza—and avoid getting crushed as the giants wrestle." Norr goes on to invoke the claims coming from research centers, such as Xerox PARC, about the virtues and inevitability of e-book technologies. He cites the PARC project to develop E-Ink, where its website offered this claim: "By the year 2003, we envision electronic books that can display volumes of information as easily as flipping a page, and permanent newspapers that update themselves daily via wireless broadcast."

33 At that moment in history, the potential size of e-book markets was unclear. Hamit (2003) reviewed Xerox's efforts in the fields of "book printing on demand" with the creation of the DocuTech 6180 "Book Factory" that prints a book in a minute. The debates about the "death of the book" and the implications of e-books were covered in a number of popular press articles. See also Murphy (2000), Carvajal (1999), and Darnton (1999).

34 Dino Felluga (2003) developed a useful set of webtexts that explained the logical architecture and use of Greimas's model for the purposes of systematic semiotic analysis.

35 I considered the two-by-two matrices as maps of the expanse of McLuhan's Gutenberg Galaxy. McLuhan (1962: 8) coined the term "The Gutenberg Galaxy" to name the social and cultural environment (including all the practices that were enabled and provoked by this environment) that was established with the advent of Gutenberg's printing press technology. For McLuhan, Gutenberg's innovation served as an "originating moment" that created a galaxy of possibility and spaces for new practices and new configurations of culture, the social, and the human. As he explains, the project (the book, *The Gutenberg Galaxy*) offers a "mosaic or field approach to its problems," which for him offered the only "practical means of revealing causal operations in history" (7). Inspired by this work, I imagined these interactives as existing at the edges of McLuhan's/Gutenberg's galaxy, where they overlapped with the outer edges of a new galaxy that had been born through a different *big bang* that the group was not yet able to apprehend. For a while the exhibit had a working title that reflected this cultural interpretation: *re:reading: Dispatches from the Edge of the Gutenberg Galaxy*. It was eventually considered much too academic as a name for the exhibit.

36 In his elaboration of a "successor metaphysics" adequate to the task of building a comprehensive theory of computation, Brian Cantwell Smith (1996) includes a

discussion of the nature of representation and the ontological foundation necessary for this project. "Ontology is the projection of registration onto the world. Representation is the projection of registration onto the subject or vehicle" (349). He goes on to assert that the distinction between "representation and ontology is indefinite, vague, unstable, etc." The critical move in his metaphysics concerns the notion of *registration*: "The original intentional act is taken to be one of registration: a process whereby the world *presents*, directly—at least as directly as is metaphysically possible . . . such presentation depends on the located 'presence' of both subject and object—presence of the subject in the sense of its being located, responsible, and aware; presence of the object in the sense of its presenting as object, as in and of the world" (350).

37 For example, I examined filmic representations of laboratories, including those of *mad scientists* (*Back to the Future*, 1985) and of *clean-room futurologists* (*Altered States*, 1980). Although the mise-en-scene of the contemporary lab has transformed to include desktop computers, printers, and new digital optical displays, the semiotic markers of *lab-ness* (in popular culture) continue to include glass beakers, lab benches, glowing lights, and bubbling liquids. Based on a suggestion from MaryKate Meyerhoffer, the graphic designer who produced the exhibit signage, Scott Minneman, started photographing actual PARC laboratories. Meyerhoffer is the principle owner and designer of SheGeek Design. See http://www.shegeekdesign.com/.

38 The 80/20 building system consists of extruded aluminum, which comes in a wide range of parts that can be combined to build all sorts of structures, and in fact is used to build structures for laboratories such as benches and equipment platforms.

39 For example, see the account of Paul Aoki's and Allison Woodruff's research on Tap Tips guidebook interface (Patch, 2001).

40 The exhibit was created through key collaborations with a group of talented people, some who were PARC colleagues, others freelance experts. Mark Meadows, an accomplished graphic comic illustrator and web artist, had been working with RED as a PAIR artist since the beginning of the discussions about the Tech exhibit in 1998. At the time, he was just starting his book project: *Pause and Effect: The Art of Interactive Narrative* (2002). Jonathan Cohen provided expert programming, including the bridging coding for RED *Dog*, and the specialized authoring environment for *The Reading Wall*. Shilajeet "Banny" Banerjee drew on his product design skills to create the design of RED *Dog* and the highly precise design for the *Glyph-O-Scope*. Maureen Stone served as color printing coordinator who painstakingly calibrated the large-scale printing of the *Walk-In Comix* exhibit (and provided endless bags of chocolates in the crucial session before opening day). Polle Zellweger, a PARC researcher who worked on the Fluid Documents project (among others), provided continuity and copy editing assistance, including the heroic task of proofreading the typographic murals of *The Reading Wall*. Bay-Wei Chang, another PARC colleague, generously worked with

Rich Gold to transform the code of his group's fluid documents application into an authoring environment for the creation of *Fluid Fiction*. Terry Murphy, principle engineer for Exhibit Engineering, Inc., was an experienced interactive exhibit fabricator who provided the specialized fabrication of signature pieces.

41 Some of the things RED didn't make included an exhibit called "Scanner Race" that would have allowed visitors to race against a scanner to see if they could read faster than a machine. "The Adventures of Red Dot" was an exhibit that was to showcase a paper-moving technology under development at PARC, which used air jets to move paper without friction. This exhibit would have featured a RED dot that would dance around a surface (propelled by air jets) based on an unfolding story. The "Walk-Up Comic Book" was planned as an interactive large comic book, which would have incorporated projectors and proximity sensors, enabling visitors to interact with architecturally scaled narrative spaces. The "Reader's Theater" would have been a performative exhibit where media-rich stories would be expertly narrated. This exhibit was also supposed to encompass expert, expressive, and provocative "readings" of some of the other XFR exhibits, such as special poetry written for RED: *Reading Eye Dog*. The "Anno-Table" was an early exhibit planned to explore the future of writing that would enable visitors to annotate the same document displayed on tables/surfaces at a distance. See RED (2001b).

42 But as the YouTube video titled "Middle Ages Tech Support" humorously demonstrates, we cannot ascribe book literacy to people of a different historical moment. This technological literacy comprises historically specific understandings and practices of the meaningfulness of the technological form that we now recognize as the book.

43 For a discussion of the way in which "things" are implicated in the creation of meaning, of the self, and of social relations, see Csikszentmihalyi and Rochberg-Halton (1981).

44 Several museum studies scholars use the term "interactives" to name that category of museum object that calls forth visitor participation in an active way. See for example, Sharon Macdonald, 1998. The XFR exhibit included fifteen interactives, two of these were multiple instances. There were two copies of the *What Haven't You Read Lately? (WHRYL?)* in the exhibit. The interactive called *Episodes in the History of Reading* comprised three wall segments, but they are considered three parts of one interactive. I count each Tilty Table as a different interactive because each table presented a different interactive logic. I count each instance of the *Listen Readers* as three different interactives as well because each used a different book.

45 John Law (2002: 2) argues that the object of technoscience needs to be decentered as a singular entity: "objects" he writes, "come in different versions." He elaborates how objects are both singular (where singularity is a consequence of practices of coherence) and plural (when coherence is methodically unpacked).

46 A representative selection of Maribeth Back's research papers on XFR exhibits are included in the bibliography (Back et al. 1999; 2001; 2002a; 2002b).

47 All the eight artists were affiliated with the San Francisco Center for the Book. Kathleen Burch was one of the co-founders; Steve Woodall was Artistic Director of the Center at the time. He was invaluable in organizing the artists' efforts before, during, and after the XFR exhibition.

48 The San Francisco Center for the Book staged its own exhibition of the artists' work: *XFB: Experiments in the Future of the Book.* The exhibit was installed from November 2001 through February 2002. For a brief review, see Silver (2001).

49 RED member Mark Chow was the principle designer for the project; Shilajeet "Banny" Banerjee, who was working as a RED intern at the time, brought considerable skills in product design and digital rendering to the project. Other RED members who worked on this interactive included Matt Gorbet and Scott Minneman. Jonathan Cohen created the program that enabled the OCR application to interact with the text-to-speech application. Terry Murphy fabricated the built form of the dog based on engineering designs by Banerjee. Mark Chow wrote a collection of sample reading pieces called "Prose and Doggerel" that were always available for RED: *Reading Eye Dog* to read.

50 In reflecting on the outcomes of these experiments, I could follow the lines of any one of these vectors, continuing to unravel a set of understandings and stories that might take form as a set of insights that came about through the design, fabrication, and installation of the XFR exhibit. And indeed, this is what I do in the website that is part of the designing culture project. See http://www.design ingculture.net.

51 In this sense, the group self-consciously committed "error 33"—the code name for doing research on one's own research.

52 Two articles written by Maribeth Back, Steve Harrison, and Rich Gold (RED, 2001a; 2001b) that listed all RED members as co-authors, described RED's genre-based research methods: the articles elaborated the "what" of XFR, and the "how" of XFR. The first described the exhibits that were included in the XFR installation, as well as some of the exhibits that weren't made (RED, 2001a). The second article explicitly develops an account of RED's genre-based design methodology (RED, 2001b). Lucy Suchman (2005) discusses the ways that a technological object acquires meaning and is implicated in the reproduction of meaning through its affiliation with relevant others (researchers, users, designers, owners).

53 At the more philosophical level there was an implicit assertion that the work of design involved several different kinds of agents, human, non-human, and cyborgian, each of which participated in the creation of the design. Following this, the term *design* was used as a shorthand term for an ontological and epistemological phenomenon that was in fact created through the sustained engagement between human actors, non-human actors, and the material world. In this sense, RED's understanding of its own methodology resonated with theoretical

observations offered by scholars in STS, feminist cultural studies of science and technology, and design-research theory. Indeed, RED member Scott Minneman's (1991) doctoral thesis (in the field of Mechanical Engineering) was an investigation of design-in-practice, and employed methods from anthropology and ethnomethodology. Some of the other "classic" sociological, STS, and cultural theory sources shared among RED members included Berger and Luckman (1966); Geertz (1973); Haraway (1986); Latour and Woolgar (1979); McLuhan (1964; 1985); Strauss (1987); Suchman (1987); Traweek (1988); Turkle (1984); and Wiener (1961).

54 We could say, now that some of the devices have been duplicated in other contexts, that RED did design the beginnings of at least two new genres. The two most commonly duplicated devices, as of 2010, are The Interactive (Reading) Wall and the Tilty Table. These devices were duplicated for other settings and clients by Onomy Labs—the company founded by former RED members—as well as by other exhibit designers and interactivity researchers. For an account of the influence of these devices, see Lee, Khandelwal, and Mazalek (2007).

55 The first public presentation of RED's speculative design research methodology occurred at the CHI conference in 2000. See Balsamo et al. (2000).

56 I had thought that the most likely candidate for duplication was the *Hyperbolic Comics*: it seemed a timely example of the recombinant possibilities of new media, merging the conventions of spatialized graphic narrative logics with hypertextually linked non-linear narrative structure. I projected that this hybrid narrative form would be replicated and eventually made available as a flash-based web application, but as of 2010 this particular new media form has not yet been duplicated.

57 In many respects the physical devices created for the XFR exhibit were much more innovative than its content, text, and narrative tropes. The Tech's museum design staff had a very clear sense of its key demographic: the group of 10–14 year-old school-age children who live in and around Silicon Valley. Consequently, they had developed strong design conventions for creating exhibits that would engage their key audiences. Moreover, as RED realized during the designing process, these interactives were not destined for an art gallery. If they had been, presumably the content could have been very different. We had to work against our own tendency sometimes to veer in the direction of the conceptual or the overly aesthetized.

58 The notion of the "narrative construction of reality" was developed by Stuart Hall (1984); Jerome Bruner (1991) develops the framework more fully.

59 In August of 1998, a few weeks after the Tech Museum's invitation was tendered, Gold sent around an email in which he reported on a "vision" he had for the main theme for the museum exhibit. (The date of the email is August 12, 1998. Although I wasn't yet on staff, it was one of the first things I was given to read when I joined the RED group.)

REDsters-

Last night I had a vision about what we might do at the S. J. Tech. This morning it still seemed like a good idea. Without apologies I offer it, both as a way of getting going (time frame is incredibly short) and of indicating the type of project I am looking for. In this regard I am looking for a project that satisfies both RED's charter (see bottom) and the needs of the Tech. We would also need explicit buy in from PARC and possibly from Xerox (for funding among other things).

Here's my proposed project for the Tech:

"New Readings"

In the future people will still read, but how they read and what they read will be different than now. At Xerox PARC researchers are working on new reading technologies, new text genres and new "reading places." Together these will change the "world of reading" as we know it. The "New Readings" exhibition will be in 3500 sq. feet of the S. J. Tech and will showcase some of these new ways of reading being developed at PARC and Xerox.

In this exhibition we will show new reading technologies and the new document genres that might exist on these technologies. We will also let people "read" these documents and even construct new ones . . .

What I like about this vision is that it still satisfies our basic RED goals:

RED's Goals:
1 Create new genres of the future by creating real documents in these genres.
2 Use the technologies of PARC (and our partners) as a platform for these genres.
3 Make this work visible to PARC and the World.
4 Work together as a team.
5 Understand in a deep way "design" in a research context.

Point (4) is critical. I believe that for this very worthy project to succeed we will need to work together as a team. That this will have to be our all-consuming work. I would be very excited about leading such a project, but only if the members of RED are willing to engage in it fully for the next nine months.

Gold proposed the topic of reading because of its relevance to the core technology of Xerox, its resonance with RED's research charter, namely the opportunity it afforded for the study and creation of new media genres, and its connection to previous research by various RED members. The Tech Museum opportunity specifically addressed all of his key objectives for RED:

1 To conduct deep research on an important social and cultural issue
2 To develop and patent new technologies
3 To use PARC technologies in new ways
4 To change Xerox's view of itself

5 To change public perception of PARC

6 To garner positive publicity for PARC

7 To stay within budget

8 To work as a team

The plan that emerged from the discussions of this email missive was that RED would design the exhibit from the ground up, which would allow the group to iterate two aspects of its *new media genres* research agenda: 1) the design and construction of new reading devices, and 2) the authoring and acquisition of appropriate content for those new devices. Gold's email suggestion that the exhibit focus on the topic of "new readings" persisted as the guiding theme of the exhibit for several weeks. But the group revised this theme several times in an effort to create a narrative frame for the development of new reading technologies. Version 2.0 (which was documented in December 1998) was titled "Reading Changes," which reflected an emergent understanding, based on the group's research into the history of reading and writing, that reading had changed dramatically throughout history not solely as a consequence of new technologies, for example, the printing press, but also as a result of changes in social and political structures. Every time the title changed, RED produced a new chapbook that represented in form and content the connotations implied by the new title.

60 Before joining the RED group at PARC, Matt Gorbet was a student at MIT in the Media Lab and the Tangible Media Group. After RED left Xerox PARC, Matt and Susan Gorbet formed Gorbet Design Inc. to continue working on innovative interactive experiences that combine art and technology. Matt Gorbet was one of the key interactivity designers for several XFR exhibits.

61 I have reinterpreted Gorbet's description of the "Red Shift" as a strategy of détournement. Debord and Wolman ([1956] 2006: 2) describe two different kinds of détournement, *minor* and *deceptive*: "Minor détournement is the détournement of an element which has no importance in itself and which thus draws all its meaning from the new context in which it has been placed. For example, a press clipping, a neutral phrase, a commonplace photograph. Deceptive détournement, also termed premonitory-proposition détournement, is in contrast the détournement of an intrinsically significant element, which derives a different scope from the new context. A slogan of Saint-Just, for example, or a film sequence from Eisenstein."

62 Another prime example of the RED Shift happened with the DataGlyph research project that was transformed into an interactive called the "Glyph-O-Scope." In this case, the original DataGlyph researchers realized some value from the collaboration with RED in creating the new interactive. RED's interest in this research stimulated renewed interest on the part of PARC management in the DataGlyph project. Consequently, some of the XFR resources funded additional work on the DataGlyph project.

63 Brenda Laurel (2003) describes a similar notion as "informance," which for her

names a design-research method that combines techniques of theatrical improvisation with ethnographic observation of users' interactions with designed products. Bonnie McDaniel Johnson (2003) further elaborates the notion of "informance."

64 Michel de Certeau (1984) claims that the narratives that circulate through the media make simulacra "real"; I think his words describe the similar move accomplished through the performance of technology demonstrations.

65 It was in the role of tour-guide that I became consciously aware of the way in which my identity was in the process of being redesigned through my work at PARC. In delivering tours of different PARC labs, I had to learn the stories to tell about the work going on in those labs that articulated the meaning of the research as "innovative" and significant. Learning those stories was very much like learning a script in preparation for a performance. And indeed, "giving the tour" was very much a performance in speaking innovation. Probably one of my most memorable tours was for William Shatner and Chip Walker who visited PARC as research for their book (Shatner and Walker, 2002).

66 In addition to drawing inspiration from Suchman's work, I also rely on insights from work by Latour (1979; 1986; 1987) and Law (2002).

67 The move to decenter the subject as a singular individual with a fixed self/identity has been a central problematic within feminist cultural theory for the past twenty-five years, and has occasioned much discussion and debate among feminist scholars who study science and technology. The crux of the debate concerns the move to deconstruct the "authority" of the subject in favor of understanding the subject-in-relation rather than as an entity with a fixed self/identity. Some feminist scholars critique this move because it could (inadvertently, perhaps) disempower women by theoretically undermining their right to be considered the "authors" of their own experience. From this perspective, the feminist agenda to create a space for the recognition of women as subjects (for example, of technological innovation) is not well served by a theoretical imperative to deconstruct the fixity of the subject, where the temptation is to locate her agency or experience as merely an effect of her positionality in overlapping social networks. I have some sympathy for this critique of the political consequences of decentering the subject. I have argued in another context that feminists need feminist heroes (Balsamo, 2000a). In a more nuanced way, feminist science/technology studies interpret the move to decenter the subject as a locus of a fixed self/ identity to mean that our analyses (especially of science-in-action) need to account for the ways in which subjects-in-relation are gendered, raced, and classed in the process of engaging in practices that also result in the "making" of scientific knowledge, of technological artifacts, and of science/technology as a domain of human effectivity. The feminist project, in this case, is to illuminate the ways in which gender identities, racial identities, and class identities are also part of the construction of a subject-in-relation, in the practice of science and technology making, rather than a priori attributes.

68 I rehearse the multiple ways that I was constituted as a subject within the PARC

research context as a way of foregrounding the impossibility of creating a fixed identity from which to author an account of the unfolding of a project of techno-logical innovation that is the objective for this chapter. Consequently, the writing is marked by a tension between the invocation of a "singular identity" (that I might construct as part of a biographical account of my life and my work), and the more contingent nature of an identity-constituted-in-relation to other social actors.

69 Latour (1996: 23) elaborates: "This tautology frees the analysis of technologies from the burden that weighs on the analysis of the sciences . . . The fact still remains that, after all the controversies, the sciences seem to have discovered a world that came into being without men and without sciences." The student of technology is freer to study engineers who have the professional job to invent "the future."

three: **The Design of Technological Literacies**

1 Macdonald describes museums of science as "cultural technologies" in that they "define both certain kinds of 'knowledge' (and certain knowledges as 'Knowl-edge' or 'Science') and certain kinds of publics" (1998: 4). This definition builds on Hooper-Greenhill's (1992) description of museums as ensembles of practices, beliefs, and structures that are constituted and in part constitute contemporary (and always shifting) histories.

2 This discussion draws on a broader conversation about the development of the science museum as a particular kind of institution that is implicated in important epistemic shifts in the constitution of knowledge over broad historical periods. This topic informs the work of several scholars who focus on the development of the "science museum" as a particular kind of museum. See, for example, Pearce (1996), Haraway (1989), Shapin (1994), and Sheets-Pyenson (1989).

3 See also Levine (1988).

4 Greg Wise (1997: 127), in his study of the founding of the Museum of Science and Industry and its constitution as a social space of communication, quotes the first director, Waldemar Kampffert, who noted the connection between the museum and the exhibition of progress: "As the visitor emerges from the museum he will understand better the spectacle that greets his eyes—electric lights, the auto-mobiles, the airplanes overhead, the towering hotels and apartment houses, the hard roads, Jackson Park itself. Chicago will seem a part of the museum—the last great exhibit in the technical progress of man."

5 Although Bennett's specific reference is to art museums in the nineteenth cen-tury, his point is applicable to other types of museums where the representational space of the museum becomes a discursive space for the creation of a narrative that provides a meaning for the objects on display.

6 Lisa Cartwright (1995: 9) describes how throughout the nineteenth century, the invention of visualization instruments was a defining characteristic of scientific

practice. As she points out, this "frenzy of the visible" reached fever pitch by the end of the nineteenth century, serving as the perfect context for the emergence of cinema as a complex techno-scientific popular medium of expression. Don Ihde (2002) traces the connections between the rise of scientific visualism (which he argues began with Leonardo Da Vinci) and contemporary preoccupations with new technologies of visuality.

7   Michelle Henning (2006) describes the major influences cited by the director of the Natural History Museum in London, in 1972, which led to the development of the museum's first installation of participatory exhibits. Among these influences were the pedagogical theory of Otto Neurath and his "International System of Typological and Pictorial Education" (Isotype system), the programmed learning approach developed by B. F. Skinner, and Frank Oppenheimer's vision for the Exploratorium in San Francisco.

8   This account comes from Peter Richards (2002).

9   Hilde Hein (1990) provides an account of the groundbreaking work of artist-created exhibits at the Exploratorium.

10   Andrew Barry (2001) offers a sustained discussion of the contradictions played out in the Exploratorium's early exhibit development. Henning (2006) discusses the role of the Exploratorium in institutionalizing a paradigm shift.

11   In 2006, I was invited by Eric Siegel at the New York Hall of Science to review the art-inspired exhibitions collected throughout the museum; my review, "A Glorious Mix: The Art of Interactive Science and Technology exhibits," serves as the introduction to a published catalog called *Intersections: Art at the New York Hall of Science* (Balsamo, 2006).

12   Edward Rothstein (2004) offers a description in his review of the opening of the expansion of the New York Hall of Science.

13   For a more complete discussion of the shift from the curator to the exhibit designer, see "A Useful Past for the Present" in Hooper-Greenhill (1992: 206–15).

14   The famous Eames "shell" chair was the result of a series of collaborations with Eero Saarinen and other designers over thirty years. Once it became popular it was always attributed to Charles Eames, such that he is often memorialized by the line that he *redefined the way that America sat* (Demetrios, 2001).

15   In describing the Eameses' work with the U.S. government, Helene Lipstadt (1997: 172) writes, "for the government's ideologues, there was no need to impress ideology on an Eames design. The idea of an ideology-free Eames production is, like the notion of their isolation from the outside world, yet another myth . . . Although they were not critical of the power structure of American society, nor of capitalism, and they did not draw Americans' attention to oppression or celebrate transgression and the oppressed, neither were the Eameses the unsuspecting tools or compliant allies of their USIA employers. If ideology was there in abundance, it was of their own making."

16   This description comes from an account by the Eameses' grandson, Eames De-

metrios, who discovered the statement in the Library of Congress Manuscript Division, Work of Charles and Ray Eames, box 218, folder no. 10.

17 According to accounts by Demetrios (2001), the Eames office staff worked on the exhibition for more than a year, drawing on visual resources from the library at Columbia University and the expertise of a well-known mathematician, Ray Redheffer. The Eameses described the process as a "learn-by-doing" activity, which is also how they described their philosophy of exhibit design. Years before the Exploratorium popularized the notion of experiential "hands-on" science exhibits, the Eameses had made the visitor's experience a central feature of several of the *Mathematica* pieces: "Like so many of the Eameses' education-related projects, *Mathematica* offers the visitor direct experiences. The purpose is to give the visitor (or the viewer, in the case of the film) a credible, direct experience to add to his or her own internal library . . . They were not just trying to make abstract order out of things, nor were they trying to make just experience without exploration . . . They bridged the gap between science and art" (2001: 188–89).

18 The original 1961 exhibit also included five short films called the IBM *Math Peep Shows*. Apparently these short 8mm filmic loops did not last as long as the other elements; they were removed because they simply wore out.

19 I recorded this quotation in my visit notes to the New York Hall of Science in June 2005 when I was there to write a review of the institution's curated collection of art and technology interactive exhibits. See Balsamo (2006).

20 In the discussion about *Mathematica* in the video *Design Q&A,* Ray Eames admits that she was conflicted about the fact that there were so few women in the history of mathematics. At the same time she asserts that they (as designers) were simply recognizing the best work and people who contributed important ideas to the development of this discipline. As she argues: If they already weren't part of this history, we were not going to lower our standards in order to include more women scientists. Clearly she wasn't thinking with much complexity about the way in which official histories get written, and how women get *written out* of those histories for all sorts of reasons.

21 To create another one of the XFR exhibits, Rich Gold explicitly acknowledged the Eameses' film *The Powers of 10* as an influence. The story Gold wrote for the *Fluid Fiction* interactive, called "Henry the Ape," is about nested universes and includes a story about microscopic amoeba, living in the stomachs of lice that live in the fur of a mouse that lives in the foot of an ape that lives on a planet that belongs to a solar system that is part of a universe that is part of the cosmos. In the creation of this interactive, Gold embraced the Eameses' edict, "innovate as a last resort." (Although they often claimed to eschew innovation, the Eameses were creative inventors when pressed [Demetrios, 2001]. For example, in working on a design for a molded plywood chair, they learned that the "honesty" of the plywood meant that it didn't lend itself to following the compound curves called for by their desired design. Charles eventually built a machine for molding plywood

called the Kazam! Machine that enabled the plywood to be shaped in certain ways. Although plywood would not be the material of their single-shell mass-produced chair, it was a material that they experimented with extensively and became part of their signature palate of materials.) Gold borrowed a narrative form from the Eames film to map onto a new mode of hypertextual annotation and display—an application that was already in development by other PARC researchers. Gold's insight was to transform this annotation application into a full-blown authoring environment.

22   This wasn't the only theoretical influence that shaped the design of this interactive. Its form factor was designed to challenge the implicit theory of culture that circulated in Silicon Valley in the late 1990s that trumpeted digital engagement as a mere mode of information exchange. This telephonic (transmission) model of communication rehearsed an old story about the asymmetrical relationship between senders and receivers; certain members of culture are cast as the intended (passive) recipients of messages (actively) created by other members of culture.

As many communication scholars attest, this model of communication has a long history, and is not easily contradicted (Carey, 1989; Roszak, 1994). *The Reading Wall* began as a way to rethink the notion of the reader as the passive recipient of historical narratives created by an omniscient anonymous author.

23   Four RED members worked on the design of *The Reading Wall*; over time the division of design and fabrication labor became more pronounced. Eventually I served as the primary author/designer of the animated digital material that appeared on the plasma display. Steve Harrison was one of the primary designers of the original idea for the history interactive. He created the first long lists of historical events to be included in the interactive, and offered the first attempt at creating a three-part structure for the material. He and Scott Minneman developed the built form and fabrication methods for the wall. Minneman not only engineered the wall's mechanical parts and designed a new sensor and braking system for the wall, he also served as art director for the overall look and feel of the entire piece. Matt Gorbet designed the typographic treatment of the static printed backgrounds. Polle Zellweger, a PARC colleague, contributed copy editing and technical writing assistance. Terry Murphy, an outside engineering contractor, fabricated the steel frame and engineered the electrical connections. It's important at least to footnote that there were no outside observers investigating and watching RED's collaborative (and interdisciplinary) process. We were both the researchers and the observers of our own research process. It would have been extremely interesting, if not a little unnerving, to have had an observational expert engaged in a parallel research effort. See, for example, Carol Ann Wald's (2004) account of her observations of the process among the interdisciplinary researchers (N. Katherine Hayles, Victoria Vesna, and James Gimzewski) who collaborated on the creation of the *nano* exhibit for the Los Angeles County Museum of Art (LACMA).

24 The digital authoring environment comprised several different computing applications, each of which has its own set of affordances and semiotic-processes. The first set of notes was (unsurprisingly) created as a word processing document in Microsoft Word. The initial set of storyboards was created in Microsoft Power-Point. The creation of the digital assets required the use of Adobe Photoshop. The animation effects were first created in an XML application; this code was compiled (using a proprietary piece of middle-ware) to create a score in Macro-media Director, where the digital assets were imported and transformed using a Director plug-in to produce certain visual effects.

25 Edward Tufte (2003: 22) forcefully argues that the presentational application PowerPoint imposes a highly constrained cognitive style on those who author and read PowerPoint slides. As he argues, "the PP slide format has probably the worst signal/noise ratio of any known method of communication on paper or computer screen" (2003: 22). In his vilification of PowerPoint, Tufte represents an extreme version of the argument for the technological determination of writing devices and applications.

26 Ian Simmons (1996: 82) suggests that this "non-linear" process has been "widely adopted in virtually all organizations which have successfully created hands-on centres." He also notes that this paradigm of exhibit design often clashes with a more traditional mode of exhibit development that begins with a curatorial research and exhibit "brief" and then proceeds linearly to the design and installation of the overarching curatorial vision. The clash of paradigms or cultures is most pronounced, he argues, in mixed-purpose institutions: museums that include "hands-on" centers.

27 In his germinal book, *Semiology of Graphics*, Jacques Bertin (1983) outlines a general theory of graphic information design. Although his book was written before the wide scale availability of digital graphic applications, he also notes that: "Electronic displays, such as the cathode ray tube, open up an unlimited future to graphics" (1983: 2).

28 I use the term *information semiologist* to name a designerly sensibility for the creation of communication in a two-dimensional planer space. When the project of information design also involves the creation of multiple spaces of information, which necessitate also the design of the relationship and navigation among these spaces of information, I use the term *information architect*.

29 The animation effects used for *The Reading Wall* drew on foundational principles of good information design as promoted by Edward Tufte. He reminds us that: "For prose, parallelism helps bring about clarity, efficiency, forcefulness, rhythm, balance" (1997: 79). Although digital information design is not the main topic of his work, Tufte presents an insightful critique of the pitfalls of much interface design, where, as he rightly asserts, "the information is the interface." For example, he shows how in several web pages only a fraction of the design space is allocated to the presentation of substantive information; most of the space is

devoted to navigation graphics or what he calls "computer administrative debris" (149).

30 In trying to describe how the elements of the text space appeared on *The Reading Wall* display, I encounter the constraints of text-based description to adequately convey the sense of animated images. Here I would direct the reader to the designing culture website that includes several the interactive wall books that I created for the xFR exhibit, as well as additional wall books created for other instances of the Interactive Wall device. See http://www.designingculture.net

For a discussion of the semiotics of motion graphic design see Goux and Houff (2003), and Bellantoni and Woolman (2001). From these books we can list key kinetic type effects: expansion; compression; speed; rotation; spin; velocity; direction. This itemizes some of the key dimensions in the choreography of motion graphics and type at play.

31 This idea also invokes Lev Manovich's (2001) notion of the "poetics of navigation." His terminology draws attention to the ontological space of the digital display as a navigable space. When he describes the logics of the bodily movements that make up the interaction, I believe that he begins to explicate not simply a poetics of navigation but more broadly a semiotics of interaction. I extend this notion to elaborate how this semiotics is culturally expressive of symbolic understandings.

32 The projection of "passivity" on the part of a reader or user of an interactive device is also repeated in claims such as the one made by Edwin Schlossberg (1988: 80–81): "Most interactive designs are misnamed. They are not based on involving the audience in a compositional or collaborative experience. Instead they are built on the capabilities of the device or computer to put some simplified story in motion. There is usually some superfluous switch or button inserted to provide the illusion of involvement." This is another facet of the discussion about passivity and interactivity. Schlossberg is right to point out that many interactive devices are merely responsive devices. If we define interactivity as a conversation between user and machine, true interactivity would allow for novel input and forms of expression on behalf of all conversational participants.

33 In her discussion of one of the other xFR exhibits, RED: *Reading Eye Dog*, Katherine Hayles (2002: 23) argues that one of the implications of the exhibit was how it demonstrated that changing the form of the (reading) artifact does not merely change the act of reading, but also "transforms the metaphoric network structuring the relation of word to world." Her observations of the importance of the "materiality" of the technotext resonates with Andrea diSessa's (2000) use of the term "material intelligence" as a substitution of the term "literacy" in discussions about computers and literacy.

34 Other experiences creating new applications for the next version of *The Reading Wall* called the *Interactive Digital Wall* provided different lessons about the process of cross-cultural design. The collaborative effort required to produce the

exhibit for the Singapore Science Center was also enlightening for me in different ways. This was my first experience in "24/7 design" where the designing process took place asynchronously in Menlo Park, California and in Singapore in a short number of days. This situation was necessitated by the very short production time we had between the signing of the contract and the required shipping date of the interactive piece. After working on the digital application in California late into the night, as is my practice, I would send the files to my colleagues in Singapore who would either receive the files in the early evening or early the next morning. They would review and revise the files during their normal business day while I slept and send them back to me in time for the start of my workday the next morning. The collaborative process in this case was very dynamic and highly coordinated. It had to be because we were producing an exhibit as remote, geographically, and temporally distant collaborators who would neither meet face-to-face nor communicate telephonically during the entire designing process.

35 In this sense, *The Reading Wall* functioned as a cultural interface—which is Lev Manovich's (2001: 70) term for a human-computer-culture interface: the interface "computers present [that] allow us to interact with cultural data." Manovich points out that new media interfaces always draw on the graphic and communicative conventions of older cultural forms.

36 In fact, Stuart Moulthrop and Nancy Kaplan (2004), two of the foremost contemporary thinkers about the nature of "literacy beyond books," argue that we should discontinue the use of the term *literacy* in favor of the term "competencies." They suggest the term "new literacy" to mean the "understanding [that] any text or writing practice is at least potentially connected to a hypertextual network . . . A new literacy also needs to consider the extension of alphabetism into social processing." See also Kaplan (1991; 1995; 2001).

37 In September 2000, near the end of the installation at the Tech Museum, I organized a symposium at Xerox PARC on the topic, "New Media, New Literacies." Thirty participants from different domains of industry, academia, and the media, including journalists, K-12 school superintendents, teachers, parents, museum exhibit designers, and artists spent the day discussing three key topics: What is the relationship between technology and literacy, historically and currently? How does one assess the cultural implications of emerging technologies? How do digital media influence the practices of reading and writing?

38 Paul Cesarini (2004) plots the historical changes in the term "technological literacy," including the way in which it became equated with "computer literacy."

39 One proponent of this view is Clifford Stoll (2000: 4), who expresses deep skepticism of "computer literacy" programs: "Learning how to use a computer—as opposed to programming a computer—is essentially a mechanical task, one that does not require or encourage creativity . . . Computer literacy doesn't demand the same level of instruction as English, American history, or physics. It doesn't require the same amount of effort either. Spending semesters teaching

computing simply subtracts time from other subjects . . . Computers encourage students to turn in visually exciting hypermedia projects, often at the expense of written compositions and hand-drawn projects."

40 Kathleen Tyner (1998: 11–12) provides a thoughtful analysis of how the construction of a new public library in San Francisco provided the occasion for a resurgence of cultural anxiety focused on the changing nature of literacy in a digital age: "But according to the critics of the New Main [library of San Francisco], library technology came at the expense of library books . . . The card catalog became the rallying post for their collective ire. To the lovers of the card catalog, the demise of the physical card catalogs was a loss of tremendous proportion that went beyond mere inconvenience. Digital records represented an irretrievable loss of knowledge, an obliteration of the past."

41 Even so, there are significant issues to address in considering the deployment of computer technologies to fix K-12 education. For example, Frederick Bennett (2002: 623) points out that "During this five-year period [1994–1999], [U.S.] schools acquired huge number of computers," yet the results of the National Assessment of Educational Progress "showed no significant change for reading, mathematics, or science for three age groups tested—nine year olds, thirteen year olds, and seventeen year olds." In arguing for the importance of the computer as a technology of literacy, Daniel Downes (2005: 81) writes that: "television therefore works against literacy in favouring image over idea, emotional response over analysis."

42 As one analyst writes, "there is no question that we will continue to invest heavily in technology in our schools, but we will never understand the most effective role for technology in K-12 education until we articulate clearly our educational goals and how we want to achieve them. If we do not articulate our educational goals and strategies first, we will never understand how to align technology with educational practice to realize the goal of improving student learning" (Rappaport, 2003).

43 Larry Cuban (2001) investigates whether or not the large-scale investment in computer hardware has improved educational practices and student learning.

44 One of the reasons I hesitate to go much further in invoking discussions about literacy and technology is that the topics and projects are proliferating in wildly productive ways. See for example the differences among the following projects: Seiter (2005); Semali (2000); Gee (2004); King (2001); Tyner (1998).

45 Taking this a step further, John Beynon and Hughie Mackay (1992: 2) suggest that the focus on "technological literacy" requires educators to "learn to 'read' technology" for its social and cultural aspects.

46 Cindy Selfe's (1999: 11) description of technological literacy comes closest to articulating what I would hope for from such a definition: "[A] complex set of socially and culturally situated values, practices, and skills involved in operating linguistically within the context of electronic environments, including reading, writing, and communicating . . . In this context, technological literacy refers to

social and cultural contexts for discourse and communication, as well as the social and linguistic products and practices of communication and the ways in which electronic communication environments have become essential parts of our cultural understanding of what it means to be literate."

47 In that the xfr interactives only focused on reading literacies, the cultural work of this exhibit was still one-sided. Andrea diSessa (2000: 113) calls this "consumer literacy," which she argues is only one aspect of literacy. "Two-way literacies," in her view, are those that involve both consuming and producing. She suggests that we don't have a wide consumer literacy of science and mathematics, unlike for novels and popular literature; but even here, we don't have wide productive literacy either. But as Kathleen Tyner (1998: 4) rightly points out, even if citizens could both "read and write the world," (her interpretation of the cultural importance of literacies), it is unlikely that this would automatically translate into an equal distribution of social power. "It is obvious that those who control both the channels of distribution and the skillful production of compatible content have access to the most favorable opportunities to influence social policy through sustained creative effort." Nonetheless, mastery of basic literacy skills is still required to even join the conversation.

48 There is some debate about whether or not the practice or field of "information design" is new. Brenda Dervin (1999) argues that information has always been designed.

49 It is fair to note that this interest in the creation of signature public interactives is prompted as much by the changing landscape of edutainment options that increase the competition for tourist and visitor attention and fees as it is by a sense of the lasting importance of these innovative technologies and sciences.

50 The use of innovative technologies in the creation of interactive exhibits has become a new design expertise. Soon after the red group left Xerox parc, another cultural institution invited two of my former red colleagues and me to build another version of *The Reading Wall*. This invitation provided the catalyst for the creation of a new company called Onomy Labs, Inc. that articulated its core philosophy as "design for culture." The early clients of Onomy Labs included museums as well as technology-transfer managers. These clients were interested in engaging Onomy Labs in the design of new exhibitions for the purposes of demonstrating innovative technologies. Onomy Labs expanded on red's research methodology to develop a more elaborate research-design-fabrication practice built on the commitment to "take culture seriously" in the creation of new technologies. Onomy Labs promoted its interactives as "narrative devices" that were designed to tell new and interesting stories about the meaning of new technologies. In this way, Onomy Labs began to build a business in "exhibiting innovation" by creating innovative narrative devices. While at Onomy Labs, I had the occasion to write two additional interactive applications for different cultural contexts, each of which offers a different historical narrative about the cultural meaning of technological development. In the process and in response to these

new design opportunities, the earlier version of the xfr *Reading Wall* was re-engineered and christened the Onomy *Interactive Digital Wall*.

four: Designing Learning

1 The notion of the Singularity was popularized by science fiction author Vernor Vinge in an article in *Omni* magazine in 1983. It was a theoretical fiction of mathematicians and early computer scientists such as John von Neumann (as credited by Ulam, 1958) and I. J. Good (1965). Ray Kurzweil (1992) has been one of the strongest contemporary proponents of the coming of the Singularity.

2 As Roy Rosensweig (2003: 739), a prominent theorist of the digital humanities, claims, "historians, in fact, may be facing a fundamental paradigm shift from a culture of scarcity to a culture of abundance." Where once it was common to worry about the loss of a culture's heritage, with the advent of new digital technologies and the World Wide Web, the products of culture are easily and often widely archived. He teases out the contradictions inherent in this shift, to argue that the abundance of digital data does not necessarily enable better historical scholarship. He makes a convincing case for the need for historians to pay attention not only to the history of the past, but also the *futures* of the past.

3 Jenkins (2006a: 243) characterizes this paradigm shift in the following way: "Convergence represents a paradigm shift—a move from medium-specific content toward content that flows across multiple media channels, toward the increased interdependence of communication systems, toward multiple ways of accessing media content, and toward ever more complex relations between two-down corporate media and bottom-up participatory culture."

4 Alvin Toffler (1981) first coined the term "prosumer." It actually has two related meanings in common usage. The first connotation suggests a consumer who participates in some way in the production of a commodity; in this way, the term relates to mass customization. More recently the term has been used to describe the phenomenon whereby media users (consumers) are also media producers (content creators and contributors).

5 While Jenkins (2006a) is careful not to paint a too rosy picture about the likely outcomes of the current paradigm shift—he reminds us that new obstacles and new modes of power will emerge on the other side of this shifting set of cultural dynamics—he does argue that the shift will likely result in new practices, new institutional forms, and new possibilities for the enactment of democracy.

6 Charles Stross (2005) explores the contours of post-Singularity human existence in his science fiction novel, *Accelerado*. Critics as well as fans identify it as one of the most elaborated thought experiments about human life after the Singularity.

7 I remind readers that Vernor Vinge was one of the first to imagine (in his fictional story "True Names") the network of computers that we would now recognize as the Internet. See Frenkel (2001). For Vinge's comments on *The Singularity*, see Vinge (1993).

8 There is also research in computer science on the development of IA's—where the acronym refers not to Vinge's notion of intelligence amplification but rather to the concept of intelligent agents. Milind Tambe, a colleague in computer science at the University of Southern California, and his research group, TEAMCORE, design software agents as members of hybrid human-computer systems. Tambe conducts research on the creation of multi-agent systems based on real-world problems such as the coordination of resources for diaster response teams. Distributed, cooperative (software) agents work collaboratively with human team members to manage complex information ecologies. See Tambe et al. (1995).

9 Much of my early work on technologies of the gendered body focused on the cultural implications of the decorporealization of post-humanist fantasies of human evolution. See Balsamo (1996).

10 In taking on this topic, I am greatly inspired by conversations with John Seely Brown. For a sample of his written work on these topics see also Brown (2002); Brown and Duguid (1998; 2000; 2002).

11 What proof can I offer that we are actually in the midst of a paradigm shift? I can offer none, really, if by proof we refer to the traditional sense of providing empirical evidence of a wide-scale change in worldview. Paradigms and paradigm shifts don't work this way. Thomas Kuhn (1962; 1970) was clear to assert that new paradigms are not adopted, initially, because of the presentation of rational evidence. If that were the case, there would be no need for a new paradigm; the evidence and the construction of "rationality" would have been sufficiently provided by the previous paradigm. Instead, Kuhn explains:

> The man [sic] who embraces a new paradigm at an early stage must often do so in defiance of the evidence provided by problem solving. He must, that is, have faith that the new paradigm will succeed with the many large problems that confront it, knowing only that the older paradigm has failed with a few . . . Something must make at least a few scientists feel that the new proposal is on the right track, and sometimes it is only personal and inarticulate aesthetic considerations that can do that . . . Rather than a single group conversion, what occurs is an increasing shift in the distribution of professional allegiances . . . Nevertheless if they are competent, they will improve it, explore its possibilities, and show what it would be like to belong to the community guided by it (1970: 158–59).

12 Even though Marc Prensky (2001a) is the one who first popularized the terms "digital natives and digital immigrants," he acknowledges the influence of Douglas Rushkoff's statement about kids as natives and adults as immigrants in a digital landscape. For his acknowledgement of Rushkoff's influence see Prensky (2001b: 414n).

13 John Seely Brown (2000) develops the notion of "growing up digital" to describe the experiences of young people who grew up with the web. Brown makes the important observation that the web for these young people is not a discrete technology but part of an emerging multimodal ecology of learning.

14 David Buckingham (2002) cautions against making grand claims about the digital literacies and experiences of children born within a particular time period—such as the dates that mark the diffusion of new media technologies. He calls for the careful investigation of the differences that play out among groups of children in their access, use, and mastery of particular new media applications (such as games) and devices (such as mobile phones).

15 See especially Danielle Bernstein (1991). There is a significant amount of feminist research that investigates the differences in experiences with technology. This was the subject of my first book (Balsamo, 1996). For more recent work on gender and technology use, see Margolis and Fisher (2002). On the topic of gender and game playing, the first major serious treatment was Cassell and Jenkins (1998). Continuing the discussion and reflecting on the rapid changes in gender and gaming experiences is Kafai et al. (2008), which focused attention on the broader media contexts that serve as the ecologies within which gaming experiences unfold.

16 Sherry Turkle's work (1984; 1997) is foundational on this topic. An early symposium on the mutability of subjectivity in virtual worlds was held at the St. Norbert Arts Center in October 1999. The organizer, Vera Lemecha, suggested that the focus of the symposium was to investigate questions such as, "What are the implications for the self-created subject as constituted on the Internet in relation to the real-time subject?" (Lemecha and Stone, 2001: 8). See also Shaviro (2003), Hayles (2005), Meadows (2008), and Boellstorff (2008).

17 A Delphi group is a large group of people used as a statistical sampling resource.

18 This section contains material excerpted from the article "A Pedagogy for Original Synners," (Anderson and Balsamo, 2007). The use of the term "synners" is an explicit reference to Pat Cadigan's novel, *Synners* (1991). For another discussion of the education of original synners in the context of creating a cultural studies curriculum within an engineering institute see Balsamo (2000b). I am not really advocating the use of the tag Original Synners as the primary identity-maker for young people who have grown up with pervasive access to digital technologies. I use it simply to mark the place of a new subject formation. While I am guilty of returning to it often, not only in this chapter, but also in other written work, I really use it tongue-in-cheek. In doing so, I am trying to avoid the generational essentialism of the "born-digital generation." It's difficult when trying to talk about an emergent sensibility that evolves through the interconnections among people (youth), technologies, cultural influences, and social practices to avoid essentialist, and of course, misleading terms.

19 In her essay, "Teaching in Your Sleep," Constance Penley (1989: 172) elaborates the psychoanalytic dynamic of teaching that shows the necessity of teachers as lifelong learners: "For learning to take place, there must always be an Other . . . Thus it cannot be said that the teacher (or student) *contains* knowledge, but that it comes about in the intersection of two partially unconscious speeches which both say more than they know . . . What we finally come to understand is both the psychical necessity and the actual contingency of these shifting and interchange-

able positions. The student becomes a teacher when he or she realizes that it is impossible to know everything, that to be a teacher one must never stop being a student. And the teacher can teach *nothing other than the way he or she learns.*"

20 While it is not the purpose of this chapter to delve into a discussion of a philosophy of learning for the digital age, suffice it to say that the time is ripe for revisiting the constructivist (or instrumentalist) learning theories of John Dewey, Paolo Freire, and Lev Vygotsky. While Dewey (1916) is one of his best known, perhaps his most relevant work on this topic is found in the later book ([1938] 1998), where he reflects on two decades of experimentation in the creation of progressive educational programs. Paolo Freire ([1970] 1998) strongly advocated for the dissolution of the dichotomy of teacher and student, in favor of a more fluid exchange between who teaches and who learns in the educational encounter. Vygotsky (1926) is a classic. For a useful introduction to Vygotsky's important essays, see Cole et al. (1978). For a more recent discussion of Vygotsky's learning theory, see Kozulin et al. (2003).

21 This insight may not be news to those community-based educators who were responsible for the creation of media literacy programs throughout the 1990s, but it is an insight that has only gained popularity more recently. Although it is difficult to determine when and where the very first community media literacy program was started, some noteworthy early efforts include the San Francisco-based program called *TILT*. Started in 1995 by video artist Lise Swenson, *TILT*'s mission is to "teach young people the fundamentals of moviemaking and media literacy through hands-on training in video production" (http://tilt.ninthstreet.org/).

22 To date Katie Salen has not published a discussion of her trenchant question, Where is school for the born digital generation? I have heard her present her work and have had the pleasure of many conversations with her during which we have discussed this question. Her published work to date focuses on game design. See, for example, Zimmerman and Salen (2003). She is currently the executive director of design for Quest to Learn which is the first public school in the United States to implement a game-based curriculum.

23 While the notion of a distributed learning network is not new, it is being revisited in light of this observation about the learning experiences of the born-digital generation. My first introduction to the term came from my sister, a sergeant in the U.S. Army, who referred me to an Army initiative called the "Advanced Distributed Learning Network" which I subsequently learned was launched in 1997 to "ensure access to high-quality education and training materials that can be tailored to individual learner needs and can be made available whenever and wherever they are required" (Downes, 2000). More recently, the MacArthur Foundation project on Digital Media and Learning includes several research efforts to study the formation and design of multi-institutional distributed learning networks. Key people involved in the MacArthur-sponsored efforts include: Diana Rhoten at SSRC, Nichole Pinkard at the University of Chicago, and Katie Salen at the Parsons School of Design.

24 This research project was sponsored by the John D. and Catherine T. MacArthur Foundation. Members of the USC research team included Susana Bautista, John Brennan, Perry Hoberman, Maura Klosterman, and Cara Wallis. The project, called "Inspiring the Technological Imagination," grew out of work from the current project on Designing Culture. I was interested in how museums and community libraries contribute to the cultivation of the technological imagination. The results of this research effort have not been formally published, but the literature review was disseminated through a series of blog posts authored by myself and members of the research team at the MacArthur Foundation sponsored web portal called DML Central. The blog postings are cited under Balsamo et al. (2009).

25 The importance of learning skills of synthesis and integration has been part of the discussion about the development of critical reading techniques for more than fifty years. See Adler and Van Dorn (1972).

26 Readers familiar with the history of cultural studies will recognize the inspiration for the creation of this diagram from Richard Johnson (1986/87). Paul duGay et al. (1997) offers an elaborated model of a circuit of culture that designates the way in which different stages of production and consumption interact and feed into one another.

27 One of the more common characterizations of lifelong learning is as the name for government programs and initiatives that address the continuing educational interests of older citizens. The Canadian government, for example, allows citizens to withdraw funds from their retirement accounts to pay for lifelong learning programs through the Lifelong Learning Plan (LLP) (http://www.servicecanada .gc.ca/). Similar programs exist in the UK and in various European countries (http://www.lifelonglearning.co.uk/).

28 As much as these projects—the programs developed at the Institute for Multimedia Literacy (IML) and the backchannel experiments at the Interactive Media Division—belong within the context of USC, they must be considered edge practices within the institution. While they were initially supported by external research funding, that funding has been spent. Continued support for further innovations has become increasingly difficult to obtain, the IML constantly teeters on being shut down, and its programs are costly to staff. I'm not singling out USC in particular, however. The precarious position of the IML points to one of the broader problems with edge practices: they may be innovative and provocative, but they are also always in danger of disappearing because they are not economically viable in the context of the contemporary fiscal priorities of the university. Most likely these practices are not going to yield patents for the university's portfolio, or new revenue streams. These projects, which directly address the university's rhetoric of innovative learner-centered pedagogy, are too expensive compared to the large lecture classroom "sage on the stage" model of education, and are often left to wither on the vine without central institutional support. Without such support, the programs disappear, the innovations dissi-

pate, and the transformative efforts lose momentum. While there are some philanthropic organizations, notably the John D. and Catherine T. MacArthur Foundation, that are stepping up efforts to fund innovative research on new digital media learning practices, this funding does not include provisions for sustaining the efforts within a particular institutional context. This is one of the intractable aspects of these new projects. While they might attract initial funding, and indeed may even articulate strongly with the institution's strategic educational mission, they require the allocation of resources to maintain over time.

29 The IML was founded by Elizabeth Daley, the dean of the USC School of Cinematic Arts, in 1998. Her vision for the IML, as developed in conversation with school alumnus George Lucas, was the creation of an educational unit that would offer programs and activities drawing on the rich visual language and dynamic modes of expression of the cinematic arts. Her vision of multimedia literacy is developed in Daley (2003). I served as the Director of Academic Programs at the IML from 2004 to 2008.

30 The IML administers two educational programs: the Honors in Multimedia Scholarship Program is a four-year, undergraduate program open to students across the university, while the Multimedia in the Core Program introduces multimedia authoring into the university's General Education program via single-semester classes designed to reach a broad segment of the USC undergraduate population. See http://iml.usc.edu/.

31 Howard Gardner (2006a; 2006b) explicitly informs the development of IML's programs and pedagogical frameworks.

32 This is clearly one of the limitations to the portability of IML's media-rich learning approach to other institutional contexts. During the first eight years of its existence while the IML enjoyed the generous support of Atlantic Philanthropies (AP), the institute employed a wide range of teachers, researchers, and media production specialists to facilitate and support the production of students' multimedia projects. The challenge facing the IML in its next phase is to create a new structure for the support and delivery of its pedagogical activities. As large-scale funding opportunities such as that provided by AP become increasingly difficult to obtain, the lessons learned by IML must be disseminated and adapted to the shifting landscapes of higher education.

33 In 2005, I organized a workshop for teachers from schools across the U.S. on the topic of "Transforming Teaching Using Multimedia." This workshop was co-facilitated by Mary Hocks (Georgia State University) and Anne Wysoki (University of Wisconsin), and incorporated many of the training exercises that had been developed by staff at the IML over the previous three years.

34 Jim Gee (2003) has established the key terms of the conversation about games and learning. Selfe and Hawisher (2007) expand the topics under discussion by including important essays on gaming and difference that consider issues such as girls and gaming, racial representations in games, sexual identity and game play, and the experience of gray (mature) game players. Early work that contributed to

the discussion on game playing and literacy include: Patricia Marks Greenfield (1984) and J. C. Herz (1997). Cassell and Jenkins (1998) carefully sorted through the facts and fictions surrounding the issue of girls and games. Marc Prensky (2001b) considers the use of video games for teaching adults in corporations and the military. More recent work that explores the relationship between gaming and the design of educational experiences include Salen (2008). Salen and the organization "Institute of Play" are involved in efforts to create a new public school in New York which would use gaming pedagogy throughout the entire school curriculum. See http://www.instituteofplay.com/.

35 Stone (2006) discussed the concept of "continuous partial attention."

36 The Interactive Media Division classroom known as the Zemeckis Media Lab (ZML) was created in 2000 by Scott Fisher and Mark Bolas. In 2010 it was dismantled as part of a massive space restructuring in the Zemeckis building.

37 The use of a "Google jockey" refutes the polemic media blitz that posited the question: "Is Google Making Us Stupid?" (Carr, 2008). When I ask students to take on the role of "Google jockey," I reframe their contribution in terms of serving as a web archeologist. The practice is the same in that they are asked to surf the web using Google (or the search engine of their choice) to uncover web-based contributions to unfolding classroom discussions.

38 The creation of this classroom space was only one of the research efforts conducted by IMD faculty to invent and implement new forms of display technologies for immersive and semi-immersive applications (Fisher et al., 2005). Another system is a rear projected 300-degree field of view cylindrical display, driven by eleven projectors with geometry correction and edge blending hardware (Bolas et al., 2006).

39 Other innovative pedagogical efforts that also explore the use of hybrid learning spaces include a project by Bruce Zuckerman (professor of religion at USC) that brought together undergraduate students from USC and the University of Illinois at Urbana-Champaign to conduct original research on ancient cylinder seals from a collection at the William R. and Clarice V. Spurlock Museum at UIUC. Educational resources were culled from Zuckerman's distributed research effort, the West Semitic Research project, that includes a distributed, digital archival database called "InscriptiFact." This database contains photographic and computer images of ancient objects and texts, such as the Dead Sea Scrolls. Zuckerman and his colleagues (Kenneth Zuckerman and Marilyn Lundberg) developed InscriptiFact to enable researchers around the world to view images of ancient documents taken under different camera and light conditions that reveal different aspects of the document pieces. The students in Zuckerman's course collaborated with UIUC students to photograph and annotate several new cylinder seals to add to the InscriptiFact database. One of the things discovered by virtue of the students' imaging efforts was the fingerprint of an ancient scribe, embedded in the surface of one of the seals. In this course, the students not only learned *about*

archeology, but were also *engaged* in the practices of archeological research and knowledge making. See Johnson (2006/7).

40 The term "applied research" is rarely elaborated as "transformative" in the various university strategic plans that now call for this kind of research effort. Here I draw on the strategic plan created by the University of Southern California (my academic employer while working on this book). First published in 2004, this document outlines a new vision to guide the university's work in the next decade. One of the strategic objectives focuses explicitly on the need to develop research programs that address societal problems. But USC isn't the only university to call for a focus on applied research. The strategic plan of my alma mater, the University of Illinois at Urbana-Champaign, includes a similar objective: "Recognize that our long-term ability to contribute to human progress comes through a balance between pursuing fundamental scholarship and research, and addressing the more immediate concerns of society" (University of Illinois at Urbana-Champaign, 2007).

41 This approach resonates with the insights developed by Graeme Sullivan (2010: 110) in his explication of art practice as transformative research.

42 The example offered by Davidson and Goldberg (2004) comes from a 2002 interview by Jeffrey D. Sachs, Professor of Economics and Director of the Earth Institute at Columbia University, who is also Special Adviser to United Nations Secretary-General on the Millennium Development Goals. Davidson and Goldberg cite a statement made by Sachs where he "insisted that interdisciplinarity was the only way to solve world problems." "The need," he said, was "to focus not on the disciplines but on the problems and to bring together five main areas in an intensive dialogue: the earth sciences, ecological sciences, engineering, public health, and the social sciences with a heavy dose of economics."

43 Bowker et al. (1997) describe the historical development of the "border crossings" between the social sciences and the computational sciences that eventually resulted in the formation of new (inter)disciplinary fields of research such as human computer interaction (HCI), computer supported cooperate work (CSCW), and, more recently, social informatics.

44 Important early work includes Suchman (1987). Other groundbreaking research includes Star (1989) and Sproull's and Kiesler (1986).

45 To promote the role of the humanities in the process of technological innovation, a group of humanities program directors, including Davidson and Goldberg, formed a virtual organization called HASTAC: *Humanities, Arts, Science and Technology Advanced Collaboratory* that has as its mission the "development of humane technologies and technological humanism." As a virtual organization for the coordination of efforts across centers and institutions, HASTAC serves as a "commons" for the exchange and dissemination of information and the coordination of collaborative activities that take place in distributed geographic locations. While each HASTAC affiliate has its specific objectives shaped by the particular

resources and sets of interests of local institutional participants, considered together, the collaborators who participate in HASTAC have initiated a broad and ambitious set of projects designed not only to reengineer the relationship between the humanities and technology innovation, but to broaden the scope of interdisciplinary technology innovation (http://www.hastac.org/).

46 The engagement between the humanities and technology has a long history. Given that philosophy has long been a key discipline within the institutional formation known in the U.S. as "the humanities," we know that this engagement dates back centuries. In tracing the more recent development of the philosophy of technology (as a humanistic endeavor), philosopher Carl Mitcham (1994) turns to the work of Lewis Mumford as one of its four founding figures. Mumford ([1934] 1962) called for humanists to pay attention to the "human values" in machinery, and to the "spiritual contributions" of the machine to culture. In addition to Mumford, Mitcham identifies three other key figures as founders of a humanistic philosophy of technology: José Ortga y Gasset; Martin Heidegger; and Jacques Ellul. Insofar as cultural studies, as another significant field of humanistic inquiry, builds on the work of an entire tradition of critical theory, especially the work of those associated with the Frankfurt School, the engagement between cultural studies and technology has a long history. Many of the figures whose work is central to the development of critical theory had also investigated cultural dimensions of science and technology. Consider, for example, the work of Marx, Marcuse, Habermas, and Polanyi (to name just a few): key theoretical terms such as "ideology," "the public sphere," and "capitalism," were debated and clarified specifically in reference to the practices of technologists and the expropriation of a scientific worldview in the development of industrial and postindustrial societies. See also Durbin (1980), Ferre (1988), Ihde (1979; 1991; 1993), Marcuse (1964), Polanyi (1958), and Winner (1977; 1986).

Out of this historical engagement between the humanities and technology, as it interfaces with the multifaceted development of critical theory and cultural studies, we can discern the emergence of a new field of study that could be identified as technohumanism. Although the emergence of this field has gained momentum during the past two decades, it is related to, but not isomorphic with, the popularization of the notion of postmodernism (as either a cultural logic or a discursive formation). I use the term technohumanism to name a field of intellectual work that has as its aim the methodological investigation of the relationship between the humanities and technology, the relationship between the human being and the technological, and the way in which these relationships take shape in different historical moments, in different geo-political contexts, and at different levels of abstraction. The creative, political, and I would emphasize, thoroughly practical aim of this field is to influence the shape of these relationships in the future.

47 Although the scholarship that is identified by the name "cultural studies" is quite diverse, and indeed, often provokes heated denouncements from the most

generously minded scholars, this body of work presents ways to critically analyze the social and cultural implications of contemporary technology. While the relationship between the project that now goes by the name of "cultural studies" and the work conducted in the name of the more traditional humanities—such as literary studies, literary history, and interpretive theory—is a fascinating story of paradigm shifts, academic politics, and the anxiety of influence, it is a story that is a bit off the topic of this book. For a discussion about the relationship between feminist literary studies and feminist cultural studies, see Balsamo (1991). For a discussion of the relationship between cultural studies and literary studies, see Balsamo and Greer (1993; 1994).

48 This shift work shares a sensibility with efforts by artists and other creative producers to foster interdisciplinary collaborative art practices. For example, artist-innovator Michael Century (2006) describes the need for the development of "studio-labs" where artists and technologists can collaborate on the construction of new media technologies as well as on the creation of new media art. Century argues that culturally significant innovation requires the creation of a new kind of institutional space: what he calls the "studio-laboratory where new media technologies are designed and developed in co-evolution with their creative application." Citing the work of the *Experiments in Art and Technology* (EAT) and various artist-in-residence programs, Century notes that people have recognized the need for these spaces for more than fifty years. In support of his assertion that artists are important (but often overlooked) initiators of technological innovation, Century offers the following example: "In 1974, pioneering electronic artist Nam June Paik assumed the role of technological forecaster and submitted a report to the Rockefeller Foundation urging the construction of a global 'broadband telecommunications infrastructure.' While critical of mandarin intellectual disdain for mass media, surprisingly Paik did not even bother to advocate spending on the avant-garde arts, or on the promotion of the work of his fellow video artists. Rather, he envisioned a two-way, high-capacity video and data network the 'electronic superhighway' that would augur a profound cultural shift."

49 For a discussion of the important role of middle managers in the incubation and support of multidisciplinary collaborative research teams, see Davidson and Goldberg (2006).

50 For a discussion of the blind spots of the humanities to consider the work going on in the sciences on specifically human capacities such as creativity and the "nature" of human nature, see Harpham (2006).

51 Mimi Ito discusses the "genres of participation" that emerge through children's use of new media. She describes the kind of social exchange that unfolds as "hypersocial" where social interactions occur on many levels and through many channels among "geographically-local peer groups, among dispersed populations mediated by the Internet, and through organized gatherings such as conventions and tournaments" (2008: 8).

52 An early example of a research project exploring new forms of digital publication is the *Labyrinth Project*. The Labyrinth Research Initiative, directed by film theorist Marsha Kinder, investigates the role of the reader/viewer as a performer of interactive narrative. Initiated in 1996, the project has published numerous works of interactive narrative on CD-ROM and DVD. The goals of the project, according to Kinder (1999), are "to expand the language, art, culture, and theory of interactive narrative and to produce emotionally compelling electronic fictions that combine filmic language with interactive storytelling." As such, it represented an early and sustained effort to prototype new genres of digital scholarship. See http://college.usc.edu/labyrinth/.

53 During the course of the publication of the first four issues, the collaborations among scholars and designers resulted in the creation of the first examples of what could be considered a new genre of digital scholarship: the animated archive. See, for example, Chun (2007); Emigh (2005); Gambrell (2005); Goldberg and Hristova (2007); and Terry (2007). As one of the emerging genres made possible by dynamic media, the animated archive employs the journal's database authoring environment as a methodology for thinking through the relationships among multimodal archival materials. No longer simply an encyclopedic enterprise, the construction of a database of archival materials requires the creation of interpretive links that connect materials to each other. Individual archival elements are tagged in different ways and invested with different properties. This structure often provokes the author/designer to think with more complexity about the interpretive meaning of the relations among individual archival elements. The meaning of the database structure is built through the interpretive practices of the author/designer, as he or she works through the processes of digitally coding and tagging archival materials. The database structure thus serves as the scaffolding for new ways of thinking and new forms of scholarly communication and presentation.

54 This history of these digital publishing efforts represents an interesting genealogy of the cross-pollination of popular culture, digital forms of entertainment, and social networking applications. For example, the development of *Kairos* grew out of early educational experiments in the creation and use of multi-user dungeons/domains (MUDS) and object-oriented MUDS (MOOS). These digital environments grew out of paper-based role-playing games such as *Dungeons and Dragons*. Officially launched in 1995, *Kairos* publishes "webtexts" that are born-digital. This means that from the beginning *Kairos* was interested not in the use of the web merely for the more expeditious distribution of print-based scholarship, but for how it might reconfigure the textual practices of scholars. As its website states, the journal seeks to "push boundaries in academic publishing at the same time we strive to bridge the gap between print and digital publishing cultures" (http://english.ttu.edu/Kairos/).

55 To assist these collaborations, the *Vectors* team developed a back-end database application that scholars use to organize and explore their research materials. The

elements of the database for any given project might include images, text, clips of dynamic media, citations, web links, analyses, interpretations, simulations, or recreations. In interacting and designing the elements of the database for their projects, author/designers rethink the relationships among research materials. In the process, new insights and interpretations emerge that were not always present in the beginning. As editor McPherson (2010: 211) explains, "As they work with a database form, scholars are exposed to flexible rule-sets and relational data. This in turn encourages iterative interaction and exploration of the connections between ideas and research elements." By working with database structures, authors/designers engage in extensive practices of relational thinking. They employ the affordances of multimodal forms of expression for the exploration of nonlinear argument. Although the creation of new authoring tools was not the primary objective of the *Vectors* publication project, what emerged during the production of the first four issues was the development of a middleware tool, called the "Dynamic Backend Generator" (DBG). Not only the need for the tool, but the design of its affordances emerged out of the deep collaborations among members of the editorial/design team and outside author/designers.

56 The National Science Foundation launched a program in 2007 called CreativeIT, which provides funding for projects that involve the participation of creative practitioners in transformative research projects in computer science, information technology, and science education (NSF, 2008).

57 See the discussion of hermeneutic reverse engineering in the introduction and chapter 1, which is a methodological approach to the study of how technologies are built, how they are implemented, and how they affect and reproduce culture.

58 The mission statement for the Massachusetts Institute of Technology is found at http://web.mit.edu/mission.html. Faculty participation in the OCW remains voluntary, but the long-term goal of the initiative is to make available the complete MIT curriculum of over eighteen hundred classes. The OCW administration assists with publishing course materials online and dealing with copyright clearances for course readings and materials; this institutional support is a crucial part of the success of this initiative.

59 MIT sought to collaborate with other institutions around the world, from early in the process. Any institution wishing to participate in OCW only had to agree to publish a minimum of ten courses under its own university's name. By late 2004, the OCW model had been adopted by several other institutions, and resulted in similar undertakings such as Carnegie Mellon University's Open Learning Initiative, Rice University's Connexions project, and the Open University's OpenLearn project, all of which shared the initial ideals of openness and ease of access established by MIT's model. During the first seven years of its existence, the MIT initiative published more than fourteen hundred graduate and undergraduate classes from the MIT curriculum. As of early 2007, MIT's Open CourseWare consortium includes universities on five continents (http://ocwconsortium .org/). The Rice University Connexions project also includes a set of open source

software tools (http://cnx.org/). The Carnegie Mellon Open Learning project includes instructional materials that draw on cognitive learning theory and offers assessment instruments of learning objectives (http://oli.web.cmu.edu/open learning/). Other projects include the Open University Learning Space, which builds on that institution's strong history in making higher education materials available to the public through partnerships with national media organizations such as the BBC (http://openlearn.open.ac.uk/).

60 One factor that contributed to the rapid rate of adoption of the Open Course-Ware movement was the broad success (in both commercial and non-commercial realms) of open source software development over the past two decades. Open source software is one mode of non-hierarchical communal programming, in which loosely affiliated networks of programmers contribute their efforts to a codebase without direct compensation. With some exceptions, members of the community at large may use the resulting software in commercial applications as long as the code remains openly available and changeable. At present, the commercial impact of open source programming on Internet-based technologies is incalculable, with the majority of network servers, databases, and operating systems utilizing some form of open source software. Although few forms of creative production lend themselves as readily to open source production as software programming, a number of similar undertakings have emerged from within other spheres of artistic, scholarly, and technical endeavor. These range from the open source cinema movements centered in the UK and the Netherlands to various open content organizations in the San Francisco Bay area, such as Creative Commons (http://creativecommons.org/), the Internet Archive (http://www.archive.org/), the Electronic Frontier Foundation (http://www.eff.org/), the Open Source Initiative (http://www.opensource.org/), and the Prelinger Library (http://www.prelingerlibrary.org/), all of which take as their point of departure the value of peer-to-peer information sharing and the support of participatory culture.

61 The Atkins, Brown, and Hammond (2007) report examines the William and Flora Hewlett Foundation's past investments in Open Educational Resources and the emerging impact of this framework. It ends with a thought-provoking exploration of future opportunities.

62 On the last point, a number of research efforts and organizations are examining ways to sustain the OER movement by creating partnerships between educational institutions and other kinds of learning organizations. Groups such as the Monterey Institute for Technology and Education (MITE) (http://www.monterey institute.org/) and the Institute for the Studies of Knowledge Management in Education (ISKME) (http://www.oercommons.org/) have begun to explore the potentials of extra-institutional learning. The aim is both to reduce the cost of the production of digital learning materials and to expand the range of the learning landscape for the purposes of equalizing access to educational opportunities across the globe.

63 Atkins, Brown, and Hammond (2007) cites the source of these figures as Sir John Daniels, President and CEO of the Commonwealth of Learning in Canada, and former Vice chancellor of the Open University, UK (http://www.col.org/).

64 The other two initiatives include the development of e-science and cyberinfrastructure-enhanced science, and cyberinfrastructure enhanced humanities. The global grand challenges are described as 1) significantly transforming the effectiveness of and participation in scientific discovery and learning; 2) enabling engaged world universities, meta-universities, and huge global increase in access to high-quality education; and 3) creating cultures of learning for supporting people to thrive in a rapidly evolving knowledge-based world (Atkins, Brown, and Hammond, 2007: 36).

65 Schwartz (2008).

66 Keeps (2008).

67 Here I'm referring to creative kits such as the PicoCricket invention kit created by Mitch Resnick's group at the MIT Media Lab (http://www.picocricket.com/). See also the range of important work coming out of Resnick's Lifelong Kindergarten Research group (http://llk.media.mit.edu/). An example of a public interactive being prototyped for use in these institutions include Onomy Lab's interactive globe.

68 Mark Hatch, the Chief Operating Office for the TechShop, identifies four major member groups: hobbyists, artists, entrepreneurs, and small business owners (personal communication). It offers a menu of monthly classes on various machines. All members must complete a basic "Safety and Basic Usage" class that covers tool and equipment safety. The company carries liability insurance to cover accidents, and requires a waiver of liability release form for use of the equipment. Children under the age of eighteen can work at the TechShop under the direct supervision of a parent or legal guardian. There are several classes available for youth as young as twelve. The TechShop has developed a viable business model that supports its services: in addition to the Menlo Park site, there are TechShops in Raleigh, North Carolina, and Portland, Oregon, with three additional sites slated for opening by the end of 2010 (http://www.techshop.ws/).

69 TELIC Arts Exchange is the creation of directors Fiona Whitton and Sean Dockray. Its mission is to "provide a place for multiple publics to engage with contemporary forms of media, art and architecture" (http://www.telic.info/). The Public School is one of several global projects such as the Peer-to-Peer University (P2PU) that are prototyping the use of social networks as one of the critical components of creating an alternative learning ecology that connects people who want to learn with people who have something to teach. It will be interesting to watch the infrastructure that develops to mediate among the interests of teachers and learners. Where formal institutions of learning employ disciplinary curricula and educational programs, these new learning systems are designed to accommodate the widest possible range of learning interests. What kind of ordering system

will be employed to allow potential learners to describe their learning interests? How do people know in advance what they want to learn? How are they to be encouraged to learn things that they aren't already predisposed to learn?

70 This section draws on my research that was generously supported by the Mac-Arthur Foundation in the form of a grant called "Inspiring the Technological Imagination: Museums and Libraries as Mixed-reality Learning Sites" (April 2008–June 2009). In October 2008, I convened a meeting on the topic of "Tinkering as a Mode of Knowledge Production in a Digital Age." The purpose of this meeting was to bring together people from different cultural institutions (museums, libraries, university research centers) and different sites of informal education (community arts programs, galleries, technology centers) to initiate a cross-domain discussion about the concept of "tinkering" as a paradigm for knowledge construction.

conclusion: The Work of a Book in a Digital Age

1 The application was first created for the online journal *Vectors* (forthcoming). It is co-authored/designed with Craig Dietrich.

2 The *Designing Culture* website includes links to other interactive maps that I've created using an application called Prezi.

3 As Jerome McGann (2003: 253) argues: "no book is one thing, it is many things, fashioned and refashioned repeatedly under different circumstances." It is exactly this nature of the book that is explored in this project by making the multiplicity which is a book manifest in different digital forms: an interactive documentary on DVD; interactive wall books; video clips; a blog for technocultural criticism; and links to related texts and projects.

4 John Law (2002) argues that scholars of technoscience need to be more critical of their focus on the object (that is, technology). He argues that "the object" needs to be decentered as a singular entity because "objects come in different versions" (2). He elaborates how objects are both singular (where singularity is a consequence of practices of coherence) and plural (when coherence is methodically unpacked).

5 The four laws were published in the book authored by McLuhan's son Eric, after Marshall's death: Marshall McLuhan and Eric McLuhan (1988).

6 As Edward Tufte (2003) is famous for asserting, the sheer character density of a print book far outweighs other media. He is especially concerned about the information paucity engendered by the over-use of digital presentation tools such as PowerPoint.

ABI Staff. 2005. "Chronicle of a Controversy." Anita Borg Institute for Women and Technology. http://anitaborg.org/.

Abrams, M. H. 1971. *A Glossary of Literary Terms.* New York: Holt, Reinhart, and Winston.

Acland, Charles, ed. 2007. *Residual Media.* Minneapolis: University of Minnesota Press.

Adams, Alison. 1998. *Artificial Knowing: Gender and the Thinking Machine.* London: Routledge.

Adler, Mortimer, and Charles Van Dorn. 1972. *How to Read a Book.* Revised edition. New York: Touchstone.

Albrecht, Donald, ed. 1997. *The Work of Charles and Ray Eames: A Legacy of Invention.* New York: Harry N. Abrams.

Allor, Martin. 2001. "Locating Cultural Activity: The 'Main' As Chronotrope and Heterotopia." *Topia* 1:42–54.

Altick, Richard D. 1983. *The English Common Reader: A Social History of the Mass Reading Public, 1800–1900.* Chicago: University of Chicago Press.

Anderson, Benedict. 1983. *Imagined Communities: Reflections on the Origin and Spread of Nationalism.* London: Verso.

Anderson, Steve, and Anne Balsamo. 2007. "A Pedagogy for Original Synners." In *Digital Young, Innovation, and the Unexpected,* edited by Tara McPherson, 241–59. Cambridge, Mass.: MIT Press.

Arnold, Ken. 1996. "Presenting Science as Product or as Process: Museums and the Making of Science." In *Exploring Science in Museums,* edited by Susan Pearce, 57–78. London: Athlone Press.

Arrington, Michael. 2006. "YouTube's Magic Number—$1.5 Billion." *TechCrunch .com*, September 21.

Atkins, Dan E., John Seely Brown, and Allen L. Hammond. 2007. "A Review of the Open Educational Resources (OER) Movement: Achievements, Challenges, and New Opportunities." Report to the William and Flora Hewlett Foundation. http://www.hewlett.org/.

Back, Maribeth, Jonathan Cohen, Rich Gold, Steve Harrison, and Scott Minneman. 2001. "Listen Reader: An Electronically Augmented Paper-based Book." In *Proceedings of CHI 2001*, 23–29. ACM Press.

———. 2002. "Speeder Reader: An Experiment in the Future of Reading." *Computers and Graphics* 26, no. 4: 623–27.

Back, Maribeth, Rich Gold, Anne Balsamo, Mark Chow, Matt Gorbet, Steve Harrison, and Scott Minneman. 2001. "Designing Innovative Reading Experiences for a Museum Exhibition." *Computer: Innovative Technology for Computer Professionals* 34, no. 1: 80–87.

Back, Maribeth, Rich Gold, and Dana Kirsch. 1999. "The SIT Book: Audio as Affective Imagery for Interactive Storybooks." In *CHI '99 Extended Abstracts*, 202–3. ACM Press.

Back, Maribeth, and Steve Harrison. 2002. "The Roads Not Taken: Detours and Dead-ends on the Design Path of Speeder Reader." In *Proceedings of Designing Interactive Systems* (*DIS 2002*), 193–99. ACM Press.

Baird, F., C. J. Moore, and A. P. Jagodzinski. 2000. "An Ethnographic Study of Engineering Design Teams at Rolls-Royce Aerospace." *Design Studies* 21, no. 4: 333–55.

Baker, Robin. 1993. *Designing the Future: The Computer in Architecture and Design*. London: Thames and Hudson.

Balsamo, Anne. 1991. "Feminism and Cultural Studies." *Journal of the Midwest Modern Language Association* 24, no. 1: 50–73.

———. 1996. *Technologies of the Gendered Body: Reading Cyborg Women*. Durham, N.C.: Duke University Press.

———. 2000a. "Teaching in the Belly of the Beast." In *Wild Science: Reading Feminism, Medicine and the Media*, edited by Janine Marchessault and Kim Sawchuk, 185–214. London: Routledge.

———. 2000b. "Engineering Cultural Studies: The Postdisciplinary Adventures of Mindplayers, Fools, and Others." In *Doing Science + Culture*, edited by Roddey Reid and Sharon Traweek, 259–74. New York: Routledge.

———. 2006. "A Glorious Mix: The Art of Interactive Science and Technology Exhibits." In *Intersections: Art at the New York Hall of Science*, 3–12. Catalog published by the New York Hall of Science.

Balsamo, Anne, Susana Bautista, Maura Klosterman, and Cara Wallis. 2009. "Inspiring the Technological Imagination: Museums and Libraries in a Digital Age." Research project, with blog postings on *DMLcentral*, http://dmlcentral.net/.

Balsamo, Anne, Matt Gorbet, Scott Minneman, and Steve Harrison. 2000. "The Methods of Our Madness: Research on Experimental Documents." *Proceedings of*

Conference on Human Factors in Computing Systems 2000. Den Hague (April): 207–8.

Balsamo, Anne, and Michael Greer. 1993. "Cultural Studies and the Undergraduate Literature Curriculum." In *Cultural Studies in the English Classroom,* edited by James Berlin and Michael Vivion, 145–64. Portsmouth, N.H.: Boynton/Cook.

———. 1994. "Displacing Literature: Cultural Studies, Pedagogy, and the Literature Classroom." In *Changing Classroom Practices: Resources for Literary and Cultural Studies,* edited by David Downing, 275–307. Urbana, Ill.: National Council of Teachers of English Press.

Bannon, Liam, and Kjeld Schmidt. 1989. "CSCW: Four Characters in Search of a Context." *ECSCW '89: Proceedings of the First European Conference on Computer Supported Cooperative Work.* London (September 13–15), 358–72.

Barad, Karen. 1998. "Getting Real: Technoscientific Practices and the Materialization of Reality." *Differences* 10, no. 2: 87–128.

———. 2000. "Reconceiving Scientific Literacy as Agential Literacy, or Learning How to Intra-act Responsibly within the World." In *Doing Science + Culture,* edited by Roddey Reid and Sharon Traweek, 221–58. New York: Routledge.

———. 2003. "Posthumanist Performativity: Toward an Understanding of how Matter comes to Matter." *Signs* 28, no. 3: 801–31.

Barr, Robert B., and John Tagg. 1995. "From Teaching to Learning—A New Paradigm for Undergraduate Education." *Change* 27, no. 6: 12–25.

Barrett, Michele. 1988. *Women's Oppression Today: The Marxist/Feminist Encounter.* Revised edition. London: Verso.

Barry, Andrew. 1998. "On Interactivity: Consumers, Citizens and Culture." In *The Politics of Display: Museums, Science, Culture,* edited by Sharon MacDonald, 99–117. London: Routledge.

Barthes, Roland. 1970. *Mythologies.* Trans. Annette Lavers. New York: Hill and Wang.

Bautista, Susana. 2009. "Museum Collections: Digitization → Dissemination → Dialogue." July 3. Blog posting on *DMLcentral,* http://dmlcentral.net/.

Behning, Ute, and Amparo Serrano Pascual, eds. 2001. *Gender Mainstreaming in the European Employment Strategy.* Brussels: European Trade Union Institute (ETUI).

Bellantoni, John, and Matt Woolman. 2001. *Type in Motion: Innovations in Digital Graphics.* New York: Rizzoli.

Belsey, Catherine. 1980. *Critical Practice.* London: Methuen.

Benamou, Michel. 1980. "Notes on the Technological Imagination." In *The Technological Imagination: Theories and Fictions,* edited by Teresa De Lauretis, Andreas Huyssen, and Kathleen Woodward, 65–75. Madison, Wisc.: Coda Press.

Bennett, Frederick. 2002. "The Future of Computer Technology in K-12 Education." *Phi Delta Kappa* 83, no. 8: 621–25.

Bennett, Tony. 1995. *The Birth of the Museum: History, Theory, Politics.* London: Routledge.

Berger, Peter L., and Thomas Luckman. 1966. *The Social Construction of Reality.* London: Penguin.

Bernstein, Danielle R. 1991. "Comfort and Experience with Computing: Are They the Same for Women and Men." *ACM SIGCSE Bulletin* 23, no. 3: 57–60.

Best, Jo. "How Eight Pixels Cost Microsoft Millions." 2004. *CNet News,* August 19.

Beynon, John, and Hughie Mackay. 1992. *Technological Literacy and the Curriculum.* New York: Falmer Press.

Bijker, Wiebe, and John Law, eds. 1992. *Shaping Technology/Building Society: Studies in Sociotechnical Change.* Cambridge, Mass.: MIT Press.

Biswas, Amitava. 2008. "Managing Art-Technology Research Collaborations." *International Journal of Arts and Technology* 1, no. 1: 66–89.

Boellstorff, Tom. 2008. *Coming of Age in Second Life: An Anthropologist Explores the Virtually Human.* Princeton, N.J.: Princeton University Press.

Bolas, Mark, J. Pair, K. Haynes, and I. McDowall. 2006. "Environmental and Immersive Display Research at the University of Southern California." *IEEE Virtual Reality Conference 2006* (March 26–29): 317.

Bolter, J. David. 1991. *Writing Space: The Computer, Hypertext, and the History of Writing.* Mahwah, N.J.: Lawrence Earlbaum Associates.

Bombardieri, Marcella. "Summers' Remarks on Women Draw Fire." 2005. *Boston.com.* January 16.

Bourdieu, Pierre. 1984. *Distinction: A Social Critique of the Judgment of Taste.* Trans. Richard Nice. Cambridge, Mass.: Harvard University Press.

Bowker, Geoffrey C., Susan Leigh Star, William Turner, and Les Gasser, eds. 1997. *Social Science, Technical Systems, and Cooperative Work: Beyond the Great Divide.* Mahwah, N.J.: Lawrence Erlbaum Associates.

Boynton, Robert. 2000. "You Say You Want an e-Book Revolution?" *Time Digital,* December: 39–48.

Brand, Steward. 1972. "Spacewar: Fanatic Life and Symbolic Death Among the Computer Bums." *Rolling Stone,* December 7.

Brantley, David. 2001. "Singapore's Biomedicine Initiative: Prescription for Growth." White Paper prepared for the Office of Technology Policy, Technology Administration, United States Department of Commerce.

Bretin, Jacques. 1983. *Semiology of Graphics: Diagram, Networks, Maps.* Madison: University of Wisconsin Press.

Brown, John Seely. 1999. Introduction to *Art and Innovation: The Xerox PARC Artist-in-Residence Program,* edited by Craig Harris, xi-xiii. Cambridge, Mass.: MIT Press.

———. 2000. "Growing Up Digital: The Web and a New Learning Ecology." *Change,* March/April, 10–20.

———. 2001. "Where Have All the Computers Gone?" *Technology Review,* January/February, 86–87.

———. 2002. "Learning in the Digital Age." In *The Internet & the University: Forum*

2001, edited by Maureen Devlin, Richard Larson, and Joel Meyerson, 65–91. Forum for the Future of Higher Education / EDUCAUSE.

Brown, John Seely, and Paul Duguid. 1998. "Universities in the Digital Age." In *The Mirage of Continuity: Reconfiguring Academic Information Resources for the 21st Century*, edited by Brian L. Hawkins and Patricia Battin, 39–60. Washington, D.C.: Council on Library and Information Resources.

———. *The Social Life of Information*. 2000. Boston: Harvard Business School Press.

———. 2002. "Local Knowledge: Innovation in the Networked Age." *Management Learning* 33, no. 4: 427–37.

Bruner, Jerome. *The Narrative Construction of Reality*. 1991. Chicago: University of Chicago Press.

Bucciarelli, Louis. 1994. *Designing Engineers*. Cambridge, Mass.: MIT Press.

Buchanan, Richard, 1992. "Wicked Problems in Design Thinking." *Design Issues* 8, no. 2: 5–21.

Buckingham, David. 2002. "The Electronic Generation? Children and New Media." In *Handbook of New Media: Social Shaping and Consequences of ICTs*, edited by Leah A. Lievrouw and Sonia Livingstone, 77–89. London: Sage.

Buderi, Robert. 2001. "Computing Goes Everywhere." *Technology Review*, January/February, 53–60.

Burton, Graham. 2001. "The Ethnographic Tradition and Design." *Design Studies* 21, no. 4: 319–32.

Cadigan, Pat. 1991. *Synners*. New York: HarperCollins.

Canto, Christophe, and Odile Faliu. 1993. *The History of the Future: Images of the 21st Century*. Trans. by Francis Cowper. Paris: Flammarion.

Carey, James. 1989. *Communication as Culture: Essays on Media and Society*. Boston: Unwin Hyman.

Carr, Nicholas. 2008. "Is Google Making Us Stupid?" *Atlantic* 302, no. 1 (July/August), 56–63.

Cartwright, Lisa. 1995. *Screening the Body: Tracing Medicine's Visual Culture*. Minneapolis: University of Minnesota Press.

Carvajal, Doreen. 1999. "Revolution Aside, Paperbacks Losing Battle for Readers." *New York Times*, March 15.

Cassell, Justine, and Henry Jenkins. 1998. *From Barbie to Mortal Combat: Gender and Computer Games*. Cambridge, Mass.: MIT Press.

Cavallo, Guglielmo, and Roger Chartier, eds. 1999. *A History of Reading in the West*. Boston: University of Massachusetts Press.

Century, Michael. 2006. "Humanizing Technology: The Studio Lab and Innovation." In *A Guide to Good Practice in Collaborative Working Methods and New Media Tools Creation*, edited by Liz Goodman and Katherine Milton. http://www.ahds.ac.uk/creating/guides/new-media-tools/.

Cesarini, Paul. 2004. "Computers, Technology, and Literacies." *Journal of Literacy and Technology* 4, no. 1: 1–6.

Chalmers, Rachel. 2000. "Surf Like a Bushman." *New Scientist* (November 11): 38–41.

Christensen, Clayton. 1997. *The Innovator's Dilemma: When New Technologies cause Great Firms to Fail.* Boston: Harvard Business School Press.

Chun, Wendy Hui Kyong. 2007. "Programmed Visions." *Vectors* 3, no. 1. http://vectors.usc.edu/.

Clark, Gordon, and Paul Tracey. 2004. *Global Competitiveness and Innovation: An Agent-Centered Perspective.* New York: Palgrave Macmillan.

Cockburn, Cynthia. 1985. *Machinery of Dominance: Women, Men and Technical Know-how.* London: Pluto.

Cohen, Noam. 2007. "A History Department Bans Citing Wikipedia as a Research Source." *New York Times* online edition, February 21.

Cole, Michael, Vera John-Steiner, Sylvia Scribner, and Ellen Souberman. 1978. *L.S. Vygotsky, Mind In Society: The Development of Higher Psychological Processes.* Cambridge, Mass.: Harvard University Press.

Coy, Peter. 2000. "Research Labs Get Real: It's about Time." *Business Week*, November 6.

Coyne, Richard. 1995. *Designing Information Technology in the Postmodern Age: From Method to Metaphor.* Cambridge, Mass.: MIT Press.

Crow, Barbara, Michael Longford, Kim Sawchuk, and Andrea Zeffiro. 2008. "Voices from Beyond: Ephemeral Histories, Locative Media and the Volatile Interface." In *Urban Informatics: The Practice and Promise of the Real-Time City*, edited by Marcus Foth, 158–78. Hershey, Pa.: Information Science Reference, IGI Global.

Csikszentmihalyi, Mihaly. 1996. *Creativity: Flow and the Psychology of Discovery and Invention.* New York: Harper Collins.

Csikszentmihalyi, Mihaly, and Eugene Rochberg-Halton. 1981. *The Meaning of Things: Domestic Symbols and the Self.* Cambridge: Cambridge University Press.

Cuban, Larry. 2001. *Oversold and Underused: Computers in the Classroom.* Cambridge, Mass.: Harvard University Press.

Curzio, Alberto Quadrio, and Marco Fortis, eds. 2005. *Research and Technological Innovation: The Challenge for a New Europe.* New York: Springer.

da Landa, Manuel. 2006. *A New Philosophy of Society: Assemblage Theory and Social Complexity.* London: Continuum Books.

Daley, Elizabeth. 2003. "Expanding the Concept of Literacy." *Educause Review* 38, no. 2 (March–April): 32–40.

Daniels, Dieter, and Barbara U. Schmidt, eds. 2008. *Artists as Inventors.* Ostfildern, Germany: Hatje Cantz Verlag.

Darnton, Robert. 1999. "The New Age of the Book. " *New York Review of Books*, March 18, 5–7.

Davidson, Cathy N. 1986. *Revolution and the Word: The Rise of the Novel in America.* New York: Oxford University Press.

Davidson, Cathy N., and David Theo Goldberg. 2004. "A Manifesto for the Humanities in a Technological Age." *Chronicle of Higher Education*, February 13, B7.

———. 2006. "Managing from the Middle." *Chronicle of Higher Education*, May 6, C1, C4.

DeBord, Guy, and Gil Wolman. (1956) 2006. "A User's Guide to Détournement." In *Situationist International Anthology*, edited and translated by Ken Knabb. Berkeley: Bureau of Public Secrets. Originally published as "Mode d'emploi du détournement" in *Les Lèvres Nues* 8 (May 1956).

de Certeau, Michel. 1984. *The Practice of Everyday life*. Trans. by Steven Randall. Berkeley: University of California.

de Lauretis, Teresa. 1980. "Signs of Wa/onder." In *The Technological Imagination: Theories and Fictions*, edited by Teresa deLauretis, Andreas Huyssen, and Kathleen Woodward, 159–74. Madison, Wisc.: Coda Press.

de Lauretis, Teresa, Andrea Huyssen, and Kathleen Woodward, eds. 1980. *The Technological Imagination: Theories and Fictions*. Madison, Wisc.: Coda Press.

Deleuze, Gilles, and Felix Guattari. 1987. *A Thousand Plateaus*. Trans. by Brian Massumi. Minneapolis: University of Minneosta Press.

Demetrios, Eames. 2001. *An Eames Primer*. New York: Universe Publishing.

Dervin, Brenda. 1999. "Chaos, Order, and Sense-Making: A Proposed Theory for Information Design." In *Information Design*, edited by Robert Jacobson, 35–58. Cambridge, Mass.: MIT Press.

Deuten, J. Jasper, and Arie Rip. 2000. "Narrative Infrastructure in Product Creation Processes." *Organization* 7, no. 1: 67–91.

Dewey, John. 1916. *Democracy and Education*. New York: Macmillan.

———. *Experience and Education*. (1938) 1998. New York: Touchstone.

DiSessa, Andrea A. 2000. *Changing Minds: Computers, Learning, and Literacy*. Cambridge, Mass.: MIT Press.

Dorst, Kees. 2006. "Design Problems, Design Paradoxes." *Design Issues* 22, no. 3: 4–17.

Downes, Daniel. 2005. *Interactive Realism: The Poetics of Cyberspace*. Montreal: McGill-Queen's University Press.

Downes, Stephen. 2000. "Advanced Distributed Learning Network." *The Technology Source* (May/June). http://technologysource.org/.

Drucker, Johanna. 1995. *A Century of Artists' Books*. Granary Books.

DuGay, Paul, Stuart Hall, Linda Janes, Hugh Mackay, and Keith Negus. 1997. *Doing Cultural Studies: The Story of the Sony Walkman*. London: Sage Publications.

Durbin, Paul, ed. 1980. *A Guide to the Culture of Science, Technology and Medicine*. New York: Free Press.

Eames, Charles, and Ray Eames. 1972. *Design Q & A*. Directed by Charles Eames and Ray Eames. Documentary short, running time 5:00.

Eckert, Claudia, and Martin Stacey. 2000. "Sources of Inspiration: A Language of Design." *Design Studies* 21, no. 5: 523–38.

Eisenstein, Elizabeth. 1980. *The Printing Press as an Agent of Change: Communications and Cultural Transformations in Early-modern Europe*. Cambridge: Cambridge University Press.

Ellsworth, Kyle, Spencer Magleby, and Robert Todd. 2002. "A Study of the Effects of Culture on Refrigerator Design: Towards Design for Culture." *Proceedings of DETC '02*. ASME 2002 Design Engineering Technical Conferences and Computer and Information in Engineering Conference, Montreal, Canada (September 29–October 2, 2002).

Emigh, Rebecca. 2005. "The Unmaking of Markets: A Composite Visual History." *Vectors* 1, no. 1. http://vectors.usc.edu/.

Febvre, Lucien, and Henri-Jean Martin. 1984. *The Coming of the Book: The Impact of Printing 1450–1800*. London: Verso.

Feenberg, Andrew. 1991. *A Critical Approach to Technology*. New York: Oxford University Press.

———. 1995. *Alternative Modernity: The Technical Turn in Philosophy and Social Theory*. Berkeley: University of California Press.

Felluga, Dino. 2003. "Modules on Greimas: On the Semiotic Square." In *Introductory Guide to Critical Theory*. http://www.cla.purdue.edu/english/theory/.

Ferre, Frederick. 1988. *Philosophy of Technology*. Englewood Cliffs, N.J.: Prentice-Hall.

Fisher, Scott S., Steve Anderson, Susana Ruiz, Michael Naimark, Perry Hoberman, and Richard Weinberg. 2005. "Experiments in Interactive Panoramic Cinema." In *Proceedings of the SPIE*, vol. 5664, Stereoscopic Displays and Virtual Reality Systems IX, edited by A. Woods, M. T. Bolas, and J. O. Merritt, 626–32.

Florida, Richard. 2002. *The Rise of the Creative Class*. New York: Basic Books.

Flynn, Elizabeth A., and Patrocinio P. Schweickart, eds. 1986. *Gender and Reading: Essays on Readers, Texts, and Contexts*. Baltimore, Md.: Johns Hopkins University Press.

Fogg, Piper. 2003. "The Gap that Won't Go Away: Women Continue to Lag Behind Men in Pay; The Reasons may have Little to do with Gender Bias." *Chronicle of Higher Education*, April 18, A12.

Freire, Paolo. [1970] 1998. *The Pedagogy of the Oppressed*. Trans. by Myra Bergman Ramos. New York: Continuum.

Frenkel, James, ed. 2001. *True Names and the Opening of the Cyberspace Frontier*. New York: Tor.

Galle, Per. 1999. "Design as Intentional Action: A Conceptual Analysis." *Design Studies* 20, no. 1: 57–81.

Gambrell, Alice. 2005. "The Stolen Time Archive." *Vectors* 1, no. 1. http://vectors.usc.edu/.

Gardner, Howard. 2006a. *Multiple Intelligences: New Horizons*. New York: Basic Books.

———. 2006b. *Five Minds for the Future*. Boston: Harvard Business School Press.

Gee, James Paul. 2004. *What Video Games have to Teach us about Learning and Literacy?* New York: Palgrave Macmillan.

Geertz, Clifford. 1973. *The Interpretation of Cultures*. New York: Basic Books.

——. "A Life of Learning." Charles Homer Haskins Lecture for 1999, *American Council of Learned Societies*, Occasional Paper, no 45. http://www.acls.org/.

Gogoi, Pallavi. 2005. "Of Gadgets and Gender." *Bloomberg Business Week*, February 14. http://www.businessweek.com/.

Gold, Rich. 1975. *The Original Goldographs*. Unpublished manuscript.

——. N.d. "How We Do Research at Xerox PARC." Unpublished manuscript.

——. 2000. "Xerox PARC at 30: Inside a Research Lab." *Dr. Dobb's Special Report*, December 1, 42–47.

——. 2007. *The Plentitude: A PowerPoint book*. Cambridge, Mass.: MIT Press.

Goldberg, David Theo, and Stefka Hristova. "Blue Velvet: Re-dressing New Orleans in Katrina's Wake." *Vectors* 3, no. 1. http://vectors.usc.edu/.

Good, I. J. 1965. "Speculations Concerning the First Ultraintelligent Machine." In *Advances in Computers*, edited by Franz L. Alt and Morris Rubinoff, 31–88. Burlington, Mass.: Academic Press.

Goux, Melanie, and James A. Houff. 2003. *On Screen In Time: Transitions in Motion Graphic Design for Film, Television and New Media*. Switzerland: RotoVision SA.

Greenfield, Patricia Marks. 1984. *Media and the Mind of the Child: From Print to Television, Video Games and Computers*. Cambridge, Mass.: Harvard University Press.

Greimas, Algirdas Julien. 1976. *On Meaning: Selected Writings in Semiotic Theory*. Trans. by Paul J. Perron and Frank H. Collins. Minneapolis: University of Minnesota Press.

Grossberg, Lawrence, Cary Nelson, and Paula Treichler, eds. 1991. *Cultural Studies*. London: Routlege.

Habermas, Jürgen. 1979. *Communication and the Evolution of Society*. Boston: Beacon Press.

——. 1981. *The Theory of Communicative Action*, vol. 1, *Reason and the Rationalization of Society*. Boston: Beacon Press.

Hagel, John, and John Seely Brown. 2005. *The Only Sustainable Edge: Why Business Strategy Depends on Productive Friction and Dynamic Specialization*. Boston: Harvard Business School Press.

——. 2008. "Student Activism can Change the World." *Bloomberg Business Week*, May 30. http://www.businessweek.com/.

Halfmann, Janet. 1999. *Greek Temples*. New York: Creative Education.

Hall, David D. 1996. *Cultures of Print: Essays in the History of the Book*. Amherst, Mass.: University of Massachusetts Press.

Hall, Justin, and Scott Fisher. 2006. "Experiments in Backchannel: Collaborative Presentations Using Social Software, Google Jockeys and Immersive Environments." *Computer and Human Interaction (CHI) Conference*, April. http://nvac.pnl.gov/.

Hall, R. M., and B. R. Sandler. 1982. "The Classroom Climate: A Chilly One for Women?" In *Student Climate Issues Packet*. Washington, D.C.: Project on the Status and Education of Women, Association of American Colleges.

Hall, Stuart. 1984. "The Narrative Construction of Reality." *Southern Review* 17, no. 1:
　3–17.
———. 1996. "On Postmodernism and Articulation: An Interview with Stuart Hall." In
　Stuart Hall: Critical Dialogues in Cultural Studies, edited by David Morley, and
　Kuan-Hsing Chen, 131–50. New York: Routledge.
Hamel, Gary. 2000. *Leading the Revolution: How to Thrive in Turbulent Times by
　Making Innovation a Way of Life*. New York: Penguin.
Hamit, Francis. 2003. "Changing the Printing Model: Digital Imaging Now Driving
　Book Business." *Advanced Imaging*, November, 35–37.
Haraway, Donna. 1985. "A Manifesto for Cyborgs: Science, Technology and Socialist
　Feminism in the 1980s." *Socialist Review* 80 (March/April): 65–108.
———. 1988. "Situated Knowledges: The Science Question in Feminism and the Privi-
　lege of Partial Perspective." *Feminist Studies* 14, no. 3: 575–99.
———. 1989. *Primate Visions: Gender, Race, and Nature in the World of Modern Science*.
　London: Routledge.
———. 1991. *Simians, Cyborgs, and Women: The Reinvention of Nature*. New York:
　Routledge.
———. 1998. *Modest_Witness@Second_Millennium.FemaleMan©Meets_OncoMouse*™:
　Feminism and Technoscience. London: Routledge.
Harding, Sandra. 1991. *Whose Science? Whose Knowledge? Thinking from Women's
　Lives*. Ithaca, N.Y.: Cornell University Press.
Harpham, Geoffrey. 2006. "Science and the Theft of Humanity." *American Scientist*
　94, no. 4: 293–98.
Harris, Craig, ed. 1999. *Art and Innovation: The Xerox PARC Artist-in-Residence Pro-
　gram*. Cambridge, Mass.: MIT Press.
Harrison, Kaesmene. 2001. "Reading the Future: E-books are Ready to Revolution-
　ize Publishing, but They Don't Mean the End for the Printed word." *San Jose Mer-
　cury News Access Magazine*, January 28, Cover, 12.
Hartley, John, ed. 2005. *Creative Industries*. Oxford: Blackwell.
Hawkes, Terrence. 1977. *Structuralism and Semiotics*. Berkeley: University of Califor-
　nia Press.
Hayles, N. Katherine. 1999. *How We Became Posthuman: Virtual Bodies in Cybernet-
　ics, Literature, and Informatics*. Chicago: University of Chicago Press.
———. 2002. *Writing Machines*. Cambridge, Mass.: MIT Press.
———. 2005. *My Mother Was a Computer: Digital Subjects and Literary Texts*. Chicago:
　University of Chicago Press.
Hein, Hilde. 1990. *The Exploratorium: The Museum as Laboratory*. Washington,
　D.C.: Smithsonian Institution Press.
Heller, Agnes. 2005. "The Three Logics of Modernity and the Double Bind of the
　Modern Imagination." *Thesis Eleven* 81 (May): 63–79.
Henning, Michelle. 2006. *Museums, Media and Cultural Theory*. Berkshire, England:
　Open University Press.

Herz, J. C. 1997. *Joystick Nation: How Videogames Ate Our Quarters, Won Our Hearts, and Rewired Our Brains.* Boston: Little, Brown.

Hiltzik, Michael. 1999. *Dealers of Lightning: Xerox PARC and the Dawn of the Computer Age.* New York: HarperCollins.

Hocks, Mary E. 1999. "Feminist Interventions in Electronic Environments." *Computers and Composition* 16:107–19.

Hocks, Mary E., and Anne Balsamo. 2003. "Women Making Multimedia: A Blueprint for Feminist Action." In *Virtual Publics: Policy and Community in an Electronic Age*, edited by Beth Kolko, 192–214. New York: Columbia University Press.

Hocks, Mary E., and Daniele Bascelli. 1998. "Building a Multimedia Program Across the Curriculum." In *Electronic Communication Across the Curriculum*, edited by Richard A. Selfe, Donna Reiss, and Art Young, 40–56. Urbana, Ill.: National Council of Teachers of English.

Honey, Margaret, Babette Moeller, Cornelia Brunner, Dorothy Bennett, Peggy Clements, and Jan Hawkins. 1991. "Girls and Design: Exploring the Question of Technological Imagination." *Technical Report: The Center for Technology and Education* no. 17.

Hooper-Greenhill, Eilean. 1992. *Museums and the Shaping of Knowledge.* London: Routledge.

Ihde, Don. 1979. *Technics and Praxis: A Philosophy of Technology.* Boston: D. Reidel.

——. 1991. *Instrumental Realism: The Interface between Philosophy of Science and Philosophy of Technology.* Bloomington: Indiana University Press, 1991.

——. 1993. *Philosophy of Technology: An Introduction.* New York: Paragon Press.

——. 2002. *Bodies in Technology.* Minneapolis: University of Minnesota Press.

——. 2008. "The Designer Fallacy and Technological Imagination." In *Philosophy and Design: From Engineering to Architecture*, edited by Pieter E. Vermaas, Peter Kroes, Andrew Light, and Steven A. Moore, 51–59. New York: Springer.

Inter-American Development Bank Newsletter. 2006. "Technological innovation called key to competitiveness for Latin America." March 29. http://www.iadb.org/.

Irigaray, Luce. 1985. *Speculum of the Other Woman.* Trans. by Gillian G. Gill. Ithaca, N.Y.: Cornell University Press.

Ito, Mizuko. 2008. "Mobilizing the Imagination in Everyday Play: The Case of Japanese Media Mixers." In *International Handbook of Children, Media, and Culture*, edited by Sonia Livingstone and Kirsten Drotner, 397–411. Thousand Oaks, Calif.: Sage.

Jameson, Fredric. 2001. *Postmoderism, or, The Cultural Logic of Late Captialism.* Durham, N.C.: Duke University Press.

Jenkins, Henry. 2006a. *Convergence Culture: Where Old and New Media Collide.* New York: New York University Press.

Jenkins, Henry, with Katie Clinton, Ravi Purushotma, Alice J. Robison, and Margaret Weigel. 2006b. "Confronting the Challenges of Participatory Culture: Media Education for the 21st Century." Occasional paper, John D. and Catherine T. MacArthur Foundation, Chicago, Ill. http://digitallearning.macfound.org/.

Jenks, Chris, ed. 1993. *Cultural Reproduction*. New York: Routledge.

Johns, Adrian. 1998. *The Nature of the Book: Print and Knowledge in the Making*. Chicago: University of Chicago Press.

Johnson, Bonnie McDaniel. 2003. "The Paradox of Design Research: The Role of Informance." In *Design Research: Methods and Perspectives*, edited by Brenda Laurel, 39–40. Cambridge, Mass.: MIT Press.

Johnson, Pamela J. 2006/7. "Technology+Teamwork=New Discoveries." USC *College of Letters, Arts and Sciences Newsletter* 7, no. 3, Cover; 6–7.

Johnson, Richard. 1986/87. "What is Cultural Studies Anyway?" *Social Text* 16:38–80.

Johnson, Steven. 2002. *Emergence: The Connected Lives of Ants, Brains, Cities, and Software*. New York: Scribner.

Julier, Guy. 2000. *The Culture of Design*. London: Sage.

Kafai, Yasmin, Carrie Heeter, Jill Denner, and Jennifer Sun, eds. 2008. *Beyond Barbie and Mortal Kombat: New Perspectives on Gender and Gaming*. Cambridge, Mass.: MIT Press.

Kaplan, Nancy. 1991. "Ideology, Technology and the Future of Writing Instruction." In *Evolving Perspectives on Computer and Composition Studies: Questions for the 1990s*, edited by Gail E. Hawisher, and Cynthia L. Selfe, 11–42. Urbana, Ill.: NCTE and Computers and Composition Press.

——. 1995. "E-Literacies: Politexts, Hypertexts, and Other Cultural Formations in the Late Age of Print." *Computer Mediated Communications Magazine* 2, no. 3 (March 1).

——. 2001. "Knowing Practice: A More Complex View of New Media Literacy." Unpublished manuscript.

Keeps, David. 2008. "Craft-making Grows in Popularity among Young Artisans." *Los Angeles Times* online edition, November 22.

Keohane, Robert. 1989. *International Institutions and State Power: Essays in International Relations Theory*. Boulder, Colo.: Westview Press, 1989.

Kinder, Marsha. 1999. "Doors to the Labyrinth: Designing Interactive Frictions with Nina Menkes, Pat O'Neill, and John Rechy." *Style* 33, no. 2: 232–45.

King, Kenneth. 2001. *Technology, Science Teaching and Literacy: A Century of Growth*. New York: Kluwer Academic.

Koelsch, Patrice. 2001. *Museums*. New York: Creative Education.

Kolko, Beth, ed. 2003. *Virtual Publics*. New York: Columbia University Press.

Kozulin, Alex, Boris Gindis, Vladimir S. Ageyev, and Suzanne M. Miller. 2003. *Vygotsky's Educational Theory in Cultural Context*. New York: Cambridge University Press.

Kramarae, Cheris, and Paula A. Treichler. 1985. *A Feminist Dictionary*. Boston: Pandora Press.

Kratzer, David. 1997. "The Practical as Instrument for Technological Imagination." *Journal of Architectural Education* 51, no. 1: 32–36.

Krippendorf, Klaus. 1995. "On the Essential Contexts of Artifacts or on the Proposi-

tion that 'Design in Making Sense (of Things).'" In *The Idea of Design*, edited by
Victor Margolin and Richard Buchanan, 156–85. Cambridge, Mass.: MIT Press.

——. 2005. *The Semantic Turn: A New Foundation for Design*. London: Taylor &
Francis.

Kroker, Arthur. 2001. "Digital Humanism: The Processed World of Marshall
McLuhan." In *Digital Delirium*, edited by Arthur Kroker and Marilousie Kroker,
89–113. Montreal: New World Perspectives.

Kuhn, Thomas. 1970. *The Structure of Scientific Revolutions*. 2nd edition. Chicago:
University of Chicago Press.

Kurtzweil, Ray. 1992. *The Age of Intelligent Machines*. Cambridge, Mass.: MIT Press.

Landau, Susan. 1991. "Tenure Track, Mommy Track." *Association for Women in Mathematics Newsletter* (May/June).

Latour, Bruno. 1987. *Science in Action*. Cambridge, Mass.: Harvard University Press.

——. 1996. *Aramis, or the Love of Technology*. Cambridge, Mass.: Harvard University
Press.

——. 2005. *Reassembling the Social: An Introduction to Actor-Network Theory*.
Oxford: Oxford University Press.

——. 2007. "Beware, Your Imagination Leaves Digital Traces." *Times Higher Education Supplement*, April 6.

Latour, Bruno, and Steve Woolgar. 1986. *Laboratory Life: The Construction of Scientific Facts*. 2nd edition. Princeton, N.J.: Princeton University Press.

Laurel, Brenda. 2001. *Utopian Entrepreneur*. Cambridge, Mass.: MIT Press.

——, ed. 2003. *Design Research: Methods and Perspectives*. Cambridge, Mass.: MIT
Press.

Law, John. 2002. *Aircraft Stories: Decentering the Object in Technoscience*. Durham,
N.C.: Duke University Press.

Lee, Hyun-Jean, Madhur Khandelwal, and Ali Mazalek. 2007. "Tilting Table: A
Movable Screen." *TEI '07* (Febuary 15–17): 93–96.

Lemecha, Vera, and Reva Stone, eds. 2001. *The Multiple and Mutable Subject*. Mani-
toba, Canada: St. Norbert Arts Center Publication.

Levine, Lawrence W. 1988. *Highbrow Lowbrow: The Emergence of Cultural Hierarchy
in America*. Cambridge, Mass.: Harvard University Press.

Levy, Steven. 2000. "It's Time to Turn the Last Page." *Time*, January 1, 96–98.

Lievrouw, Leah A. 2002. "Determination and Contingency in New Media Develop-
ment: Diffusion of Innovations and Social Shaping of Technology Perspectives."
In *Handbook of New Media: Social Shaping and Consequences of ICTs*, edited by
Leah A. Lievrouw and Sonia Livingstone, 183–200. London: Sage.

Lievrouw, Leah A., and Sonia Livingstone. 2002. "Introduction: The Social Shaping
and Consequences of ICTs." In *Handbook of New Media: Social Shaping and Consequences of ICTs*, edited by Leah A. Lievrouw and Sonia Livingstone, 1–21. London: Sage.

Lipstadt, Hélène. 1997. " 'Natural Overlap': Charles and Ray Eames and the Federal

Government." In *The Work of Charles and Ray Eames: A Legacy of Invention*, edited by Donald Albrecht, 150–77. New York: Harry N. Abrams.

Lloyd, Peter. 2000. "Storytelling and the Development of Discourse in the Engineering Design Process." *Design Studies* 21, no. 4: 357–73.

Lopez-Claros, Augusto, Michael E. Porter, and Klaus Schwab. 2006. *The Global Competitiveness Report 2006–2007*. Hants, U.K.: Palgrave Macmillan.

Louridas, Panagiotis. 1999. "Design as Bricolage: Anthropology Meets Design Thinking." *Design Studies* 20, no. 6: 517–35.

Love, Terrence. 2000. "Philosophy of Design: A Meta-theoretical Structure for Design Theory." *Design Studies* 21, no. 3: 293–313.

———. 2002. "Constructing a Coherent Cross-disciplinary Body of Theory about Designing and Design: Some Philosophical Issues." *Design Studies* 23, no. 3: 345–61.

Lovink, Geert, and Ned Rossiter, eds. 2007. *MyCreativity Reader: A Critique of Creative Industries*. Amsterdam: Institute of Network Cultures.

Löwgren, Johan, and Erik Stolterman. 2004. *Thoughtful Interaction Design: A Design Perspective on Information Technology*. Cambridge, Mass.: MIT Press.

Luhmann, Niklas. 1998. *Observations on Modernity*. Trans. by William Whobrey. Stanford, Calif.: Stanford University Press.

Lunenfeld, Peter. 2002. *The Digital Dialectic: New Essays on New Media*. Cambridge, Mass.: MIT Press.

MacDonald, Sharon, and Roger Silverstone. 1990. "Rewriting the Museums' Fictions: Taxonomies, Stories and Readers." *Cultural Studies* 4, no. 2: 176–91.

Macdonald, Sharon. 1998. Introduction to *The Politics of Display: Museums, Science, Culture*, edited by Sharon Macdonald, 1–24. London: Routledge.

Machor, James L., ed. 1993. *Readers in History: Nineteenth-century American Literature and the Contexts of Response*. Baltimore, Md.: Johns Hopkins University Press.

Malloy, Judy, ed. 2003. *Women, Art and Technology*. Cambridge, Mass.: MIT Press.

Manguel, Alberto. 1996. *A History of Reading*. New York: Penguin Books.

Manovich, Lev. 2001. *The Language of New Media*. Cambridge, Mass.: MIT Press.

Marchessault, Janine. 2007. *Fluid Screens, Expanded Cinema*. Toronto: University of Toronto Press.

Marcuse, Herbert. 1964. *One-Dimensional Man: Studies in the Ideology of Advanced Industrial Society*. Boston: Beacon Press.

Margolin, Victor. 2002. *The Politics of the Artificial: Essays on Design and Design Studies*. Chicago: University of Chicago Press.

Margolin, Victor, and Richard Buchanan, eds. 1998. *The Idea of Design*. Cambridge, Mass.: MIT Press.

Margolis, Jane, and Allan Fisher. 2002. *Unlocking the Computer Clubhouse: Women in Computing*. Cambridge, Mass.: MIT Press.

Markoff, John. 1999. "Not a Great Equalizer After All?: On the Web, as Elsewhere, Popularity is Self-Reinforcing." *New York Times*, June 21.

Markussen, Randi. 1996. "Politics of Intervention in Design: Feminist Reflections on the Scandinavian Tradition." *AI & Society* 10, no. 2: 127–41.

Marshall, Cathy. N. d. "Subverting the Link." Unpublished manuscript.

———. 2004. "No Bull, No Spin: A Comparison of Tags with Other Forms of User Metadata." *ACM Conference '04* (January/February): 241–50.

Martin, Henri-Jean. 1988. *The History and Power of Writing*. Chicago: University of Chicago Press.

Marvin, Carolyn. 1990. *When Old Technologies Were New: Thinking about Electric Communication in the Late Nineteenth Century*. New York: Oxford University Press.

Massachusetts Insititute of Technology (MIT). 2001. "Mission." web.mit.edu/mission.html.

Matyas, Marsha Lakes, and Linda Skidmore Dix, eds. 1992. *Science and Engineering Programs: On Target for Women?* Washington, D.C.: National Academy Press.

McCaffery, Larry. 1990. *Across Wounded Galaxies: Interviews with Contemporary American Science Fiction Writers*. Urbana: University of Illinois Press.

McGann, Jerome. 1991. *The Textual Condition*. Princeton, N.J.: Princeton University Press.

———. 2002. "Dialogue and Interpretation at the Interface of Man and Machine: Reflections on Textuality and a Proposal for an Experiment in Machine Reading." *Computers and the Humanities* 36, no. 1: 95–107.

———. 2003. "Textonics: Literacy and Cultural Studies in a Quantum World." In *The Culture of Collected Editions*, edited by Andrew Nash, 245–60. New York: Palgrave Macmillan.

McKenzie, Gordon. 1986. *Orbiting the Giant Hairball*. New York: Viking Press.

McLuhan, Marshall. 1951. *The Mechanical Bride: Folklore of Industrial Man*. Boston: Beacon Press.

———. 1962. *The Gutenberg Galaxy: The Making of Typographic Man*. Toronto: University of Toronto Press.

———. 1964. *Understanding Media: The Extensions of Man*. New York: Signet Books.

McLuhan, Marshall, and Eric McLuhan. 1988. *Laws of Media: The New Science*. Toronto: University of Toronto Press.

McPherson, Tara, ed. 2008. *Digital Youth, Innovation, and the Unexpected*. Cambridge, Mass.: MIT Press.

———. 2010. "Vectors: An Interdisciplinary Digital Journal." In *The Oxford Handbook of Interdisciplinary*, edited by Robert Frodeman, Julie Thompson Klein, and Carl Mitcham, 210–11. Oxford: Oxford University Press.

McQuire, Scott, Meredith Martin, and Sabine Niederer, eds. 2009. *Urban Screens Reader*. Amsterdam: Institute of Network Cultures.

Meadows, Mark Stephen. 2002. *Pause and Effect: The Art of Interactive Narrative*. New York: New Rider's Press.

———. 2008. *I, Avatar: The Culture and Consequences of Having a Second Life*. Berkeley: New Riders Press.

Meluch, Wendy. 2000. "*XFR Summative Evaluation*." Unpublished Visitor Study report prepared for the Tech Museum of Innovation, April.

Mills, C. Wright. 1959. *The Sociological Imagination*. London: Oxford University Press.

Minneman, Scott L. 1991. "The Social Construction of A Technical Reality: Empirical studies of Group Engineering Design Practice." Ph.D. dissertation, Department of Mechanical Engineering, Stanford University. Reprinted as Xerox PARC research document # SSL-91–22, December 1991.

Mitcham, Carl. 1994. *Thinking Through Technology: The Path between Engineering and Philosophy*. Chicago: University of Chicago Press.

Mitcham, Carl, and Robert Mackey, eds. 1972. *Philosophy and Technology: Readings in the Philosophical Problems of Technology*. New York: Free Press.

Mitchell, William J., Allen S. Inouye, Marjory S. Blumenthal, eds. 2003. *Beyond Productivity: Information Technology, Innovation, and Creativity*. Washington, D.C.: National Academies Press.

Mitter, Swasti, and Umit Efendioglu. 1997. "Teleworking in a Global Context." In *Virtually Free: Gender, Work and Spatial Choice*, edited by Ewa Gunnarsson, 13–20. Stockholm: Nutek.

Morris, Meaghan. 2005. "Humanities for Taxpayers: Some Problems." *New Literary History* 36, no. 1: 111–29.

Morse, Margaret. 2003. "The Poetics of Interactivity." In *Women, Art & Technology*, edited by Judy Malloy, 16–33. Cambridge, Mass.: MIT Press.

Moulthrop, Stuart, and Nancy Kaplan. 2004. "New Literacies and Old: A Dialogue." *Kairos* 9, no. 1. http://kairos.technorhetoric.net/.

Mumford, Lewis. (1934) 1962. *Technics and Civilization*. New York: Harcourt, Brace & World.

Murphy, Kim. 2000. "Electronic Literature: Thinking Outside the Book." *Los Angeles Times*, July 24.

Naimark, Michael. 1999. "Art at Interval." Speech for the Opening of the Tech Museum of Innovation, San Jose, California. (March 2). http://www.naimark.net/.

———. 2003. "Truth, Beauty, Freedom, and Money: Technology-based Art and the Dynamics of Sustainability." (May). http://www.artslab.net/.

———. 2005. "Two Unusual Projection Spaces." In "Immersive Projection Technology," ed. Carolina Cruz-Niera, special issue, *Presence* 14, no. 5: 597–605.

National Science Foundation (NSF). 2002. *Program for Gender Equity in Science, Technology, Engineering, and Mathematics: A Brief Retrospective 1993–2001*. Arlington, Va.: National Science Foundation. NSF 02–107. http://www.nsf.gov/.

———. 2008. "Creative IT Program Solicitation." Arlington, Va.: National Science Foundation. http://www.nsf.gov/.

Nelson, Donna. 2005. "Harvard President's Comments Demonstrate Need for Commitment to Equality for Women in Science and Technology." January 21. National Organization for Women. http://www.now.org/.

Nelson, Theodor Holm. 1990. *Literary Machines*. 2nd edition. Sausalito, Calif.: Mindful Press.

Newsletter of the Knowledge Initiative, 2001. "PARC Researchers Study Knowledge Sharing and Work Practices at Kinko's to Improve a Transition to the Digital Age." *Knowledge Newsline*, March 23.

Norr, Henry. 2000. "E-Books Not a Good Read Yet." *SFGate*, September 4. http://www.sfgate.com/.

Nunberg, Geoffrey, ed. 1996. *The Future of the Book*. Berkeley: University of California Press.

Office of Advocacy, U.S. Small Business Administration, 2003. "Dynamics of Women-Operated Sole Proprietorships, 1990–1998." March. http://www.sba.gov/advol/.

Oppenheimer, Frank. 1968. "Rationale for a Science Museum." *Curator*, November, 1–3.

Organization for Economic Cooperation and Development (OECD). 2004. "Science, Technology and Innovation for the 21st Century: Final Communique." http://www.oecd.org/.

Pake, George E. 1985. "Research at Xerox PARC: A Founder's Assessment." *IEEE Spectrum*, 54–61.

———. 1986. "From Research to Innovation at Xerox: A Manager's Principles and Some Examples." *Research on Technological Innovation, Management and Policy* 3:1–32.

Palfrey, John, and Urs Gasser. 2008. *Born Digital: Understanding the First Generation of Digital Natives*. New York: Basic Books

Papert, Seymour. 1980. *Mindstorms: Children, Computers, and Powerful Ideas*. New York: Basic Books.

PARC: Palo Alto Research Center. "Research at the Intersections." Promotional brochure. http://www.parc.com/.

Patch, Kimberly. 2001. "PDA Interface Keeps a Low Profile." *TRN (Technology Research News)*, February 21.

Pearce, Susan, ed. 1996. *Exploring Science in Museums*. London: Athlone.

Penley, Constance. 1989. *The Future of an Illusion: Film, Feminism, and Psychoanalysis*. Minneapolis: University of Minnesota Press.

Penny, Simon. 2008. "Bridging Two Cultures: Towards an Interdisciplinary History of the Artist-Inventor and the Machine Artwork." In *Artists as Inventors*, edited by Dieter Daniels and Barbara U. Schmidt, 142–57. Ostfildern, Germany: Hatje Cantz Verlag.

Perrow, Charles. 1984. *Normal Accidents: Living with High-risk Technologies*. New York: Basic Books.

Peters, Thomas, and Robert Waterman. 1982. *In Search of Excellence*. New York: Warner Books.

Polanyi, Michael. 1958. *Personal Knowledge: Toward a Post-Critical Philosophy*. Chicago: University of Chicago Press.

Prensky, Marc. 2001a. "Digital Natives, Digital Immigrants." *On the Horizon* 9, no. 5.

———. 2001b. *Digital Game-based Learning*. New York: McGraw Hill.

Probyn, Elspeth. 2005. *Blush: Faces of Shame*. Minneapolis: University of Minnesota Press.

Radway, Janice. 1984. *Reading the Romance: Women, Patriarchy and Popular Literature*. Chapel Hill: University of North Carolina Press.

Rappaport, Richard. 2003. "Why We've Failed to Integrate Technology Effectively in Our Schools." *e-School News Online*. (August 1). http://www.eschoolnews.com/.

Research in Experimental Documents (RED). 2001a. "The What of XFR: Experiments in the Future of Reading." *Interactions* (May/June): 21–30.

———. 2001b. "The How of XFR: Experiments in the Future of Reading: Genre as a Way of Design." *Interactions* (May/June): 31–41.

Richards, Peter. 2002. "The Greater Good: Why We Need Artists in Science Museums." *ACTC Dimensions*. (July/August). http://www.astc.org/.

Rosenfeld, Rachel A. 1984. "Academic Career Mobility for Women and Men Psychologists." In *Women in Scientific and Engineering Professions*, edited by Violet B. Haas and Carolyn C. Perrucci, 89–134. Ann Arbor: University of Michigan Press.

Rosensweig, Roy. 2003. "Scarcity or Abundance? Reserving the Past in a Digital Age." *American Historical Review* 108, no. 3: 735–62.

Ross, Andrew. 1991. *Strange Weather: Culture, Science and Technology in the Age of Limits*. London: Verso.

———. 2003. *No-Collar: The Humane Workplace and Its Hidden Costs*. New York: Basic Books.

Rosser, Sue V. 1990. *Female-Friendly Science: Applying Women's Studies Methods and Theories to Attract Students*. New York: Pergamon Press.

Rossiter, Ned. 2006. *Organized Networks: Media Theory, Creative Labour, and New Institutions*. Rotterdam: NAi Publishers.

Roszak, Theodore. 1994. *The Culture of Information: A Neo-Luddite Treatise on High-Tech, Artificial Intelligence, and the True Art of Thinking*. Berkeley: University of California Press.

Rothstein, Edward. 2004. "Museum Review: From Internet Arm Wrestling to the Magic of Math." *New York Times*, November 24.

Salen, Katie. 2008. *The Ecology of Games: Connecting Youth, Games and Learning*. Cambridge, Mass.: MIT Press.

Sawchuk, Kim. 1999. "Wounded States: Sovereignty, Separation, and the Quebec Referendum." In *When Pain Strikes*, edited by Bill Burns, Cathy Busby, and Kim Sawchuk, 96–115. Minneapolis: University of Minnesota Press.

Schlossberg, Edwin. 1998. *Interactive Excellence: Defining and Developing New Standards for the Twenty-First Century*. New York: Library of Contemporary Thought.

Schmoch, Ulrich, Christian Rammer, and Harald Legler, eds. 2006. *National Systems of Innovation in Comparison: Structure and Performance Indicators for Knowledge Societies*. Dordrecht: Springer.

Schon, Donald. 1985. *The Design Studio: An Exploration of Its Traditions and Potential*. London: RIBA Publications.

Schrage, Michael. 2001. "That's a Brilliant Business Plan—But is it Art?" *Fortune,* March 5, 226.

Schwartz, John. 2008. "This, From That." *New York Times* online edition, May 13.

Seiter, Ellen. 2005. *The Internet Playgound: Children's Access, Entertainment, and Miseducation.* New York: Peter Lang.

Selfe, Cynthia. 1999. *Technology and Literacy in the Twenty-first Century: The Importance of Paying Attention.* Carbondale: Southern Illinois University Press.

Selfe, Cynthia, and Gail Hawisher. 2007. *Gaming Lives in the Twenty-First Century: Literate Connections.* New York: Palgrave Macmillan.

Semali, Ladislaus M. 2000. *Literacy in Multimedia America: Integrating Media Education Across the Curriculum.* New York: Falmer Press.

Sennett, Richard. 2008. *The Craftsman.* New Haven, Conn.: Yale University Press.

Shapin, Steven. 1994. *A Social History of Truth: Civility and Science in Seventeenth-Century England.* Chicago: University of Chicago Press.

Shatner, William, with Chip Walker. 2002. *Star Trek: I'm Working on That: A Trek from Science Fiction to Science Fact.* New York: Pocket Books.

Sheets-Pyenson, S. 1989. *Cathedrals of Science: The Development of Colonial Natural History Museums During the Late Nineteenth Century.* Montreal: McGill University Press.

Shaviro, Steven. 2003. *Connected, or What it Means to Life in the Network Society.* Minneapolis: University of Minnesota Press.

Silver, Karen. 2001. "Printed Matter." *San Francisco Weekly,* December 19. http://www.sfweekly.com/.

Simmons, Ian. 1996. "A Conflict of Cultures: Hands-on Science Centres in UK Museums." In *Exploring Science in Museums,* edited by Susan M. Pearce, 79–94. London: Athlone Press.

"Singapore on its way to achieve Intelligent Nation vision by 2015." 2007. September. http://www.designsingapore.org/.

Slack, Jennifer Daryl. 1989. "Contextualizing Technology." In *Rethinking Communication,* Vol. 2, *Paradigm Exemplars,* edited by Brenda Dervin, Lawrence Grossberg, Barbara J. O'Keefe, and Ellen Wartella, 324–39. Newbury Park, Calif.: Sage.

Slack, Jennifer Daryl, and J. Macgregor Wise. 2002. "Cultural Studies and Technology." In *The Handbook of New Media: Social Shaping and Consequences of ICTs,* edited by Leah Lievrouw and Sonia Livingstone, 485–501. London: Sage.

———. 2005. *Culture and Technology: A Primer.* New York: Peter Lang.

Smith, Douglas K., and Robert C. Alexander. 1988. *Fumbling the Future: How Xerox Invented, Then Ignored, the First Personal Computer.* New York: William Morrow.

Smith, Keith A. 1995. *Text in the Book Format.* Rochester, New York: Keith A. Smith Books.

Snow, C. P. 1963. *The Two Cultures: and a Second Look.* New York: Cambridge University Press.

Sparke, Penny. 1992. *An Introduction to Design and Culture [1900 to the present].* 2nd edition. London: Routledge.

Sproull, Lee, and Sara Kiesler. 1986. "Reducing Social Context Cues: Electronic Mail in Organizational Communication." *Management Science* 32:1492–1512.

Stanley, Autumn. 1995. *Mothers and Daughters of Invention*. New Brunswick, N.J.: Rutgers University Press.

Star, Susan Leigh. 1989. *Regions of the Mind: Brain Research and the Quest for Scientific Certainty*. Stanford, Calif.: Stanford University Press.

Star, Susan Leigh, and Geoffrey C. Bowker. 2002. "How to Infrastructure." In *The Handbook of New Media: Social Shaping and Consequences of ICTs*, edited by Leah A. Lievrouw and Sonia Livingstone, 151–62. London: Sage.

Star, Susan Leigh, and K. Ruhleder. 1996. "Steps Toward an Ecology of Infrastructure: Design and Access for Large Information Spaces." *Information Systems Research* 7:111–33.

"State of the Union: American Competitiveness Initiative." 2006. Press release, Office of the Press Secretary of the President of the United States. January 31. http://georgewbush-whitehouse.archives.gov/.

Steedman, Carolyn Kay. 1987. *Landscape for a Good Woman: A Story of Two Lives*. New Brunswick, N.J.: Rutgers University Press.

Sterling, Bruce. 2005. *Shaping Things*. Cambridge, Mass.: MIT Press.

Stoll, Clifford. 2000. *High-Tech Heretic: Reflections of a Computer Contrarian*. New York: Anchor.

Stone, Linda. 2006. "Attention: the *Real* Aphrodisiac." Talk delivered at the 2006 Emerging Technology Conference. http://radar.oreilly.com/.

Strathern, Marilyn. 1992. *Reproducing the Future: Anthropology, Kinship, and the New Reproductive Technologies*. New York: Routledge.

Strauss, Anselm. 1985. "Work and the Division of Labor." *Sociological Quarterly* 26, no. 1: 1–19.

———. 1987. *Qualitative Analysis for Social Scientists*. Cambridge: Cambridge University Press.

Strickland, Rachel. 2003. "Spontaneous Cinema as Design Practice: How to Walk Without Watching Your Step." In *Design Research: Methods and Perspectives*, edited by Brenda Laurel, 118–28. Cambridge, Mass.: MIT Press.

———. N.d. "Portable Effects: A Design Vocabulary for Everyday Life." http://adaweb.walkerart.org/~dn/a/enfra/rstrickland.html.

Stross, Charles. 2005. *Accelerando*. New York: Ace Books.

Suchman, Lucy. 1987. *Plans and Situated Actions: The Problem of Human Machine Communication*. Cambridge: Cambridge University Press.

———. 1994. "Do Categories have Politics? The Language/Action Perspective Reconsidered." *Computer Supported Cooperative Work* 2:177–90.

———. 1996. "Supporting Articulation Work." In *Computerization and Controversy: Value Conflicts and Social Choices*, edited by Robert Kling, 407–23. 2nd edition. San Diego: Academic Press.

———. 2002. "Located Accountabilities in Technology Production." *Scandinavian Journal of Information Systems* 14, no. 2: 91–105.

———. 2005. "Affiliative Objects." *Organization* 12, no. 3: 379–99.

———. 2007. *Human-machine Reconfigurations: Plans and Situated Actions.* Cambridge: Cambridge University Press.

Sullivan, Graeme. 2010. *Art Practice as Research: Inquiry in Visual Arts.* 2nd edition. Thousand Oaks, Calif.: Sage.

Summers, Lawrence. 2005a. "Remarks at NBER Conference on Diversifying the Science and Engineering Workforce." Talk delivered to National Bureau of Economic Research Conference. January 14. http://www.president.harvard.edu/.

———. 2005b. "Letter from President Summers on Women and Science." January 19. http://www.president.harvard.edu/.

Sun, Chih-Yuan, and Donna Benton. 2008. "The Socioeconomic Disparity in Technology Use and Its Impact on Academic Performance." In *Proceedings of the Society for Information Technology and Teacher Education International Conference,* edited by Karen McFerrin, Roberta Weber, Roger Carlsen, and Dee Anna Willis, 1025–28. Chesapeake, Va.: Society for Information Technology and Teacher Education.

Tambe, Milind, W. L. Johnson, R. M. Jones, F. Koss, J. E. Laird, P. S. Rosenbloom, and K. Schwamb. 1995. "Intelligent Agents for Interactive Simulation Environments." AI *Magazine* 15, no. 1: 15–39.

Tavares, Ana Teresa, and Aurora Teixeira, eds. 2006. *Multinationals, Clusters and Innovation: Does Public Policy Matter?* New York: Palgrave Macmillan.

Taylor, Chris. 2000. "Team Xerox." *TIME,* December 4, 96–99.

Taylor, Jonathan. 2000. "The Need for the Journal of Literacy and Technology." *Journal of Literacy and Technology: An Academic Journal.* (May). http://www.literacyandtechnology.org/.

TELIC Arts Exchange. N.d. "The Public School." http://www.telic.info/.

Terry, Jennifer. 2007. "Killer Entertainments." *Vectors* 3, no. 1, http://vectors.usc.edu/.

Thackara, John, ed. 1988. *Design After Modernism: Beyond the Object.* Gloucester: Thames and Hudson.

———. 2005. *In the Bubble: Designing in a Complex World.* Cambridge, Mass.: MIT Press.

Thomas, Douglas, and John Seely Brown. 2007. "The Play of Imagination: Extending the Literary Mind." *Games and Culture* 2, no. 2: 149–72.

———. 2008. "The Power of Dispositions." *Ubiquity* 9 (November). http://ubiquity.acm.org/.

Thomas, Gillian, and Tim Caulton. 1996. "Communication Strategies in Interactive Spaces." In *Exploring Science in Museums,* edited by Susan M. Pearce, 107–22. London: Athlone Press.

Toffler, Alvin. 1981. *The Third Wave.* New York: Bantam.

Traweek, Sharon. 1988. *Beamtimes and Lifetimes: The World of High Energy Physics.* Cambridge, Mass.: Harvard University Press.

Treichler, Paula A. 1990. "Feminism, Medicine and the Meaning of Childbirth." In

Body/Politics: Woman and the Discourses of Science, edited by Mary Jacobus, Evelyn Fox Keller, and Sally Shuttleworth, 113–38. New York: Routledge.

———. 1999. *How to Have Theory in an Epidemic: Cultural Chronicles of AIDS.* Durham, N.C.: Duke University Press.

Tufte, Edward R. 1997. *Visual Explanations: Images and Quantities, Evidence and Narrative.* Cheshire, Conn.: Graphics Press.

———. 2003. *The Cognitive Style of PowerPoint.* Cheshire, Conn.: Graphics Press.

———. 2006. *Beautiful Evidence.* Cheshire, Conn.: Graphics Press.

Tuman, Myron C., ed. 1992. *Literacy Online: The Promise (and Peril) of Reading and Writing with Computers.* Pittsburgh, Penn.: University of Pittsburgh Press.

Turkle, Sherry. 1984. *The Second Self.* New York: Simon and Schuster.

———. 1997. *Life on the Screen: Identity in the Age of the Internet.* New York: Simon and Schuster.

Turner, Mark. 1998. *The Literary Mind.* New York: Oxford University Press.

Tyner, Kathleen. 1998. *Literacy in a Digital World: Teaching and Learning in the Age of Information.* Mahwah, N.J.: Lawrence Erlbaum Associates.

Ulam, Stanislaw. 1958. "Tribute to John von Neumann." *Bulletin of the American Mathematical Society* 64, no. 5, pt. 2: 1–49.

University of Illinois at Urbana-Champaign. 2007. *Creating a Brilliant Future for the University of Illinois.* http://www.uillinois.edu/.

University of Southern California. 2004. *USC Strategic Plan: USC's Plan for Increasing Academic Excellence: Building Strategic Capabilities for the University of the 21st Century.* (September). http://www.usc.edu/.

Vinge, Vernor. 1983. "First Word." *Omni* (January): 10.

———. 1993. "The Singularity." Talk presented at VISION-21 Symposium sponsored by NASA Lewis Research Center and the Ohio Aerospace Institute. (March 30–31). http://mindstalk.net/.

Vygotsky, Lev. 1926. *Educational Psychology.* Boca Raton, Fla.: St. Lucie Press.

Wakefield, Nina, and Kris Cohen. 2008. "Fieldwork in Public: Using Blogs for Research." In *The Sage Handbook of Online Research Methods*, edited by Nigel Fielding, Raymond M. Lee, and Grant Blank, 307–26. London: Sage Press.

Wald, Carol Ann. 2004. "Working Boundaries on the Nano Exhibition." In *Nanoculture: Implications of the New Technoscience*, edited by N. Katherine Hayles, 83–108. Bristol, England: Intellect Books.

Waters, Donald, and John Garrett. 1996. *Preserving Digital Information: Report on the Task Force on Archiving of Digital Information.* Washington, D.C.: Commission on Preservation and Access.

Weiser, Mark, Rich Gold, and John Seely Brown. 1999. "The Origins of Ubiquitous Computing Research at PARC in the Late 1980's." *IBM Systems Journal* 38, no. 4: 693–96.

Wiener, Norbert. 1961. *Cybernetics.* Cambridge, Mass.: MIT Press.

Williams, Raymond. 1961. *The Long Revolution.* New York: Columbia University Press.

———. 1981. *Sociology of Culture.* New York: Schocken Books.

Winner, Langdon. 1977. *Autonomous Technology: Technics-Out-of-Control as a Theme in Political Thought.* Cambridge, Mass.: MIT Press.

———. 1986. *The Whale and the Reactor: A Search for Limits in an Age of High Technology.* Chicago: University of Chicago Press, 1986.

Winograd, Terry. 1986. "A Language / Action Perspective on the Design of Cooperative Work." *CSCW '86 Proceedings,* 203–20. Conference on Computer-Supported Cooperative Work, December 3–5, Austin, Texas.

Winograd, Terry, and F. Flores. 1986. *Understanding Computers and Cognition: A New Foundation for Design.* Norwood, N.J.: Ablex.

Wise, J. Macgregor. 1997. *Exploring Technology and Social Space.* Thousand Oaks, Calif.: Sage Publications.

Women in Science and Engineering Leadership Institute (WISELI). 2005. "Response to Lawrence Summers' Remarks on Women in Science." http:// wiseli.engr.wisc.edu/.

Wood, K. C., H. Smith, and D. Grossniklaus. 2001. "Piaget's Stages of Cognitive Development." In *Emerging Perspectives on Learning, Teaching and Technology,* edited by M. Orey. http://projects.coe.uga.edu/.

Woodward, Kathleen, ed. 1980. *The Myths of Information: Technology and Post-industrial Culture.* Madison, Wisc.: Coda Press.

Zimmerman, Eric, and Katie Salen. 2003. *Rules of Play: Game Design Fundamentals.* Cambridge, Mass.: MIT Press.

Born-digital generation (*cont.*) 241n13, 242n14; "conceptual blending" of, 143; differences of, 139; digital learning spaces and, 143–45, *145*, 154; dispositions of, 142–43, 154–55, 182, 195–96; importance of historical context for, 181–82; learning and, 140–43, 195–96; as mutable subjects, 142; on-line gaming and, 142–43, 154–55, 182; as "Original Synners," 141–43, 146, 182–83, 242n18; self-fashioning in, 140–41; teaching of, 150–51

Bourdieu, Pierre, 203n18

Brown, John Seeley, 21, 57, 142–43, 154, 173, 196, 209n45, 241n13

Bucciarelli, Louis, 12, 207n37

Buchanan, Richard, 168

Buckingham, David, 139, 242n14

California Museum of Science and Industry, 103

Carey, James, 40, 214n21

Center of the Edge Gallery, 59–60, 68, 221n28

"Christmas Tree Balls" (artwork, Miller), 101

Collaboration and multidisciplinary collaboration, 8, 24–25, 61, 101, 137, 166, 209n44, 224n40, 249n49; creative thinking and, 36; in design, 36–37; disciplinary specialists in, 160–61; ethical principles of, 163; RED@PARC and, 59–61; Singapore Science Center and, 236n34; technocultural innovation and, 12–13, 22; in universities, 147, 158–62

Comic books, 78, 79

Communities of interest: in museums, 146; tinkering and, 178–79

"Conceptual blending," 143

"Consumption communities," 134–35, 182

Convergence, 134–35, 182, 240n3

Creativity: collaboration and, 36; culture and, 166–68; technological imagination and, 164–65, 167–68; transdomain, 167–68

Critical reading of multimedia, 152–53

Csikszentmihalyi, Mihaly, 167, 225n43

Cultural technologies, 95, 132, 231n1. *See also* Science/Technology museums; XFR interactives

Culture and technology index, 1. *See also* Technocultural innovation

DataGlyphs, 80

Davidson, Cathy, 158–59

de Certeau, Michel, 69–70, 91, 109, 117–18, 122, 230n64; on space versus place, 143

Dell (computer company), 30

Delphi groups, 141

Demetrios, Eames, 103, 232n16

Design and designing, 6, 12, 35–36, 206nn35–36, 207n37; agency in, 33–34; articulation, 9–10, 20, 43, 193, 205n26; cultural reproduction and, 10, 197, 203n18; failure and, 25; hermeneutic reverse engineering and, 13–16, 206n30, 208nn38–40; intra-actions in, 34–35, 43, 47; material objects in, 65, 225n45; as meaning-making, 197, 205n25; metaphor in, 204n24; multidisciplinary teams in, 36–37; "paradox of design," 89; presuppositions of, 36; of *The Reading Wall*, 110–12; self-conscious versus unselfconscious, 212n13; technocultural reproduction and, 11–13, 170; technological imagination skills and, 168–72; technological literacy and, 129–30; of *Women of the World Talk Back*, 43–47. *See also* Eames, Charles; Eames, Ray; RED@PARC

Designing Culture book (Balsamo), 192,

197–98; *designingculture.net* website and, 23, 193–97; as EKOS, 198; as transmedia book, 22–23, 192, 254n3

Designingculture.net website, 23, 72, 193–97, 236n30, 254n2; *Designing Culture* book and, 193–97; digital learning objects and, 196; *Interactive Digital Wall*, 194; video primers on, 196–97; XFR interactives and, 23, 72, 193–95

Dewey, John, 142, 168, 182, 243n20

Digital humanities, 7, 148–51, *149*, 196, 240n2, 248nn46–47, 249n50; model of creativity in, 167–68; new forms of scholarship and outreach in, 165–66, 192, 200n6, 250nn52–54; new literacies and, 166–72; new technology research and, 149–50; technological innovation in, 137, 159–60, 247n45; transformative research in, 158–63. *See also* Learning and education in digital age; Universities

Digital learning objects, 190–91, 196

Distributed learning networks, 243n23

DIY (do it yourself) movement and projects, 2, 131, 177

Eames, Charles, 20, 96, 102–5, 232n15, 233n17; influence on "Henry the Ape" interactive, 233n21; shell-chair of, 232n14. *See also Mathematica: A World of Numbers and Beyond* (exhibit)

Eames, Ray, 20, 96, 102–5, 233n17; influence on "Henry the Ape" interactive, 233n21; shell-chair of, 232n14; on woman in mathematics, 233n20

Education. *See* Learning and education in digital age

Employment choices for women, 29

Engineering, gender imbalance in, 27–29

Ethics: in multidisciplinary collaboration, 161; in technocultural innova-tion, 31, 46–47; technological literacy and, 129–30

Evocative knowledge objects (EKOS), 19, 70–72, 170, 198

Exhibits. *See Mathematica*; Science / Technology museums; XFR interactives

Exploratorium (San Francisco), 20, 96, 100–102, 232n10; artist in residence at, 101, 232n9; *Seeing the Light* exhibit at, 101

Facebook, 2, 143

Feenberg, Andrew, 11, 206n34

Feminist technoculture studies and activism, 18, 31, 37, 41–43, 48–49, 193. *See also Women of the World Talk Back*

Fluid Fiction (XFR interactive), 78, *79*

Fumbling the Future: How Xerox Invented, the Ignored the First Personal Computer (Smith and Alexander), 54

Galton, Sir Francis, 104

Games, 242n15; non-Barbie games, 39; *Telephone* (children's game), 81. *See also* Online game players

Gasser, Urs, 138

Geertz, Clifford, 14, 209n41

Gender and technology, 30–37, 47–49, 210n2, 211n7, 211n10, 230n67, 241n9; biological essentialism, 31, 36; educational programs in science and math and, 38, 214n20; employment choices and, 29; feminist technoculture studies and activism, 18, 37, 41–43, 48–49, 193; games and, 242n15, 245n34; gendered pronouns in Visual Thesaurus, 186, *188*, 188–89; male identity in, 32; Ray Eames on, 233n20; in science and mathematics, 27, 210n5, 233n20; STEM programs and, 29, 210n4; "strong objectivity" and, 44; in tech-

Anne Balsamo is Professor of Interactive Media at the School of Cinematic Arts and Professor of Communication in the Annenburg School of Communications and Journalism at the University of Southern California. She is the author of *Technologies of the Gendered Body: Reading Cyborg Women* (1996).

Library of Congress Cataloging-in-Publication Data

Balsamo, Anne Marie, 1959–
Designing culture : the technological imagination at work / Anne Balsamo.
p. cm.
Title of accompanying DVD: Women of the world talk back
Includes bibliographical references and index.
ISBN 978-0-8223-4433-9 (cloth : alk. paper)
ISBN 978-0-8223-4445-2 (pbk. : alk. paper)
1. Technological innovations—Social aspects.
2. Technological literacy.
3. Civilization, Modern.
4. Creation (Literary, artistic, etc.)
I. Title. II. Title: Women of the world talk back.
HM846.B35 2011
306.4'6—dc22   2010054445